LEGAL DESIGN FOR SOCIAL-ECOLOGICAL RESILIENCE

Theories of social-ecological resilience have developed over the past decades and rapidly become an important framework for governance of complex non-linear environmental problems. This book explores the resilience theories and their compatibility with law, it identifies corresponding legal features. The legal features identified, including legal measures, mechanisms, principles and approaches, form a legal design for social-ecological resilience. A legal design that can be applied to different governance situations. It can be a tool both for designing new laws, as well as for assessing the effectiveness of current laws and legal systems. In many ways environmental law has adjusted and developed new approaches to meet complex environmental problems, but law is still challenged by the complexity that characterize environmental problems and the environmental change connected with the Anthropocene. This book provides a comprehensive review of the most fundamental components of the governance framework for social-ecological resilience and the role of law.

Brita Bohman is LL.D. and Senior Lecturer in Environmental Law at the Faculty of law at Stockholm University, Sweden. Her dissertation on law and resilience from 2017 includes a case study of the environmental governance of the Baltic Sea and was conducted in a transdisciplinary research environment, in cooperation with Stockholm Resilience Centre and the Baltic Sea Centre at Stockholm University. Bohman has been a researcher at Åbo Akademi University in Finland and postdoctoral researcher in Ocean Governance Law at the University of Gothenburg, Sweden (2017–2019). Her research mainly addresses legal issues related to ecological complexity, resilience and ecosystem approach.

Legal Design for Social-Ecological Resilience

BRITA BOHMAN
Stockholm University

CAMBRIDGE
UNIVERSITY PRESS

CAMBRIDGE
UNIVERSITY PRESS

Shaftesbury Road, Cambridge CB2 8EA, United Kingdom

One Liberty Plaza, 20th Floor, New York, NY 10006, USA

477 Williamstown Road, Port Melbourne, VIC 3207, Australia

314–321, 3rd Floor, Plot 3, Splendor Forum, Jasola District Centre, New Delhi – 110025, India

103 Penang Road, #05–06/07, Visioncrest Commercial, Singapore 238467

Cambridge University Press is part of Cambridge University Press & Assessment, a department of the University of Cambridge.

We share the University's mission to contribute to society through the pursuit of education, learning and research at the highest international levels of excellence.

www.cambridge.org
Information on this title: www.cambridge.org/9781108793841

DOI: 10.1017/9781108879101

First published 2021

A catalogue record for this publication is available from the British Library

ISBN 978-1-108-84017-0 Hardback
ISBN 978-1-108-79384-1 Paperback

Contents

Preface and Acknowledgments

The following book is in a field of environmental law, which combines law with theories of so-called social-ecological resilience. The purpose of combining law with these theories is to explore new legal methods and approaches to complex environmental problems. In a time where the environment is rapidly degrading and even eroding our basic conditions for life, finding a better role or way for law to contribute to sustainability is more important than ever. The increasing complexity of environmental issues and the polycentric development of institutions and legal regimes present the legal system with new challenges. New regulatory approaches are taking form. In the connection between social and ecological systems, law could play a vital role as a driver for change. The aim of the study presented in this book is to identify legal concepts, mechanisms and approaches that contribute to successful and effective operationalization of social-ecological resilience. This means that what is to be explored and defined is the role of law in a governance system designed to promote social-ecological resilience. The intent is to examine the extent to which law may contribute to achieving social-ecological resilience and the sustenance of resilience governance structures, and how law may do this. Doing so involves not only seeking parallels and synergies but also exploring whether there are any significant obstacles or conflicts connected with integrating law with such governance and, if so, where these obstacles can be found.

The goal of the book is to create a theoretical model of a legal system, a legal design, that corresponds to a governance system for social-ecological resilience. The concrete result is a proposed legal design that will contribute to social-ecological resilience. The legal design will be a model or a tool for how to adjust legal systems for such governance. It will also be a tool for evaluating whether existing legal instruments meet the requirements and provide the prerequisites for effective ecosystem governance. The book contributes to a better understanding and perception of the legal mechanisms in regard to their effectiveness and compatibility with the concept of resilience. In addition, researching and elaborating these ideas and terms in a legal context can contribute to further development of the theories and concepts of social-ecological resilience.

This book is based on a doctoral dissertation. Compared to the dissertation, the book is more concise but takes a wider approach, with the aim of creating a general tool that can be applied in many different settings. In relation to the original dissertation, I am grateful to my former supervisors Professor Jonas Ebbesson and Professor David Langlet. David has, in addition, been helpful, giving good advice throughout the process of developing this book. I am also indebted to Professor Ellen Hey, who provided much valuable advice on how to transform the dissertation into a book aimed at a wider audience. While working with parts of the manuscript, I was fortunate to have a postdoctoral position at the Department of Law at the University of Gothenburg, Sweden. I owe much gratitude for this opportunity and the time for research that it provided me with.

Table of Treaties and International Instruments

1945 The Charter of the United Nations, signed on June 26, 1945, in San Francisco, USA, 1 UNTS XVI, 145.

1950 Convention for the Protection of Human Rights and Fundamental Freedoms (the European Convention on Human Rights) 213 UNTS 221.

1969 Convention on the Law of Treaties (the Vienna Convention), UN Doc. A/Conf.39/27; 1155 UNTS 331.

1972 United Nations Declaration on Human Environment, Stockholm, June 16, 1972 (the Stockholm Declaration), 11 ILM 1972, p. 1416.

1979 Convention on Long-Range Transboundary Air Pollution (LRTAP), 1302 UNTS 217.

1982 United Nations Convention of the Law of the Sea (LOSC), 1833 UNTS 3.

1985 Vienna Convention for the Protection of the Ozone Layer, 1513 UNTS 323.

1987 Montreal Protocolon Substances that Deplete the Ozone Layer (the Montreal Protocol), 1522 UNTS 3, adopted under the Vienna Convention for the Protection of the Ozone Layer.

1989 Basel Convention on the Control of Transboundary Movements of Hazardous Wastes and Their Disposal (the Basel Convention), 1673 UNTS 126.

1992 Convention on the Protection of the Marine Environment of the Baltic Sea Area (the Helsinki Convention), 2099 UNTS 195.

1992 Convention for the Protection of the Marine Environment of the North-East Atlantic (OSPAR Convention), 2354 UNTS 67.

1992 United Nations Declaration on Environment and Development, Rio de Janeiro June 4–13, 1992 (the Rio Declaration), 31 ILM 1992, p. 876.

1992 United Nations Environment and Development Agenda, "Agenda 21," adopted at the 1992 UN Rio Conference on Environmental and Development, UN GAOR, 46th Sess., Agenda Item 21, UN Doc A/Conf.151/26 (1992).

1992 Convention on Biological Diversity, 1760 UNTS 79.

1992 United Nations Framework Convention on Climate Change (the UNFCCC), 1771 UNTS 107.

1998 Aarhus Convention on Access to Information, Public Participation in Decision-Making and Access to Justice in Environmental Matters (the Aarhus Convention), 2161 UNTS 447.

2002 The United Nations 2002 Johannesburg Declaration on Sustainable Development (The Johannesburg Declaration), UN doc nr: A/CONF.199/20.

2003 Kiev Protocol on Pollutant Release and Transfer Registers (the PRTR Protocol) under the UNECE Convention on Access to Information, Public Participation in Decision-Making and Access to Justice in Environmental Matters (the Aarhus Convention), Official UN doc nr: Doc. MP.PP/2003/1.

2010 UNEP Guidelines for the Development of National Legislation on Access to Information, Public Participation and Access to Justice in Environmental Matters (the Bali Guidelines).

2015 Paris Agreement, adopted under the United Nations Framework Convention on Climate Change (the UNFCCC).

2016 Treaty on European Union (Consolidated version 2016) (TEU), OJ C 202, 7.6.2016, p. 13–388 (EN).

2016 Treaty on the Functioning of the European Union (Consolidated version 2016) (TFEU), OJ C 202, 7.6.2016, p. 1–388 (EN).

2016 The Revised African Convention on the Conservation of Nature and Natural Resources (the African Convention on the Conservation of Nature).

2018 The ECLAC Regional Agreement on Access to Information, Public Participation and Justice in Environmental Matters in Latin America and the Caribbean (the Escazú Agreement).

Table of EU Law

1992 Council Directive 92/43/EEC of May 21, 1992, on the conservation of natural habitats and of wild fauna and flora (the Habitats Directive), OJ L 206, pp. 7–50.

2000 Directive 2000/60/EC of the European Parliament and of the Council of October 23, 2000, establishing a framework for community action in the field of water policy (the Water Framework Directive), OJ L 327, pp. 1–73.

2003 Council of Europe Recommendation 1614 (2003), Environment and Human Rights.

2003 Directive 2003/4/EC of the European Parliament and of the Council of January 28, 2003, on public access to environmental information (the Directive on Environmental Information) and repealing Council Directive 90/313/EEC, OJ L 41, p. 26–32.

2003 Directive 2003/35/EC of the European Parliament and of the Council of May 26, 2003, providing for public participation in respect of the drawing up of certain plans and programmes relating to the environment (the Public Participation Directive) and amending with regard to public participation and access to justice Council Directives 85/337/EEC and 96/61/EC – Statement by the Commission, OJ L 156, p. 17–25.

2005 Council Decision 2005/370/EC of February 17, 2005, on the conclusion, on behalf of the European Community, of the Convention on access to information, public participation in decision-making and access to justice in environmental matters (the Aarhus Decision), OJ L 124, p. 1–3.

2006 Regulation (EC) No 166/2006 of the European Parliament and of the Council of January 18, 2006, concerning the establishment of a European Pollutant Release and Transfer Register (E-PRTR) and amending Council Directives 91/689/EEC and 96/61/EC, OJ L 33, p. 1–17.

2006 Regulation (EC) No 1367/2006 of the European Parliament and of the Council of September 6, 2006, on the application of the provisions of the Aarhus Convention on Access to Information, Public Participation in Decision-Making and Access to Justice in Environmental Matters to Community Institutions and Bodies (the Aarhus Regulation), OJ L 264, p. 13–19.

2008 Directive 2008/50/EC of the European Parliament and of the Council of May 21, 2008, on ambient air quality and cleaner air for Europe (the Air Quality Directive), OJ L 152, p. 1–44.

2008 Directive 2008/56/EC of the European Parliament and of the Council of June 17, 2008, establishing a framework for community action in the field of marine environmental policy (Marine Strategy Framework Directive), OJ L 164, pp. 19–40.

2009 Directive 2009/147/EC of the European Parliament and of the Council of November 30, 2009, on the conservation of wild birds (the Birds Directive), OJ L 20, p. 7–25.

2010 Directive 2010/75/EU of the European Parliament and of the Council of November 24, 2010, on industrial emissions (integrated pollution prevention and control) (the Industrial Emissions Directive), OJ L 334, p. 17–119.

2011 Directive 2011/92/EU of the European Parliament and of the Council of December 13, 2011, on the assessment of the effects of certain public and private projects on the environment (the EIA Directive), OJ L 26, pp. 1–21.

2014 Directive 2014/52/EU of the European Parliament and of the Council of April 16, 2014, amending Directive 2011/92/EU on the assessment of the effects of certain public and private projects on the environment, OJ L 124, p. 1–18.

2014 Directive 2014/89/EU of the European Parliament and of the Council of July 23, 2014, establishing a framework for maritime spatial planning (Maritime Spatial Planning Directive), OJ L 257, pp. 135–145.

2014 Document 52014XC0521(01), Withdrawal of obsolete Commission Proposals (2003/0246/COD and 2014/C 153/03), OJ C 153, p. 3–7.

Table of Cases

The Trail Smelter Arbitration Case (United States *v.* Canada) 1941, UN Reports of International Arbitral Awards, Vol III, p. 1905 (1949). UN Reports of International Arbitral Awards, Vol III, LIX, pp. 1905–1982, Trail smelter case. United States of America, Canada. April 16, 1938 and March 11, 1941. See more at http://legal.un.org/riaa/cases/vol_III/1905–1982.pdf.

Case 26/62 van *Gend and Loos*, ECLI:EU:C:1963:1

Case 6/64 Costa *v.* ENEL, ECLI:EU:C:1964:66

Legality of the Threat or Use of Nuclear Weapons (Nuclear Weapons Advisory Opinion), Advisory Opinion, ICJ Reports 1996, p. 226.

Gabcikovo-Nagymaros Project (Hungary *v.* Slovakia), Judgment, ICJ Reports 1997, p. 7.

The MOX Plant Case (Ireland *v.* United Kingdom), ITLOS, Request for provisional measures, order (December 3, 2001), International Legal Materials, Vol. 41, no. 2, 2002, pp. 405–437.

The MOX Plant Case, Ireland *v.* United Kingdom, ITLOS, Order No 3, Suspension of Proceedings on Jurisdiction and Merits, and Request for Further Provisional Measures. June 24, 2003 (Permanent Court of Arbitration – Case Repository).

Dispute Concerning Access to Information under Article 9 of the OSPAR Convention, Final Award (Ireland *v.* the United Kingdom) (July 2, 2003), ITLOS, Permanent Court of Arbitration, International Legal Materials, Vol. 42 (2003), p. 1118.

Taşkın and Others *v.* Turkey (Application no. 46117/99) [2004] ECHR 621, Judgment of November 10, 2004.

Okyay and others *v.* Turkey (Application no. 36220/97), Judgment of July 12, 2005.

Joined Cases T-236/04 and T-241/04 European Environmental Bureau (EEB) and Stichting Natuur en Milieu *v.* Commission ECLI:EU:T:2005:426.

The MOX Plant Case, Ireland *v.* United Kingdom, ITLOS, Order No 6, Termination of Proceedings. June 6, 2008 (Permanent Court of Arbitration – Case Repository).

Case T-91/07 WWF-UK Ltd *v.* Council of the European Union, ECLI:EU:T:2008:170.

ACCC/C/2005/17, submitted by the non-governmental organization Association Kazokiskes Community (Lithuania) alleging non-compliance by the European Community with its obligations under article 6, paragraphs 2 and 4, and article 9, paragraph 2, of the Convention, Report by the Compliance Committee, Third Meeting of the Parties, Riga, June 2008, ECE/MP.PP/2008/5/Add.10.

Case C-355/08 P WWF-UK Ltd *v.* Council of the European Union and the Commission of the European Communities, ECLI:EU:C:2009:286.

Case C-427/07 Commission *v.* Ireland, ECLI:EU:C:2009:457.

Case C-263/08 Djurgården-Lilla Värtans Miljöskyddsförening, ECLI:EU:C:2009:631.

Tatar *v.* Romania (Application no. 67021/01), Judgment of January 27, 2009.

Pulp Mills on the River Uruguay (Argentina *v.* Uruguay), Judgment, I.C.J. Reports 2010, p. 14.

ACCC/C/2008/32 (Part I), Report of the Compliance Committee: Findings and recommendations with regard to communication concerning compliance by the European Union, adopted on April 14, 2011, ECE/MP.PP/C.1/2011/4/Add.1.

Case C-240–09 Lesoochranárske zoskupenie VLK *v.* Ministerstvo životného prostredia Slovenskej republiky, "Slovak Brown Bears Case" ECLI:EU:C:2011:125.

ACCC/C/2010/54 concerning compliance by the European Union, prepared by the Compliance Committee and adopted on June 29, 2012, ECE/MP.PP/C.1/2012/12.

ACCC/C/2010/54, communication alleging a failure by the European Union (EU) to comply with its obligations under articles 5 and 7 of the Convention, in relation to Ireland's renewable, especially wind, energy policy, ECE/MP.PP/2014/2/Add.1, Decision V/9 g.

Whaling in the Antarctic (Australia *v.* Japan: New Zealand intervening), Judgment, I.C.J. Reports 2014, p. 226.

Joined Cases C-401/12 P to C-403/12 P Council of the European Union and Others *v.* Vereniging Milieudefensie and Stichting Stop Luchtverontreiniging Utrecht ECLI:EU:C:2015:4.

Abbreviations

ACCC	Aarhus Convention Compliance Committee
CBD	Convention on Biological Diversity
CLOS	Convention on the Law of the Sea
COP	Conference of the Parties
EAP	Environmental Action Programme
EC	European Community
ECJ	European Court of Justice
ECLAC	Economic Commission for Latin America and the Caribbean
EIA	Environmental Impact Assessment
EQS	Environmental Quality Standards
EU	European Union
HELCOM	Helsinki Commission
ICJ	International Court of Justice
IED	Industrial Emissions Directive
IGO	intergovernmental organization
IPPC	Integrated Pollution Prevention and Control
ITLOS	International Tribunal for the Law of the Sea
LRTAP	Convention on Long-Range Transboundary Air Pollution
MOP	Meeting of the Parties
MSFD	Marine Strategy Framework Directive
NGO	nongovernmental organization
OSPAR	Convention for the Protection of the Marine Environment of the North-East Atlantic
PRTR	Protocol on Pollutant Release and Transfer Registers
TEU	Treaty on European Union

TFEU	Treaty on the Functioning of the European Union
UN	United Nations
UNECE	United Nations Economic Commission for Europe
UNEP	United Nations Environment Program
UNFCCC	United Nations Framework Convention on Climate Change
WFD	Water Framework Directive

1

Introduction

Despite the fast development of environmental governance and environmental law over the past decades, the world is facing fundamental threats to the environment and the earth system. Some of the most urgent problems today are both huge threats on their own, as well as being interconnected and creating an even more problematic situation together, as in, for example, climate change; biodiversity loss; pollution to air, water and oceans; as well as chemical pollution. Many scholars argue that the world is entering the Anthropocene, a new geological epoch represented by the fact that the earth now in an unprecedented way is shaped by human activities.[1] In addition to reflecting the global scale of the environmental problems, this perspective also emphasizes the complex and intertwined relationship between the human and the natural systems (i.e., the social and the ecological). Human activities are both driven by, and themselves affecting, the environment and the natural resources. The human impact shapes the conditions provided by the ecosystems; at the same time, the conditions created are unpredictable and affect the

[1] The concept of the Anthropocene was first introduced by Crutzen, P. J., "Geology of Mankind," *Nature*, Vol. 415, no. 6867, 2002, p. 23. See also e.g. Steffen, W., Crutzen, P. J. and McNeill, J. R., "The Anthropocene: Are Humans Now Overwhelming the Great Forces of Nature?," *Ambio*, Vol. 36, No. 8, 2007, p. 614; Steffen, W., et al., "The Anthropocene: From Global Change to Planetary Stewardship," *Ambio*, Vol. 40, No. 7, 2011, p. 739; Biggs, R., Schlüter, M. and Schoon, M. L., "An Introduction to the Resilience Approach and Principles to Sustain Ecosystem Services in Social-Ecological Systems," in Biggs, R., Schlüter, M. and Schoon, M. L. (eds.), *Principles for Building Resilience: Sustaining Ecosystem Services in Social-Ecological Systems*, Cambridge University Press, 2015b, pp. 4–5; Stephens, T., "What Is the Point of International Environmental Law Scholarship in the Anthropocene?," in Pedersen, O. W (ed.), *Perspectives on Environmental Law Scholarship: Essays on Purpose, Shape and Direction*, Cambridge University Press, 2018a; Kotzé, L. (ed.), *Environmental Law and Governance for the Anthropocene*, Hart Publishing, 2017; Benson, M. H. and Craig, R. K., *The End of Sustainability: Resilience and the Future of Environmental Governance in the Anthropocene*, University Press of Kansas, 2017.

conditions for human activities in turn. In the Anthropocene, we cannot assume that the earth system will continue in the same predictable manner as in the Holocene, and this has consequences for law and governance.[2] In this respect, the Anthropocene can also be a concept that describes the complexity of environmental problems, with sudden and unpredictable changes, chain reactions in ecosystems across scales, elements of surprise, and in addition, it describes an intertwined and connected system where human impact is no longer having foreseeable or linear effects on the ecosystems. Given this view of the earth system and the biosphere, the idea of sustainability or sustainable development is increasingly viewed as an ill-fitting description of what needs to be accomplished. The sustainability concepts seem to build on an assumption of some level of predictability in the system governed.[3] Against this background, it is clear that the general legal concepts, approaches and goals are tested.

If environmental law is to stay relevant, it must develop in line with the knowledge that is provided by these perspectives on the earth system and the environment. It is a fact, of course, that law always develops and changes its applicability in relation to the development of society and that environmental law generally extends its interpretation in line with new scientific knowledge. However, the perspectives presented above raise a demand for other changes and pose new questions – questions of the effectiveness of environmental law and governance in this new context. Some scholars even argue that we need to reassess the entire content and effectiveness of environmental treaty regimes and take the lead to change law beyond its normative scope.[4] Either way, these new perspectives call for new legal approaches and pose significant challenges for legal design and for legal scholars to explore. New concepts and theories for effective laws are necessary.

The purpose of this book is to partake in that exploration of new theories and concepts, with a focus on international and EU environmental law. The aim is not to suggest a redesign of law as such. In fact, the aim, which is threefold, is (1) to explore the possibilities at hand within the scope of already existing legal regimes, (2) to propose a tool for assessing the potential effectiveness or vulnerability of environmental laws and legal systems, and (3) to reveal the

[2] Stephens, T., "Wishful Thinking? The Governance of Climate Change-Related Disasters in the Anthropocene," in Lyster, R. and Verchick, R. R. M. (eds.), *Research Handbook on Climate Disaster Law: Barriers and Opportunities*, Elgaronline, 2018b, p. 45.

[3] Benson, M. H. and Craig, R. K., 2017, p. 24, pp. 48–49 and pp. 48ff.

[4] Stephens, T., 2018a, pp. 124 and 137–138. See also Kotzé, L. J. and Kim, R. E., "Earth System Law: The Juridical Dimensions of Earth System Governance," *Earth System Governance*, Vol. 1, 2019.

necessary components for designing environmental laws or legal regimes equipped for an increasingly unpredictable earth system. The subject of this book is in a field of environmental law, which combines law with theories of social-ecological resilience (resilience theories). Social-ecological resilience is a transdisciplinary theoretical field within environmental science with close connections to policy and governance (see further in Section 1.1). The resilience theories are centered in the dynamic and complex interconnectedness that exists between human social systems and ecosystems, as described previously. The theories on social-ecological resilience provide an environmental governance framework with principles that take into account many crucial aspects that characterize such complex environmental problems (resilience governance).[5] This kind of governance represents 'effectiveness' in this study. Effectiveness is in this context understood as the ability of law and governance to safeguard or manage ecosystems and natural resources in the pursuit of human activities, so that the ecosystems remain resilient or in a 'sustainable' state. Understanding the role of law in resilience governance provides guidance on how law should be designed and operationalized in such environmental issue areas that are characterized by nonlinearity and complexity. Hence, exploring the role of law in resilience governance can provide answers to the challenges and questions posed here on the effectiveness of environmental law in the era of the Anthropocene with increasingly complex threats to the earth system.

Areas characterized by nonlinearity are areas that law generally has had trouble dealing with in a satisfactory manner.[6] This is why new legal methods and approaches need to be explored to find solutions. Complexity and nonlinear environmental problems are beyond the more traditional scope or assumptions of law. Besides the fact that the earth system may have been more predictable, or have been perceived as such, thus shaping laws that build on this assumption, law

5 See e.g. Biggs R., Schlüter M. and Schoon M. L. (eds.), *Principles for Building Resilience: Sustaining Ecosystem Services in Social-Ecological Systems*, Cambridge University Press, 2015a; Chapin, F. S., Kofinas, G. P. and Folke, C., (eds.), *Principles of Ecosystem Stewardship – Resilience-Based Natural Resource Management in a Changing World*, Springer, 2009; Reyers, B., et al., "Social-Ecological Systems Insights for Navigating the Dynamics of the Anthropocene," *Annual Review of Environment and Resources*, Vol. 43, 2018, pp. 267–289; Lebel, L., Anderies, J. M., Campbell, B., et al., "Governance and the Capacity to Manage Resilience in Regional Social-Ecological Systems," *Ecology and Society*, Vol. 11, No. 1, 2006.

6 See inter alia environmental law theories on this matter in Westerlund, S., *Miljörättsliga Grundfrågor* 2.0, IMIR Institutet för miljörätt, Åmyra förlag, Uppsala 2003, at pp. 56–70, and pp. 95–100; and Westerlund, S., *Fundamentals of Environmental Law Methodology*, Uppsala: Uppsala University, Department of Law, 2007, electronic version at http://uu.diva-portal.org/smash/get/diva2:903401/FULLTEXT01.pdf [2020-08-18], pp. 156ff.

is also based on its own need or assumption of predictability in relation to the principles of rule of law and legitimacy. The latter are also issues that must be taken into account when combining law with the theories of social-ecological resilience with the aim to explore new legal methods and approaches for complexity. In addition to the purpose of developing a proposed legal design that can deal with the complexity and interconnectedness of social-ecological systems and to the development of more effective environmental laws, reasons for writing a book where law is combined with and compared to theories on social-ecological resilience are also to contribute to an increasingly diverse transdisciplinary theoretical framework. To this end, it is an additional secondary aim to contribute to the practical application of the resilience theories. The book aims to be a practical guide besides its theoretical approach to the issues investigated. Many law scholars have explored the connection between law and social-ecological resilience from different perspectives, and much of that research enlightens the analysis in this study. The focus and method in this study are, however, reversed from most previous research (Section 1.2)

The theoretical approach chosen can provide answers to the questions and problems of environmental law for earth system governance characterized by complexity. However, the new conditions provided by an unpredictable and intertwined social-ecological earth system also create fundamental changes to the conditions for human activities and the basics of human life. The consequences for human activities, human lives and living conditions are also dimensions of social-ecological systems where law generally has an important role in creating stability and security. When natural resources are limited and the changes in the earth system also change the living conditions for large groups of people, then the access and distribution of such resources and the rights for those groups become central. Social stability is an issue of so-called social resilience (Section 1.1). It is definitely a task for law to control and regulate such rights and access to resources, and thus in this context, there is a central role for law in achieving social resilience.[7] Equity and fair distribution of

[7] This can be addressed in many different perspectives, see e.g. Raworth, K., "A Safe and Just Space for Humanity: Can We Live within the Doughnut?" Oxfam Discussion Paper, *Oxfam Policy and Practice: Climate Change and Resilience*, Vol. 8, No. 1, 2012, pp. 1–26; Dearing, J. A., et al., "Safe and Just Operating Spaces for Regional Social-Ecological Systems," *Global Environmental Change*, Vol. 28, 2014, pp. 227–238; Craig, R. K., et al., "Balancing Stability and Flexibility in Adaptive Governance: An Analysis of Tools Available in U.S. Environmental Law," *Ecology and Society*, Vol. 22, No. 2, 2017, p. 3; Folke, C., et al., "Transnational Corporations and the Challenge of Biosphere Stewardship," *Nat. Ecol. Evol.*, Vol. 3, 2019, pp. 1396–1403; Gonzales, C. G., "Global Justice in the Anthropocene," in Kotzé, L. J. (ed.), *Environmental Law and Governance for the Anthropocene*, Bloomsbury Publishing, 2017, eBook.

resources not only is a question of ethics but may also become a question of stability and of avoiding human disasters. However, these questions need to be covered by a separate study and will not be dealt with in depth in this book, although it is an equally important issue.

The resilience theories have developed over the past decades and rapidly become important at different levels of policy. They are also important for governance and management in many parts of the world, including in European and international environmental cooperation. The theoretical framework of social-ecological resilience is transdisciplinary; the study of and development of these theories include both ecology or other natural sciences, as well as different branches of humanity and social science, such as law, political science and sociology. The book builds on this previous research; it is both a stepping stone for this study as well as the backdrop against which the chosen perspectives are tested.

1.1 SOCIAL-ECOLOGICAL RESILIENCE

Resilience in social-ecological systems is a theoretical framework for research on environmental governance and management with a transdisciplinary perspective. There is no single theory on resilience, but resilience is generally described as a concept for assessing the resistance to pressures within a system. In an environmental context, this is seen as a state where a system can cope with threats, such as pollution or depletion of biological resources, and sustain its main structures and functions, thus avoiding a collapse or abrupt change. In this respect, a social-ecological resilience perspective generally takes a broad approach to the environment and mirrors a complex relationship between human social systems and natural ecological systems, where human beings and the social systems are seen as an integrated part of the biosphere or the earth system. The social-ecological system is then characterized as a complex adaptive system. Put simply, this means that environmental problems do not act in a linear or foreseeable way – as described in the introduction. Instead, they are characterized by irregular responses like surprise and cascading effects.[8]

[8] On the theoretical framework of Social-Ecological Resilience and its origin, see inter alia Biggs, R., Schlüter, M. and Schoon, M. L., (eds.), *Principles for Building Resilience: Sustaining Ecosystem Services in Social-Ecological Systems*, Cambridge University Press, 2015; Folke, C., "Resilience: The Emergence of a Perspective for Social-Ecological Systems Analysis," *Global Environmental Change*, Vol. 16, No. 3, 2006, pp. 253–267; Walker, B. and Salt, D., *Resilience Thinking – Sustaining Ecosystems and People in a Changing World*, Island Press, 2006; Folke, C., et al., "Resilience and Sustainable Development: Building Adaptive Capacity in a World of Transformations," *Ambio*, Vol. 31, No. 5, 2002, pp. 437–440; Liu, J., et al.,

A state of resilience entails prerequisites for a system to resist external pressures and retain its basic functions. From the perspective of ecology, this means a state where the ecosystem is able to continue developing and maintain the production of what we generally call ecosystem services.[9] The theories on resilience were originally developed by ecologists as a way to describe changes and interactions of ecological dynamics in and between ecosystems. In more elaborate terms, resilience in this context is the ability of a system to endure or absorb disturbances and external shocks in a way that makes it possible for the ecosystem to still maintain its particular dynamics, structure and functions. The connection made with social-ecological systems means a state where the social and ecological systems together create a resilient interconnected system. A resilient social-ecological system is, in simple terms, a state where the social system can gain from ecosystems services to maintain its basic needs and functions, and at the same time create prerequisites for ecosystem resilience and thus not overharvest and not create disturbances that pushes the ecosystems beyond the border of a resilient state. At the same time, acknowledging this interconnectedness also creates unpredictable and spontaneous changes that need to be accounted for in governance.

Beyond the connection and prerequisites created by ecosystem services for the state of social resilience, it must also be further explored what social resilience means. The knowledge on social resilience and how it is accomplished is less explored than ecological resilience. However, it seems easy to establish that law must have an important role in creating social resilience, beyond its dependence on resilient ecosystems. Not least issues of justice, access to resources and social justice are increasingly the focus of environmental governance. If these issues are not addressed, social resilience will not be achieved. What social resilience means and includes can be discussed, but generally social resilience is a prerequisite for social-ecological resilience (see Sections 3.3 and 3.4). Although the main focus in this study is on the role of law for governance of ecosystems, some aspects of the role of law for social resilience in connection to ecosystem governance are also further discussed.

"Complexity of Coupled Human and Natural Systems," *Science*, Vol. 317, No. 5844, 2007, pp. 1513–1516; Folke, C., et al., "Resilience Thinking: Integrating Resilience, adaptivity and Transformability," *Ecology and Society*, Vol. 15, No. 4, 2010, pp. 20–28; Folke, C., Jansson, Å., Rockström, J., et al., "Reconnecting to the Biosphere," *Ambio*, Vol. 40:719, 2011; Carpenter, S., et al., "From Metaphor to Measurement: Resilience of What to What?," *Ecosystems*, Vol. 4, 2001.

9 Ecosystem services are generally seen to be the material or energy outputs from ecosystems, including food, water and other resources or necessary functions of the ecosystem.

Effective environmental governance structures should aim to create resilience in social-ecological systems. The descriptions of the complex changes and interactions of ecological and social dynamics that are included in the resilience theories should constitute the basis for the governance approach and measures chosen – especially in the light of the Anthropocene. The resilience perspective and research on social-ecological resilience provide an important framework for identifying how to regulate environmental problems that are characterized by complexity and nonlinearity. As mentioned, these are also problems that create scenarios where the legal system is often challenged, since law originally builds on an idea of more linear causal relationships.[10] Moreover, the concept of social-ecological resilience creates a frame for a more integrated perspective on the operationalization of sustainable development. Many have argued for law and governance based on the principle of sustainable development and that it should be the ecological factors, which set the prerequisites for any other development (i.e., social and economic development in the concept of sustainable development).[11] The concept of social-ecological resilience also acknowledges that the environment sets the base and boundaries for any social-ecological system; however, it also acknowledges that the relationship between the different elements of social-ecological systems is complex.[12] It provides, as suggested, tools for how to manage these systems accordingly.

1.2 COMBINING SOCIAL-ECOLOGICAL RESILIENCE AND LAW

Because of the urgent need to find new solutions and new perspectives on sustainability, the theories on resilience and resilience governance are

10 See e.g. Westerlund, S., 2003, at pp. 56–70, and pp. 95–100; and Westerlund, S., 2007, electronic version at http://uu.diva-portal.org/smash/get/diva2:903401/FULLTEXT01.pdf [2020-08-18], pp. 156ff.

11 That is, the social system elements of sustainable development as discussed in, for example, the UN Report on Sustainable Development Report of the World Commission on Environment and Development: Our Common Future, 1987 (the Brundtland Report), Transmitted to the General Assembly as an Annex to document A/42/427 – Development and International Co-operation: Environment. The report laid out the concept of sustainable development as containing environmental, economic and social aspects. See e.g. Bosselmann, K., *The Principle of Sustainability: Transforming Law and Governance*, Ashgate, 2008, eBook [accessed 2016-09-11], generally and pp. 22ff.; and Bosselmann, K., Engel, R. and Taylor, P., *Governance for Sustainability: Issues, Challenges, Successes*, UCN Environmental Policy and Law Paper No. 70, IUCN, Gland, Switzerland, 2008 [accessed 2016-11-26], pp. 3ff. Cf. Benson, M. H. and Craig, K. R., 2017, where the authors argue that sustainability is no longer a useful concept in light of increasing complexity and unpredictability of the earth system.

12 Chapin, F. S., Folke, C. and Kofinas, G. P., "A Framework for Understanding Change," in Chapin, F. S., Kofinas, G. P., Folke, C., (eds.), Principles of Ecosystem Stewardship – Resilience-Based Natural Resource Management in a Changing World, Springer, New York, 2009, p. 6; Folke, C., et al., 2002.

receiving growing attention, from many directions – not least in policy making. Resilience theories also have an important connection to more general ideas of adaptive governance. As described, the concept of resilience was initially developed by ecologists and further on in transdisciplinary contexts, by environmental science, social science, humanities, and not least within political science. Law scholars are also exploring this field of research and have approached these topics with increasing interest in the past decade.[13] The study in this book builds on this previous research that has contributed and extended the resilience theories, both transdisciplinary and legal research. Much of the previous legal research on resilience governance and adaptive governance establishes the foundation of and adds to the understanding of the different components of governance that are identified and discussed here. However, much of the research done on resilience draws conclusions based on case studies. The approach taken in this study is the opposite; it aims to propose a legal design with a general applicability to any given case and does not take any specific case as its stepping stone.

The conclusions that other researchers have drawn based on case studies have provided a set of principles and features that are important in resilience

[13] Some of the most significant pieces of work in the field of integrating legal research with research on social-ecological resilience specifically are Arnold, C. A. and Gunderson, L. H., "Adaptive Law and Resilience," originally printed in *Environmental Law Reporter*, Vol. 43, No. 10427, 5–2013, Reprinted with copyright to Environmental Law Institute, Washington DC, 2013, University of Louisville, Legal Studies Research Paper Series, Paper No. 2104-04; Cosens, B. A., "Transboundary River Governance in the Face of Uncertainty: Resilience Theory and the Columbia River Treaty," *University of Utah Journal of Land Resources, and Environmental Law* Vol. 30, No. 2, 2011, pp. 229ff.; Cosens, B. and Gunderson, L. H., (eds.), *Practical Panarchy for Adaptive Water Governance – Linking Law to Social-Ecological Resilience*, Springer International Publishing AG, 2018; Ebbesson, J., "The Rule of Law in Governance of Complex Socio-Ecological Changes," *Global Environmental Change*, Vol. 20 (3), 2010, pp. 414–422; Garmestani, A. S., Allen, C. R. and Cabezas, H., "Panarchy, Adaptive Management and Governance: Policy Options for Building Resilience," *Nebraska Law Review*, Vol. 87, 2008, pp. 1036ff.; Garmestani, A. S. and Allen, C. R. (eds.), *Social-Ecological Resilience and Law*, Columbia University Press, 2014a; Green, O. O., et al., "Barriers and Bridges to the Integration of Social–Ecological Resilience and Law," *Frontiers in Ecology and the Environment*, Vol. 13, 2015a, pp. 332–337; Special Feature in *Ecology and Society* (two parts/issues): Part I – Garmestani, A. S., Allen, C. R. and Benson, M. H. (guest editors), "Special Feature on Law and Social-Ecological Resilience, Part I: Contributions from Resilience 2011," *Ecology and Society*, 2013, Vol. 18(2); and Part II – Ebbesson, J. and Hey, E. (guest editors), "Part II: Contributions from Law for Social-Ecological Resilience Symposium, Stockholm, Sweden, 2010," *Ecology and Society*, 2013, Vol. 18(3); Special Feature in *Ecology and Society*, Chaffin, B., Gunderson, L. and Cosens, B. C. (guest editors), "Practicing Panarchy: Assessing Legal Flexibility, Ecological Resilience, and Adaptive Governance in U.S. Regional Water Systems Experiencing Climate Change," *Ecology and Society*, 2018, Vol. 23(1).

governance. The study in this book builds on these principles for governance and explores how they are represented in law and legal systems, or how law in other ways can contribute to their role in the wider governance system. In this analysis, previous legal studies of social-ecological resilience are included as support and substantial understanding of how law can be seen in this context. The study also investigates potential obstacles or limits of the role of law in resilience governance based on these given governance principles. With the basis in this investigation, the study analyses the role of law in resilience governance structures and concludes on what components a legal design for resilience governance should include. The result is a proposed legal design or tools for the assessment of legal design with a broad application. Of course, that being said, all cases are unique and demands specific adjustments – the proposed components for legal design are not fixed, they must be seen as part of bigger system. As the study will show, the legal components or features discussed and presented are inter-dependent, and so the legal design with its different components will in the end also depend on how the other components are designed or function in each specific case. However, it will provide some answers to what kind of environmental laws, legal mechanisms and regimes may be necessary to approach such unpredictable and complex environmental problems that are characteristic of the Anthropocene.

In this book, a model for a legal system compatible with resilience theories and governance is created through comparing the main principles of resilience governance with law, legal principles and other law mechanisms. Mechanisms in this sense means functions of law and legal regulatory constructions. The study both reviews the fundaments of law and its principles as such, and addresses legal institutional frameworks or structures as they normally are constituted, both in terms of deliberate functions and features, and in how they have come to be developed in perhaps a more dynamic and spontaneous way to adopt certain functions and features. Such a legal system model, as suggested, will represent a structure for how law should be designed and combined in order to serve the same purpose as, and otherwise contribute to, resilience governance. To this end, the book provides a comprehensive review of some of the most fundamental components of the governance framework for social-ecological resilience and their compatibility with law – more specifically, the compatibility with international and EU law. As such, it presents a theoretical analysis of how these main components of resilience governance compare to and can be integrated in law, as well as how they can be operationalized in a legal structure. The main focus is put on the theoretical basis for the design of such legal system, but it will be illustrated and exemplified by examples from case law and contemporary regulatory structures.

1.3 THE CHALLENGES FOR ENVIRONMENTAL LAW AND GOVERNANCE

International environmental law started to develop in the late 1960s with the United Nations Conference on the Human Environment (the Stockholm Conference) in 1972 as a first milestone. Its development was both a response to and in parallel with increasing environmental concerns. It is increasingly acknowledged and accepted that laws can be regarded as one component in a network of institutions, steering instruments and measures included in governance and management.[14] Environmental law has thus developed beside and partly together with developments in theories on environmental governance. International environmental law is also continuously developing as a response to changing knowledge and perception of environmental problems and environmental values – and has provided more and less precise answers to the need for governing transboundary international commons and other shared resources of environmental concern.

Environmental law is primarily characterized by its aim to balance significant scientific uncertainties in the dynamics and complexity of environmental problems with other more direct values and measures in the social system, such as the fundamental values of legal systems and the rule of law. Additionally, environmental law must balance or value economic and political dimensions in connection to environmental protection. These aspects are also connected to the role of law for social resilience. As discussed in the introduction, the growing environmental complexity confronts the legal system with new challenges; this also opens the matter to other viewpoints and disciplinary fields in a manner similar to that of governance for social-ecological resilience. This is displayed through adjustments in the legal approaches to environmental challenges and changes. Environmental law instruments aim to be dynamic, holistic and adaptive in response to the environment. As a result, however, questions also increasingly arise about effectiveness, legitimacy in relation to the choice of legal instrument, legal design and new approaches. Furthermore, these concepts of law may include

14 See e.g. the definition of global governance in: Commission on Global Governance, *Our Global Neighbourhood – The Report of the Commission on Global Governance*, Oxford University Press, 1995, p. 2f.

or entail both legal and extra-legal measures or mechanisms, all with the aim of matching environmental governance and management structures.[15]

The resilience perspective views humans as part of the biosphere or the earth system and assumes that the resulting intertwined social-ecological systems behave as so-called complex adaptive systems.[16] Social-ecological resilience has developed since the 1970s as a school of interdisciplinary research on the interplay and integration of social and ecological systems, searching for factors that promote social-ecological resilience. Law has developed in parallel. Already in the 1972 Declaration of the United Nations Conference on the Human Environment[17] (the Stockholm Declaration), a scenario similar to that of the Anthropocene was described, stating that "through the rapid acceleration of science and technology, man has acquired the power to transform his environment in countless ways and on an unprecedented scale."[18] This highly important issue has continued to receive attention but remains insufficiently addressed.

The ultimate goal for sustainable development is a world where the prerequisites for social and economic development are coherent with an environmental frame and thus the limits of the biosphere.[19] In the same way, social-ecological resilience inter alia signifies the state described previously – a state in which the interdependence between social and ecological systems is at a level where the ecosystem can resist pressures, and retain its function and structure despite these pressures. Ecosystems must retain their functions and structures for many different reasons. It is important with regard to the ecosystem itself and with regard to social systems, as with regard to sustaining

15 See e.g. de Sadeleer, N., *Environmental Principles – From Political Slogans to Legal Rules*, Oxford University Press, 2002, pp. 305ff.; Bodansky, D., Brunnée, J. and Hey, E., "International Environmental Law – Mapping the Field," in Bodansky, D., Brunnée, J. and Hey, E. (eds.), *The Oxford Handbook of International Environmental Law*, Oxford University Press, 2007b, generally and at pp. 21–23.

16 Biggs, R., Schlüter, M. and Schoon, M. L., 2015b, p.1.

17 11 ILM 1972, p. 1416.

18 Declaration of the United Nations Conference on the Human Environment (the Stockholm Declaration), Preamble, paragraph 1.

19 See World Commission on Environment and Development: Our Common Future, 1987, Chapter I – Section 3, Para 27, stating: "Humanity has the ability to make development sustainable to ensure that it meets the needs of the present without compromising the ability of future generations to meet their own needs. The concept of sustainable development does imply limits – not absolute limits but limitations imposed by the present state of technology and social organization on environmental resources and by the ability of the biosphere to absorb the effects of human activities." More on how this concept has developed as a general principle, its interpretation and legal status can be found in Barstow Magraw, D. and Hawke, L. D., "Sustainable Development," in Bodansky, D., Brunnée, J. and Hey, E., (eds.), 2007, pp. 613 ff.

social-ecological resilience. One particular factor that is often brought to attention with regard to ecosystem functions, however, is the connection to so-called ecosystem services in resilient ecosystems. Ecosystem services are the aspects of the ecosystem functions that are directly important, or even absolutely necessary, for social welfare and development on a number of levels and in many different ways.[20]

As a reaction to this transformational, all-encompassing environmental impact, and the large-scale human transformations of the earth system, environmental research is now focusing on identifying boundaries or buffer zones for environmental transformations of the earth system. Seeking to avoid catastrophic risks for society and irreversible environmental change on both regional and a global, planetary scale, this research strives to find limits to the use of environmental resources – through pressures and ecosystem services – which humans must keep within. So far, this research has suggested nine specific areas of planetary boundaries as particularly important.[21] These nine planetary boundaries are climate change, changes in biosphere integrity, stratospheric ozone depletion, ocean acidification, biogeochemical flows, land-system change, freshwater use, atmospheric aerosol loading and novel entities (new substances, new forms of existing substances and modified life-forms that have the potential for unwanted geophysical and/or biological effects – like chemical pollution etc.). The research on planetary boundaries shows that some of the boundaries are connected and that several already are transgressed. Although these planetary boundaries are quantified primarily on a global scale, they must be controlled and governed to the greatest extent on the regional and local scale.[22] The operationalization of such goals in political and global institutional structures may meet obstacles.[23] The resilience governance must aim to keep the earth system within these boundaries – hence, this is also the new role of law on a global scale.

In the situation as it is pictured here, almost all these global environmental problems are connected to regional and sometimes local scales. To a large extent, global problems are the sum of degradation in different regions. Not

[20] Biggs R., Schlüter, M. and Schoon, M. L., 2015b, pp. 13ff.

[21] More specific definition of these are found in Rockström, J., et al., "Planetary Boundaries: Exploring the Safe Operating Space for Humanity," *Ecology and Society*, Vol. 14(2):32, 2009.

[22] Rockström, J., et al., 2009; Biermann, F., et al., "Navigating the Anthropocene: Improving Earth System Governance," *Policy Forum, Science*, Vol. 335, No. 6074, 2012; Steffen, W., et al., "Planetary Boundaries: Guiding Human Development on a Changing Planet," *Science*, Vol. 347, No. 6223, 2015.

[23] Saunders, F., "Planetary Boundaries: At the Threshold . . . Again: Sustainable Development Ideas and Politics," *Environment, Development and Sustainability: A Multidisciplinary Approach to the Theory and Practice of Sustainable Development*, Vol. 17(4), 2015, pp. 823–835.

many of the global scale problems confronting the world today will be solved only through cooperation on a global scale. While global communication and cooperation through universal agreements are necessary in many issue areas, in creating prerequisites for action around the world, the solutions will mainly be found on smaller spatial scales. The global issues will be narrowed down to regional cooperation and national or local action.[24] Through cooperation on common-pool resources or common-pool problems, on all scales, we can also bridge the boundaries set up by State borders, of which pollution and environmental damage take no notice. Therefore, success in solving the crucial global problems facing us today will depend greatly on how we manage our international cooperation both globally and especially on a regional scale. If we find mechanisms, structures and tools that work and spread incentives for action, it is most likely that they will be implemented and successful on a regional scale. That is why it is also relevant to discuss the design of international environmental law, environmental legal agreements, international treaty regimes, as well as EU law – with great significance for the whole European region. This is also why it is important not only to scrutinize existing structures to find solutions to obvious problems, but also to identify the components that may make the difference. It is not least important, then, to identify the role of law, and legal mechanisms, that plays a part in these processes and in successful institutions.

This book introduces a theoretical perspective on how law should be designed to provide a suitable institutional structure for the promotion of social-ecological resilience and to keep the earth system within the planetary boundaries. The chosen perspective on law in this book is part of a new, rapidly growing, theoretical area of interest in law and environmental governance. Increasing internationalization and globalization make the causes and effects of environmental problems more difficult to define, just as the different actors involved, and thus the problems are more difficult to control. They are difficult to control since they are complex environmental problems, and complexity is generally due to nonlinear causality in the relationships between societies and ecosystems. It all reflects an increasingly plural, polycentric world order and societies with many different operators and stakeholders, including both polluters and regulators, which complicates the interconnected relationship between humans and the environment and makes the context of legal rules more difficult to overview. Altogether, this creates a situation with many dimensions that blurs the possibility for traditional foreseeability, strict rules, and strict control. As a consequence, environmental problems must be seen in new

[24] See also Folke, C., et al., 2010.

perspectives; other forms of legislation techniques, as well as other forms of compliance review, may be called for. In addition, the concept of the ecosystem approach is becoming a common approach within many modern environmental law instruments. The theories presented on social-ecological resilience can provide support to the interpretation and implementation of an ecosystem approach in legal systems. The study also includes a discussion on the connection between social-ecological resilience and the concept of ecosystem approach. There are strong similarities between typical features in a governance system reflecting characteristics for social-ecological resilience and features and governance principles constituting the concept of ecosystem approach. The resilience theories therefore also form an interesting basis for evaluating the implementation of an ecosystem approach.

1.4 OUTLINE

The book can thematically be seen as divided in two different parts. The first part (Chapters 1–4) introduces the subject and the foundations that the study will be built on, or take as stepping stones. The second part (Chapters 5–9) analyzes the compatibility between law and social-ecological resilience based on a range of features that are defined and discussed in the first part (Chapter 4).

So, after this first general introduction to the subject and purpose (Chapter 1), the book continues to engage more specifically with the different foundations that form the study. The characteristics of environmental law are reviewed (Chapter 2). The general objectives and approaches of international and EU environmental law are presented and the overall scope of environmental law today is analyzed. The study aims to compare law with resilience governance and build a matching legal design; therefore it is necessary to start looking at the building blocks that environmental law provides us with. The core of this study is the role of law in governance and specifically in resilience governance, and thus the next chapter reviews the connection between environmental governance, law and social-ecological resilience (Chapter 3). This is an evaluation and analysis of the relationship between law and governance, and includes the important task of placing law in the theoretical framework of governance for social-ecological resilience. With these ground stones laid out, the following chapter reviews more specifically the theories of social-ecological resilience and resilience governance (Chapter 4). This review of the theories of social-ecological resilience includes analyzing and defining some core principles or features for resilience governance. These features for governance set the structure for further study.

In the second part, law is analyzed based on the defined resilience features. In this way, the components of a legal design for social-ecological resilience are being shaped and assessed and the role of law for resilience governance is analyzed. The features analyzed are adaptivity, flexibility and transformability; multidimensional and polycentric structures; stakeholders and structures for participation; and operationalization, monitoring, compliance and trust building. The chapter on adaptivity, flexibility and transformation reviews the ability and potential obstacles for law to include adaptive and flexible legal mechanisms in the same manner as resilience governance (Chapter 5). Multidimensional and polycentric structures is a chapter that reviews to what extent law reflects the resilience governance aim of multilevel governance, redundant approaches and cross-scale interaction, with the aim to match the dynamics of the ecosystem (Chapter 6). The resilience theories address many important aspects of including stakeholders in the governance and the reflection of these features is reviewed in the chapter on stakeholders and structures for participation (Chapter 7). Finally, the ultimate aim of all environmental governance – the ability to actually make change and steer the ecosystem toward a more sustainable or resilient state – is also discussed. In the context of law and legal terms, this is analyzed in terms of operationalization, monitoring, compliance and trust building (Chapter 8). The last chapter summarizes the finding of the review of resilience features and the legal design for social-ecological resilience (Chapter 9). It also presents some final aspects that are important to take into account when applying the legal model created.

2

Environmental Law

Before going further with the study on the compatibility of law and resilience governance, the general features of environmental law will be presented. Over time, environmental law has developed its own legal techniques, norms, approaches and principles with the aim to match the dynamic and holistic perspectives of the ecosystem. However, law also have features that match ecosystem dynamics or resilience governance, although based in functions that are not deliberately designed in such way. These different functions of environmental law are important since they are the pieces of law that will form the legal components that will be scrutinized and that can be compatible with and reflect the different features of social-ecological resilience governance. It also entails that it is important to understand the basic fundaments of how law works.

Environmental law has been in constant development since it started to form as its own field of law in the late 1960s, often as a reflection of the current understanding of the environment and the environmental problems at each point in time. In the 1980s and the 1990s, the concept of sustainable development informed and influenced the shape and role of environmental laws. In recent years, new perspectives on the environment and the understanding of environmental problems include ideas and theories on more complex problems and connections.[1]

Now focus is on this more fundamental shift in the view of the impact that human activities have on the environment and the entire earth system. The resilience theories connect to a focus on complex problems, earth system change, a shift to the Anthropocene and the research on planetary boundaries.

[1] On the general development of international environmental law, see e.g. Sands, P., "The Evolution of International Environmental Law," in Bodansky, D., Brunnée, J. and Hey, E. (eds.), *The Oxford Handbook of International Environmental Law*, Oxford University Press, 2007.

This, of course, are changes that must also be reflected in law and the legal approaches to governance.

The purpose of the study in this book is to examine how law can be designed to match and contribute to social-ecological resilience. This builds on the current state of environmental law and legal systems as they are created and function today. Although the aim is to present a new framework for creating and assessing environmental law in relation to resilience theories, the components as such will be based in current laws and legal systems – only in a new setting. The extent to which law is equipped to adjust to these circumstances and contribute to governance for social-ecological resilience will in part depend on how we interpret and identify different forms of measures, regulatory approaches and other mechanisms in environmental law. This chapter aims to explain some of the fundaments of environmental law and pinpoint approaches techniques, norms, approaches, principles and other mechanisms that are characteristic for environmental law. These characteristic mechanisms will be important components of the legal constructions and designs as the focus of this study.

2.1 INTERNATIONAL ENVIRONMENTAL LAW

International environmental law is a field within international law. This means that beyond the specific environmental law principles and characteristics, the general features and principles that apply to the creation and interpretation of international law also apply to international environmental law. Formally, the field of international environmental law started to form after the Stockholm Conference in 1972, making it a rather young field of international law. A basic general foundation in international law is the principle that all States are sovereign and thereby independent in relation to other States when it comes to legal authority and political decisions within the State territory. This is important to keep in mind, since it creates the prerequisites for cooperation and the development of legal instruments. When States adopt international agreements, this principle stipulates that each State that becomes a Party to the agreement in question must expressively agree to and accept the provisions before becoming a Party. As a result, provisions on treaty bodies and especially structures for dispute settlement are agreed on separately. This is a foundation or prerequisite that also imbues international law with its specific nature and characteristics. Moreover, it represents both the most obvious obstacles as well as the most obvious prerequisites for international cooperation and compliance. The obstacles can be connected to the difficulties involved in agreeing on concrete and purposeful provisions when many States negotiating an agreement must manage to agree to a final text.

Moreover, it is an obstacle to the possibility to force any State into external dispute settlement or into agreeing to transfer a claim of alleged noncompliance for review by an international court. A positive view of what is provided by this system, on the other hand, is related to the fact that it could also be seen as a prerequisite of genuine engagement. Any State can choose to withdraw from its intention to enter into an agreement and thereby deny cooperation if it does not consider the text agreed upon as relevant and reasonable. All States are of course sovereign and have the basic freedom to act according to their own will in the international community. The international legal system also builds on an international system of rule of law.[2]

Most modern environmental agreements have their own independent treaty bodies that form separate institutional structures with competence to lead the work among the Parties and to develop the provisions of the agreement. It is important to realize why such structures for decision-making have been developed. An institutional structure with the possibility to take new decisions, and adapt and develop the contents of an agreement, is necessary due to the dynamic and continuous development of environmental problems.[3] This aspect of international agreements is also important when discussing the interpretation of international law. Opinion is divided on how to view international agreements. Although the 1969 *Vienna Convention on the Law of Treaties*[4] (the Vienna Convention) has formalized a set of rules for the interpretation of agreements, there is no one clear answer on the correct way to pursue such interpretation. The different views can be described as being on a spectrum, where one end is described as a strictly legal realm where a treaty interpretation will have a determinate result and law is seen as a self-contained regime. The other end consists of the opinion that international law is dynamic and affected by other agreements and political statements. From this point of view, legal norms are not capable of constraining political judgment.[5] However, especially

[2] For a general review of the development and status of international environmental law, see e.g. Birnie, P., Boyle, A. and Redgwell, C., *International Law and the Environment*, 3rd ed., Oxford University Press, 2009, pp. 1–42.

[3] See e.g. Gehring, T., "Treaty-Making and Treaty Evolution," in Bodansky, D., Brunnée, J. and Hey, E. (eds.), 2007, p. 473, and pp. 474–475; Ulfstein, G., "Treaty Bodies," in Bodansky, D., Brunnée, J. and Hey, E. (eds.), 2007, pp. 880ff. See also Churchill, R. and Ulfstein, G., "Autonomous Institutional Arrangements in Multilateral Environmental Agreements: A Little-Noticed Phenomenon in International Law," *The American Journal of International Law*, Vol. 94, No. 4, 2000, pp. 623–659.

[4] 1155 UNTS 331.

[5] See more about this in Linderfalk, U., *On the Interpretation of Treaties – The Modern International Law as Expressed in the 1969 Vienna Convention on the Law of Treaties*, Springer, 2007, pp. 4 and 373ff.

Article 31 of the Vienna Convention is of interest when reviewing and assessing the interpretation and application of an agreement that has developed over time. This Article establishes principles for interpretation that includes subsequent practices and other agreements between the Parties. Such principles of interpretation are relevant for the development of international law and new management approaches.[6]

2.2 ENVIRONMENTAL LAW AND THE EUROPEAN UNION

EU law is based on the principle of conferred powers, meaning that the EU can only act in areas where a legal base has been established through a transfer by the Member States of competence to act.[7] This means that there has to be a legal base provided for the EU to create and adopt legal acts in different areas. This structure makes the EU a supranational regime rather than an international legal system, although the EU does not have a full veto in regard to its Member States. The structure builds on majority and qualified majority voting. As in international law, environmental regulation and environmental law principles also are central to the legal regime of the EU. Environmental law was not mentioned in the original Treaties of the EU. It emerged later in parallel with increased environmental concern and the developments on the international scene after the Stockholm Conference in 1972. The environmental policies were then first addressed by a line of Environmental Action Programmes (EU EAPs). It was first in 1987 that a specific environmental legal base was created within the EU legal regime.[8]

Today the EU is a key driver of environmental policy in Europe, with important impacts on domestic law. EU environmental law is based mainly on principles found in Articles 191–193 of the Treaty on the Functioning of the EU (TFEU). According to Article 191(2) TFEU, the EU environmental law aims at a high level of environmental protection. Furthermore, in the Treaty on the European Union (TEU) it is stated that "it [the Union] shall work for the sustainable development of Europe" and "a high level of protection and improvement of the quality of the environment."[9] In addition to the basic

6 See especially the Vienna Convention, Article 31(3).

7 See Articles 1 and 5(2) TEU and Article 2, TFEU. See also Craig, P. and de Búrca, G., *EU Law – Text, Cases, and Materials*, 5th ed., Oxford University Press, 2011, pp. 73ff.

8 Articles 191–193 TFEU was introduced in the Maastricht Treaty on the European Union as Articles 130r, 130s and 130t EEC. See further in Jans, J. H. and Vedder, H. H. B., *European Environmental Law after Lisbon*, 4th ed., Europa Law Publishing, 2012, pp. 6ff. See also Langlet, D. and Mahmoudi, S., *EU Environmental Law and Policy*, Oxford University Press, 2016, pp. 27ff.

9 Article 3(3) TEU.

environmental values in TFEU, the environmental law principles developed in international environmental law are the cornerstones of EU environmental law (Section 2.4.1).[10] Particularly the precautionary principle, the polluter pays principle and the no-harm-principle (although mentioned as the principle of preventive action) were established as a base for the EU environmental law in Article 191(2). Although their impact is in doubt, the principles still influence EU environmental laws.[11] Thus, environmental law principles are creating a framework for not only environmental protection under international law but also for environmental law of the EU.

The EU also plays a significant role in the international community, where the EU is a Party to a multitude of different agreements. As a Party and actor in the field of international law, the EU takes part in both the creation and implementation of international law. According to the TEU, the EU shall contribute to "the strict observance and the development of international law" as well as to "the sustainable development of the Earth."[12] When negotiating and entering into international (or regional) agreements, the EU can be an important actor, pushing for strict agreements. When these agreements are transposed into EU law, it follows that the rules emanating from the EU obligations generally become more strictly enforced than in relation to international law.[13] This is connected to the much stricter compliance control structures found in the EU due to the conferred competence and the supranational regime that constitutes the EU, compared to most international legal regimes. As a result, the EU legal acts typically have more tangible effects for the Member States in comparison to international legal regimes.[14]

Shared competence, with minimum harmonization, on which the EU environmental law is based, constitutes an important feature of EU environmental legislation since this means that the Member States are allowed to take more, but not less, protective measures compared to the EU rules. Legislation based on the EU's environmental policy entails only this minimum harmonization. Individual Member States may thus decide on more far-reaching protective measures as long as they are compatible with the aim of the EU

[10] Langlet, D. and Mahmoudi, S., 2016, pp. 28ff.

[11] See e.g. Jans, J. H. and Vedder, H. H. B., 2012, p. 41; Krämer, L., *EU Environmental Law*, 7th ed., Sweet and Maxwell, 2011, pp. 14–16.

[12] Article 3(5) TEU.

[13] The structure for enforcing laws is stricter in the EU compared to international law, but it must also be noted that legal research shows that the number of cases and the repetitive nature of infringements brought to the commission rather implies that it is not effective. See Wennerås, P., *The Enforcement of EC Environmental Law*, Oxford University Press, 2007, p. 251.

[14] Langlet, D. and Mahmoudi, S., 2016, pp. 131ff.; Wennerås, P., 2007, pp. 251ff.

law and its objectives in the specific area. Other criteria are also set through general EU law principles; national legislation must then be proportional and not arbitrarily discriminatory in its effects on trade between the Member States.[15] There is, however, a strong tendency among Member States to regard EU environmental legislation as setting a standard that national legislation should not exceed, for fear of harming the individual States' economic interests.[16]

2.2.1 *Implementation and Enforcement of EU Law*

Implementation and enforcement of EU legislation is generally a responsibility of the Member States. In comparison with international law that must first be accepted and ratified by the State before it becomes binding, the supranational structure of the EU legal order entails that the laws adopted become binding on the Member States without prior approval or ratification. It is already indirectly accepted with the transfer of competence. In this way, the individual Member States have abandoned the ability to block legislation adopted by the EU, although the Member States do vote on new legislation.[17] Legislation by the EU takes different forms, however, depending on the issue area and the competence given. The main forms of legislative instruments are regulations, directives and decisions.[18] Regulations are the most direct and detailed form of legislation in the EU. They are binding in their entirety and are directly applicable within all Member States. Directives differ from regulations in that they are only binding with regard to what is to be achieved, they leave the choices of methods, measures or mechanisms to the Member States. Directives thus have to be implemented and are not directly applicable. The third alternative, decisions, are just like regulations in that they are binding in their entirety, but are only binding on those to whom the decision is addressed.[19]

In the field of environmental law, the EU has also developed a legislating technique or approach that aims to adapt to the diversity and different prerequisites and pressures provided in different regions in the EU. It is a legislative

15 Measures adopted by an individual Member State have to be consistent with the EU treaties, not least the rules on free movement of goods set out in Articles 34 to 36 TFEU and the case law of the EU Court. On harmonization and minimum harmonization generally, see e.g. Jans, J. H. and Vedder, H. H. B., 2012, pp. 97ff.

16 Jans J.H., et al., "'Gold Plating' of European Environmental Measures?," *Journal for European Environmental and Planning Law*, Vol. 6(4), 2009, pp. 417–435.

17 According to Article 192 TFEU, it is only legislation that is supported by consensus, or a qualified majority of Member States representing a qualified majority of the EU citizens that can be adopted.

18 TFEU Article 288.

19 See a more detailed description in Craig, P. and de Búrca, G., 2011, pp. 104ff.

structure that is open to local response and regional differences in the environment. This approach to regulating environmental problems has been imposed primarily by so-called framework directives and is partly a product of what has been called new governance, which started to emerge in the EU in the 1990s. A general call for more open institutions, and participation by the general public, together with increased accountability and effectiveness of policies taken, was published in a white paper on European governance in 2001 (the EU Commission White Paper on Governance).[20] Framework legislation is found also in other areas of EU law as a response to a call for more open and flexible governance in the EU in general. The most significant and prominent examples have been developed in EU environmental law, where there was an apparent need for this kind of legislation – laws that are flexible and adjustable not only to the different regions and countries but also to environmental variations.[21] Directive 2000/60/EC, establishing a framework for Community action in the field of water policy, the Water Framework Directive,[22] was one of the first and most significant legal acts of this kind. What this entails with regard to legislation and governance perspectives will be discussed further later in this chapter.

The EU regime is based on a structure of independent EU institutions and bodies. Some of the most significant institutions are the Commission, the Council, the European Council and the European Parliament. In addition, the EU regime has a specific court system, which includes the Court of Justice (the EU Court).[23] Through this institutional system, the EU provides for relatively strong monitoring and enforcement. The EU Commission is independent from the Member States and has a special role in the EU institutional structure. Not only does it have the exclusive role of proposing new legislation; it also has the task of supervising and enforcing compliance.[24] To ensure compliance by individual Member States, the EU Commission has the responsibility to make a primary review of implementation and enforcement of the EU laws.[25] The work of the EU Commission is supported by agencies

[20] EU White Paper (2001), Communication from the EU Commission, "European Governance – A White Paper," Brussels, 25.7.2001, EU COM (2001) 428 final, OJ Document: 2001/C 287/01.

[21] EU White Paper (2001), pp. 11f, "Proposals for change"; Jänicke, M. and Jörgens, H., "New Approaches to Environmental Governance" in Jänicke, M. and Jacob, K. (eds.), *Environmental Governance in Global Perspective: New Approaches to Ecological Modernisation* (FFU Report 01–2006) Freie Universität, Berlin, 2006; and Von Homeyer, I., "The Evolution of EU Environmental Governance," in Scott, L. (ed.), *Environmental Protection – European Law and Governance*, Oxford University Press, 2009.

[22] OJ L 327, pp. 1–73.

[23] Langlet, D. and Mahmoudi, S., 2016, p. 11.

[24] Article 17(1) and (2) TEU.

[25] Article 17 TEU.

and directorates organized in different issue areas. As part of this responsibility, the Commission also has the exclusive right to initiate (and determine) infringement procedures in the EU Court.[26] The EU Court makes judgments regarding the correct interpretation and implementation of EU law. The channels otherwise available for judicial review under EU law, in general, are rare. National courts have the firsthand role of testing national law in relation to EU legislation, but they also have the choice to refer a case from a national court to the EU Court, in order to receive a more authoritative interpretation. The most direct way for a natural or legal person to have judicial review according to the EU law is to initiate a case in a national court directly supported by EU law and the principle of direct effect.[27] A secondary alternative is to ask for a preliminary ruling according to 267 TFEU, in the national court.[28] If the court finds that a State is non-compliant with the EU law, it will demand that implementation and application are changed, and in addition, severe fines may be levied.

This system means that EU law stands a better chance of being effectively enforced than do purely international agreements. At the same time, EU legislation – particularly that based on the rationale of the internal EU market – has much more potential than international law to restrain individual States that want to take protective measures on their own.[29]

2.2.2 *The EU as an Actor in International Environmental Law*

The EU has the competence to enter into international agreements.[30] The external policies of the EU are primarily expressed in Article 21 TEU. The article articulates a common, overarching set of principles or a framework with

26 Article 17(1) TEU, and additionally Article 258 TFEU about the right to take a Member State to the EU Court.

27 Together with the principle of Primacy of EU law, the principle of Direct Effect regulates the relationship between EU law and national legal systems. Well-established case law gives EU law priority over national law; it also establishes that this principle can be invoked by concerned individuals and companies if the provisions are unconditional (i.e., do not require any additional measures) and are sufficiently clear and precise (Case 6/64 *Costa v ENEL* ECLI:EU:C:1964:66 and Case 26/62 van *Gend and Loos* ECLI:EU:C:1963:1). A Declaration (no. 17) concerning primacy is now also confirming this principle as part of the Lisbon Treaty, in the Annex to the Final Act of the Intergovernmental Conference, which adopted the Treaty of Lisbon. See further in Langlet, D. and Mahmoudi, S., 2016, pp. 17ff.

28 Article 19 TEU.

29 This is regarding the secondary legislation based on article 113 TFEU or its predecessor article 95 in the previous EC Treaty.

30 Article 47 TEU creates a first prerequisite since it declares that the EU has a legal personality, which is a formal requirement.

objectives for EU international relations. Beyond general principles such as the rule of law, human rights and a respect for the Charter of the United Nations (the UN Charter),[31] it furthermore sets out that the EU inter alia shall seek to develop relations with third countries and international, regional or global organizations. The EU shall also define and pursue common policies and actions that foster for example environmental development, and furthermore help develop measures to improve environmental quality and sustainable management of natural resources, in order to ensure sustainable development. To some extent, the EU now has exclusive competence to enter into international agreements, according to 3(2) TFEU.[32]

Just like any Party to an international agreement, the EU becomes obligated when it ratifies a treaty. This obligation to enforce agreements is independent of the different Member States, which may also be Party to the agreement, in parallel with the EU. As a result of its international obligations, the EU regularly transforms international law into provisions of EU law. This is particularly important because the EU also has mechanisms for compliance control and adjudication that resemble those of a State more than those generally found in international law. A significant aspect of EU law is that all obligations and principles adopted by the EU must be transposed into concrete obligations for the EU Member States. This means that the general principles of international environmental law not only set a framework for regulation in EU law but also become the object of a more direct implementation or application, influenced by the precedents of international environmental law.[33] In a case of non-compliance with an international agreement, or rather an EU legal act that followed as an adoption of an international obligation, the EU Court might also indirectly interpret the international law obligations.[34]

As stated, the EU has the competence to create binding legislation in many areas. In addition, the EU has exclusive competence in some areas and the possibility to impose full regulatory harmonization in certain issue areas. However, the issues regulated with the environment as a primary base are not in a field of such harmonization or of exclusive competence; the

[31] The Charter of the United Nations and Statute of the International Court of Justice, signed on 26 June 1945 in San Francisco, USA.

[32] See more in e.g. Jans, J. H. and Vedder, H. H. B., 2012, pp. 64 ff.

[33] Langlet, D. and Mahmoudi, S., 2016, pp. 128f.

[34] A similar argument is developed in Ebbesson, J., "Implementing and Enforcing the Baltic Sea Convention through European Community Law," in Führ, M., Wahl, R. and von Wilmowsky, P. (eds.), *Umweltrecht und Umweltwissenschaft – Festschrift für Eckhard Rehbinder*, Erich Schmidt Verlag, 2007b, pp. 693–704.

environment is an area of shared competence between the EU and the Member States. Only a minimum harmonization is required, providing some opportunity for a Member State to have more far-reaching environmental legislation (Section 2.2). Still, if the EU has used its competence, there is little room for the States to act beyond this.

In addition to the general aspects of the EU as a Party in the international community, an important aspect is that it may entail a possibility for the EU to introduce its own legal mechanisms. Because the EU is an important and active participant in many international constellations, effective EU measures and mechanisms could be transferred into, and indirectly develop, the international principles and agreements. Many of the EU obligations placed on Member States in the environmental field are more far-reaching in some aspects compared to obligations of international law. Furthermore, as a result of the EU environmental law developments, the environmental policy agenda of the EU Member States is now largely determined by the need to implement European environmental law and to anticipate and shape European measures and action plans. The EU is Party to a number of international law agreements and thus as a Party has implemented or transferred much of these obligations into EU legislation, which also contributes to the agenda setting for national environmental laws and policy in the EU Member States.[35]

2.3 THE SCOPE OF ENVIRONMENTAL LAW

Environmental law can simply be defined as an area of law that aims to protect the environment and human health as well as regulating the use of natural resources. However, even if environmental law is seen as an area of law on its own, environmental law touches upon and combines many different fields of law. The common denominator for these different fields of law where environmental law can make claims is that they also in some aspect regulate natural resources and the protection of the environment and human health, or at least include aspects that play an important role for these objectives of environmental law. Environmental law can in this way take many different forms. Whether it concerns national, regional or international legislation, the area of law or legal approach chosen will primarily reflect the instrument, the aim and focus on what to achieve as well as the field in which it is placed.

Beyond the focus and aim on the environmental problem to be solved, it is noteworthy that an applicable legal instrument or legal structure may also

35 Jans, J. H. and Vedder, H. H. B., 2012, pp. 64ff.; Jänicke, M. and Jörgens, H., 2006, p. 173; von Homeyer, I., 2009.

include completely different functions or considerations than those directly relevant for the environmental goal. Such other considerations can be found in a diverse range of societal issues that need to be taken into account in addition to the environmental issues at stake, but which are also to be regarded as part of environmental law. These issues can include factors such as important stakeholder and interest group positions, as well as inter alia politically or economically motivated measures or goals. In a way, these kinds of aspects are also interesting to discuss in relation to the concept of social-ecological resilience. They reflect another role of law in this interplay between social and ecological. Besides contributing to effective governance of ecosystem and the environment, law also has an important role in establishing a legitimate and stable State or regime, building on the rule of law. Hence, this contributes more directly also to creating social resilience as discussed above (Section 1.1), which is just as important as a prerequisite for social-ecological resilience as ecological resilience.

Environmental law, forming its own area of international law, furthermore includes a number of area-specific principles, norms and legislation techniques that have developed at different levels in the environmental law field. These developments have been a result of the kind of change and adjustments that the environmental law field has undergone in its aim to focus on the specific nature and dynamics of the object of protection – thus a result of the changes in knowledge and perceptions of environmental problems and environmental governance. The principles and norms that are particularly applicable for the environmental law field, as well as an increasing number of legal concepts, mechanisms and legal acts are holistic, adaptive and flexible.[36]

Theories, ideas and insights regarding environmental governance and management approaches are central to environmental law, seen from the perspective that law is an inherent and important part of governance structures. One needs to understand the complexity of international environmental problems that the legal instruments aim to solve, in order to design applicable legal instruments and tools. This knowledge is also necessary to be able to understand the intentions behind international environmental law structures and design, and to be able to analyze their effectiveness and applicability. One prerequisite, then, is to understand the structures and approaches of environmental governance, such as the features for resilience governance that will be presented and discussed in the following chapters. This is important since such features for governance are developed to reflect, handle or somehow

[36] See e.g. de Sadeleer, N., 2002, pp. 305ff; Bodansky, D., Brunnée, J. and Hey, E., 2007b, generally and at pp. 21–23, and Sands, P., 2007, pp. 29 ff.

meet the characteristics of environmental complexity. It should thus also influence the choice of legal instrument or legal design.

2.4 ENVIRONMENTAL LAW APPROACHES AND MECHANISMS

Because of the nature and focus of environmental law and the dynamic problems it aims to solve, it lies within the structure of environmental law itself to include knowledge and information from other disciplines in the legal analysis and application. This is not unique for environmental law. Rather, the impression is that many fields of law have to turn to other disciplines to find answers regarding aim achievement and effectiveness. However, it becomes perhaps more apparent in the field of the environment. It also becomes a specific feature with regard to demands in environmental law principles or concepts such as the ecosystem approach, for example (as discussed later in this chapter), or best environmental practices, best available technique, and the precautionary principle (Section 2.4.1). All these legal principles are defined through environmental and technical knowledge and research.

The legal approaches that have generally been applied to environmental issues are usually environmental laws of precaution and preventive measures or standards. Such legal approaches are often bluntly called *traditional law approaches* or *command-and-control*. These traditional legal approaches are increasingly challenged due to increased environmental complexity, or increasing knowledge on complexity, as described in Chapter 1. Substantial distances or delays between causes and effects, diverse diffuse pollution sources, unpredictable cascading feedbacks and problematic additive impacts are factors characterizing these kinds of problems. Together with factors like many different actors being involved over many different scales, predictability and linear approaches are impossible. Altogether, it makes these problems difficult to pin down with detailed laws.[37] Thus effectively regulating diffuse pollution sources, or biodiversity threats and complex environmental responses, are the main issues in solving or reducing many modern environmental problems, as those described as connected to earth system change and the Anthropocene.

Slow environmental changes are typical of the kind of environmental problems described. Such slow change means that an ecosystem can sustain external pressures for a long time without reacting until a rather sudden change appear, but also that there is a time lapse between the release of pollution, habitat destruction, reduction of natural resources, or other harm

[37] See e.g. Jänicke, M. and Jörgens, H., 2006, pp. 169ff.

to the ecosystems, until it actually reaches the ecosystem on a level that affects the environmental status. Climate change, eutrophication in marine waters and the collapse of the cod stock in the Baltic Sea are all examples of such problems that appear suddenly after a long time of appearing resistant to pressures. The view that ecosystems in themselves show variations and continuous dynamic change, in addition to the factors described previously, has caused critique against applying too rigid and detailed legal approaches to environmental issues and ecosystem protection. Such regulatory approaches have received much criticism for not allowing or providing space for natural variations and complexity. Based on this disparity, many scholars argue that ecosystems become less resilient and that the legal regulations are too focused on controlling specific aspects of the problem instead of providing for wider ecosystem management and governance. It is argued that law needs to break with this approach in order to become more effective, and that legal institutions must thus become more flexible and adaptive. Law must meet the features developed with regard to adaptive governance, as opposed to an idea of command-and-control regulation.[38] It could be argued that this development is already well on its way, with the development of a range of principles and concepts, not least the ecosystem approach that signals a changed focus. Additionally, also the scale of the legal system applied will impact the level of detail. International law is rarely as detailed as national laws can be. EU law is sometimes detailed and could form so-called command-and-control laws. However, especially the EU environmental laws are generally designed to take a more overarching goal-based approach, where details will be adjusted to the specific area of implementation. Nevertheless, there is still much more knowledge needed to answer how or with what kinds of mechanisms environmental law would become more effective. Moreover, while attempting to be more holistic, law is still rather sector specific as opposed to taking a wider ecosystem perspective. In the following discussion, some of the more specific environmental law characteristics and mechanisms developed to take a more adaptive or holistic approach are introduced.

[38] See Tarlock, A. D., "The Nonequilibrium Paradigm in Ecology and the Partial Unraveling of Environmental Law," *Loyola of Los Angeles Law Review*, Vol. 27, 1994. See also e.g. Coleman, W. T., "Legal Barriers to the Restoration of Aquatic Systems," *Vermont Law Review*, Vol. 23, 1998, pp. 177ff. and at p. 186; Holling, C. S. and Meffe, G. K., "Command and Control, and the Pathology of Natural Resource Management," *Conservation Biology*, Vol. 10, No. 2, 1996, pp. 328–337. See also Sands, P., et al., *Principles of International Environmental Law*, Cambridge University Press, 2012, pp. 121ff., where a distinction is made between direct regulation (command-and-control) meaning regulation by environmental standards and regulation by economic incentives (economic instruments).

2.4.1 *Environmental Law Principles*

Some of the main environmental law characteristics that are significant in relation to the role of law in environmental governance are the environmental law principles. These principles have developed over time; some were stated primarily in declarations such as the Stockholm Declaration and the Declaration adopted in 1992 at the United Nations Conference on Environment and Development[39] (the Rio Declaration) but have since then successively gained further acknowledgment. The environmental law principles have often successively grown to become internationally acknowledged and integrated into international agreements. The principles could be described as a number of flexible features that will steer actors toward better environmental practices and further protection of the environment in different respects and situations. To a large extent, they are considered as fundamental features of environmental law today. Although their binding force may be debated, the principles generally reflect what could be regarded as minimum standards and general norms regarding how and to what extent actors should take into consideration the different aspects of potential environmental risks and effects tied to their actions. The environmental law principles, such as *the precautionary principle, the polluter pays principle, the principles on the use of best available technique*, and *best environmental practices*, are a regulatory response to the need for proactivity and precaution in relation to the environment. Contrary to rules, and command-and-control-regulation, the general principles rather give direction without stating an exact predetermined or specific action.[40]

Environmental law principles are designed to further adaptive and flexible approaches in law (Sections 2.4.3 and 2.4.4). To a large extent, they reflect a knowledge-based approach, where requirements will change with new knowledge about the problem at hand. An example is that precautionary measures will vary with the extent of knowledge about risks. The principles of best available technique and best environmental practice also reflect knowledge-based requirements. They thus represent a first step toward forms of regulation that set a framework for the peculiarities of environmental law and provide room for environmental change and flexibility. The development of the environmental law field during the past decades has laid important grounds for specific environmental legislation techniques, and these principles are essential for the application and pursuit of modern environmental

39 31 ILM 1992 p. 876.
40 Sands, P., et al., 2012, pp. 187ff.

law.[41] The environmental law principles are important flexible and adaptive elements in environmental law.

These overarching environmental law principles, with no precise definition, reflect a general shift from positivist law approaches. A transformation that entails a wider and, to some extent, more pragmatic approach in environmental law, it is also a shift which, both deliberately and as a consequence, changes the approaches, measures and methods adopted in environmental law.[42] Moreover, other important and to some extent moral environmental principles have formed in the international community. They largely regulate the level of responsibility of States in preventing environmental harm. In this context, the most significant principles are stipulated in the concepts of the *no-harm principle*,[43] and in the overlying aim or *principle of sustainable development* that govern most environmental regimes today.[44]

Nevertheless, environmental law principles are meant only as guiding or complementary features within a regulatory regime. When environmental problems are dynamic and caused by diffuse transboundary sources, or other forms of transboundary harmful activities, environmental principles do not suffice as the sole adaptive element. They are important and not least normative for actors, but cannot embrace all aspects of environmental problems. When it comes to pollution, for example, the increased complexity in environmental issues means that it may not always be possible even to identify who the polluter is, because the pollution is diffuse or stems from a very large number of separate polluters. Moreover, each one of the pollution sources may not be considered as harmful to the environment on its own. The no-harm-principle means that States have a responsibility to ensure that activities

41 On the environmental principles and their application in environmental law, see inter alia Sands, P., et al., 2012, pp. 187–237; de Sadeleer, N., 2002, generally; Sands, P. H., 2007, pp. 31ff.; Beyerlin, U., "Different Types of Norms in International Environmental Law: Policies, Principles and Rules," in Bodansky, D., Brunnée, J. and Hey, E. (eds.), 2007.

42 de Sadeleer, N., 2002, p. 371.

43 The no-harm principle was first formulated as Principle 21 of the 1972 UN Stockholm Declaration: "States have, in accordance with the Charter of the United Nations and the principles of international law, the sovereign right to exploit their own resources pursuant to their own environmental policies, and the responsibility to ensure that activities within their jurisdiction or control do not cause damage to the environment of other States or of areas beyond the limits of national jurisdiction." This simply means that States have the sovereign right to exploit their own natural resources, and in parallel they have the responsibility, or obligation, not to cause damage to the environment of other States or of areas beyond the limits of national jurisdiction. This is a fundamental component in international environmental law. See further in Sands, P., et al., 2012, pp. 190f.

44 See more on the Principle of Sustainable Development in inter alia: Bosselmann, K., 2008; Barstow Magraw, D. and Hawke, L. D., 2007; Sands, P., et al., 2012, pp. 206ff.; Birnie, P., Boyle, A. and Redgwell, C., 2009, pp. 125–164.

in their jurisdiction do not cause damage to the environment of other States or of areas beyond the limits of national jurisdiction.[45] This implies that States should anticipate and act to reduce pollution or other harmful activities with transboundary effects. When it comes to pollution, the question is how the no-harm-principle applies to a shared common area, or a shared problem, where it is not the discharges from a single State that are harming the rights of others, but instead the accumulated effects of discharges from many States. It could be argued that the principle of no harm may apply simply because of the fact that these accumulated effects of pollution are harmful, but then the question arises again of how to best restrict the pollution from such diversity of sources. This is the reason why other, generally more directly ecosystem-based features are being increasingly promoted. In this context, it should be mentioned that acknowledged problems relating to accumulated transboundary pollution of different kinds are often also directly regulated through international environmental agreements.

Similarly, international conflicts may arise if a single State does harm to the environment within its own territory, with effects that would be transboundary. This could appear in relation to the interest in biodiversity if important habitats or species are threatened. A striking example would be the conflicts surrounding the problems with the Brazilian governance of the Amazon that peaked in 2019.[46] In relation to the case of biodiversity loss, the *principle of common concern* is activated in addition to the no-harm principle. The principle of common concern relates to specifically such problems that are global and that cannot be resolved unless States collaborate and where all States will benefit from protective action. It is applicable to areas both within and outside national jurisdiction. Actually, it is not the areas as such that are subject of common concern; it is the protective actions. In this way, it creates a way around sovereignty. In modern environmental agreements, such as the 1992 United Nations Framework Convention on Climate Change (the UNFCCC)[47] and the International Convention of Biological Diversity (the CBD),[48] the common concern is expressed in the treaties.[49] In the CBD, it is the actual conservation of biological diversity that is seen as a common concern.[50] In a way, this means that the no-harm principle is

45 According to Principle 2 of the 1992 Rio Declaration.

46 See e.g. Carvalho, W. D., et al., "Deforestation Control in the Brazilian Amazon: A Conservation Struggle Being Lost as Agreements and Regulations Are Subverted and Bypassed," *Perspectives in Ecology and Conservation*, Vol. 17, No. 3, 2019, pp. 122–130.

47 1771 UNTS 107.

48 1760 UNTS 79.

49 Brunnée, J., "Common Areas, Common Heritage, and Common Concern," in Bodansky, D., Brunnée, J. and Hey, E. (eds.), *The Oxford Handbook of International Environmental Law*, Oxford University Press, 2007, pp. 564–565.

50 CBD, preamble.

extended to include also harm to biodiversity within State territories, if it is in an area where it is of common concert to protect the biological diversity

2.4.2 *Goal-Based Laws and Combined Approaches*

Law has often been accused of being rigid and using "command-and-control" approaches. In a general sense, the term *command-and-control regulation* is imprecise and not well chosen for discussing alternative regulatory approaches. Based on its wording, this term could just as well be compared to goal-oriented approaches, where the command could for example be "good ecological status" or "favourable conservation status" to take examples from EU law.[51] It is also not a good description for international law, which is rarely very detailed. Goal-based regulatory models can generally leave much room for adaptive and flexible measures, which must be controlled by the governing agencies if they are commanded by law. The question posed above of how to best restrict and regulate the pollution from a diversity of sources, diffuse pollution sources or other complex factors, remains though. An important factor is that the causes of these environmental problems often lie outside the traditional domain of environmental law; these kinds of environmental pressures are often a product or result of everyday routines in other sectors. Climate change is, of course, the most obvious example of this. This fact implies that the activities causing problems are directed and regulated – as well as motivated – by other laws and desired results.[52]

The areas where a more direct, linear form of regulation is usually applied – as suggested by the term command-and-control – are sectors were the environmental situation is less complex in this way and the environmental law situation is thus less problematic. In regard to governance approaches, it has been argued that while a first assessment may paint a picture where adaptive models or approaches offer very different recipes for governance compared to more general legal regulation, this does not mean that one approach is right and the other is wrong. Instead, the question of which is right is a question regarding the conditions under which each approach is applied. Different approaches have different domains of validity and can

[51] "Good environmental status," "good chemical status" and the like are the overarching goals set up for the EU Water Framework Directive [OJ L 327, p. 1–73] – the goals that all measures taken are to aim for. In a similar way, Directive 92/43/EEC on the conservation of natural habitats and of wild fauna and flora [OJ L 206, p. 7–50] (the Habitats Directive) have formulated the goal of "favourable conservation status" in Article 2(2).

[52] See also Jänicke, M. and Jörgens, H., 2006, pp. 169–171; Stewart, R. B., "Instrument Choice," in Bodansky, D., Brunnée, J. and Hey, E. (eds.), 2007.

therefore benefit from being combined. In coping with these kinds of governance challenges, a carefully differentiated strategy seems to offer better prospects than one relying entirely on only one of these models.[53]

It should be noted that the shape, role and application of law vary. Scale has serious impact on legal application, and the law will thus vary due to the geographical, demographical, ecological and other aspects bound to the different circumstances. Primarily, it will vary depending on whether it is applied in an international, regional, national or local context. Transferring it into general statements will thus be difficult. In international and regional levels of regulation, in a context of searching for effective regulatory approaches, it is important to adopt the idea articulated previously – that different approaches have different domains and function differently, depending on the setting in which regulation is applied. Just as with the governance approaches, more generally applicable regulatory approaches are called for. In summary, this means that depending on the source and nature of the environmental problem and the level of scale and complexity of the situation, different regulatory approaches can be applied and play a significant role. In the area of environmental law, area-specific principles, norms and legislation techniques go far beyond the idea of strict and detailed regulation as implied by command-and-control.[54]

2.4.3 *Adaptive Law*

A main challenge for the legal system in the changing environmental conditions is to address uncertainty. New legal approaches in environmental law are primarily focused on more adaptive and flexible approaches with all that this entails. They are designed to incorporate mechanisms for increased flexibility, for participation, and to foster experimentation and deliberation, as well as to accommodate regulation by multiple levels of government. The success and effectiveness of these new approaches have varied, however. A common denominator for all approaches has been decentralization, from the perspective of environmental governance, a positive aspect is that the decentralized nature of these legal instruments allows policies and decisions to be implemented

[53] Underdal, A., "Complexity and Challenges of Long-Term Environmental Governance," *Global Environmental Change*, Vol. 20, No. 3, 2010, pp. 389–390.

[54] Bodansky, D., *The Art and Craft of International Environmental Law*, Harvard University Press, 2010, p. 84, and for a general description of regulatory instruments and approaches, see pp. 57ff. See also Gunningham, N. and Holley, C., "Next-Generation Environmental Regulation: Law, Regulation, and Governance," *Annual Review of Law and Social Science*, Vol. 12:1, 2016, pp. 273–293.

more adaptively and more locally (i.e., closer to the source of the problem). This, it is believed, will facilitate a more responsive, flexible continuum of reactions to the regulatory challenges of the future.[55]

In the aim to approach ecological uncertainty the law has been influenced by adaptive governance and thus adopted different forms of ecosystem-based legislation with a basis in environmental governance strategies. It aims to include strategies that can better address intractable, transboundary problems with a large variety of policy levels, sectors, vested interests and competing policy instruments.[56] Many modern environmental law instruments are designed to achieve specific environmental quality objectives through a diversity of measures.[57] In this way, the international legal and institutional system has undergone a change, just as the perspectives on ecosystems and governance of common resources have changed. As a result, international environmental law has become both a product of and – in part – a cause of a transformation of governance approaches. By integrating adaptive approaches, including specific measures or mechanisms, as well as those institutional structures and strategies that aim to meet complexity, law could also be better adjusted to deal with complexity. The idea is that these legal structures could bridge some of the gaps that occur in application of excessively strict legal measures to complex problems.[58]

A flexible and adaptive response, as is typical of the general comprehension of adaptive governance, is also the goal of most of the new approaches applied in environmental law.[59] Since these ideas were first introduced, wider and more developed concepts have appeared within law, with a more direct focus on adaptive governance and environmental concerns. The examples found, all primarily reflect national law and national legal systems. They thus reflect regulation set out on levels other than those that are the primary focus in this study. Despite this, they still reflect most of the regulatory strategies that are also embraced or aimed for within the new legal governance approaches at higher governance levels.

55 Ruhl, J. B., "Regulation by Adaptive Management – Is It Possible?," *Minnesota Journal of Law, Science and Technology*, Vol. 7, No. 1, 2006. See also Chaffin, B. C., Gosnell, H. and Cosens, B. A., "A Decade of Adaptive Governance Scholarship: Synthesis and Future Directions," *Ecology and Society* Vol 19(3): 56, 2014.

56 Jänicke, M. and Jörgens, H., 2006, p. 171.

57 Stewart, R.B., 2007, p. 149.

58 See also Cosens, B. A., et al., "The Role of Law in Adaptive Governance," *Ecology and Society*, Vol. 22(1):30, 2017.

59 See also Ruhl, J. B., "Thinking of Environmental Law as Complex Adaptive System: How to Clean Up the Environment by Making a Mess of Environmental Law," *Houston Law Review*, Vol. 34, No. 4, 1997, generally and at p. 996.

A significant feature of adaptive law, or law matching adaptive management and governance, compared to standard regulation at all regulatory levels, is for example a system for monitoring ecosystem responses followed by evaluation of the efforts and proposals for remedial action, in a cyclical fashion. This implies that after the implementation of specific activities and procedures, the status of the ecosystem is regularly and systematically reassessed in relation to the actions taken. It is therefore emphasized that adaptive management requires new institutional structures for monitoring-adjustment, frameworks that allow reevaluation and adjustments in decisions.[60] It is also stated that some of the obstacles to making this work effectively are administrative agencies and legislators, which have become accustomed to the more traditional and linear style of regulation that has dominated for decades.[61] The question, however, is how far away the so-called traditional approaches are from monitoring-adjustment frameworks, since legal measures are generally evaluated continuously. Although such evaluations are not the same as a circular adaptive system, the idea that the regulatory efforts must be adjusted to the problem is not new.

Still, it has often been held that such adaptive forms of regulation would be counteractive to legal systems that rely on firm rules of law.[62] Some even argue that while adaptive management has gained much support and recognition among scientists, regulators, resource managers and even legal scholars, it has not quite been fully embraced and properly integrated into law and legal structures.[63] Rather, it is argued, environmental law decisions must be better connected to environmental science. Universities and other research institutions are still the primary contributors to the development of new scientific ideas and approaches in environmental law, while in practice these ideas have not quite been applied and developed as well as they could and should have been. One reason for this is likely the significant methodological gap in the methods and purposes used in law and science, respectively.[64]

One important critique toward adaptive approaches in environmental law is that the scholars arguing for this are missing the point of goals and substantive law, and instead are relying too much on process and procedural law. It is

60 See e.g. Ruhl, J. B., 2006; Angelo, M. J., "Harnessing the Power of Science in Environmental Law: Why We Should, Why We Don't, and How We Can," *Texas Law Review*, Vol. 86, 2007–2008, pp. 1546ff.

61 Ruhl, J. B., 2006, pp. 36 ff.

62 Angelo, M. J., 2007–2008, p. 1548; Profeta, T. H., "Managing without a Balance: Environmental Regulation in Light of Ecological Advances," *Duke Environmental Law and Policy*, Vol. 7, 1996, pp. 86ff.; see also Tarlock, A. D., 1994, pp. 1139ff.

63 Angelo, M. J., 2007–2008, pp. 1530ff.

64 Ibid., p. 1573.

argued that the goal of long-term environmental protection may be better achieved through the more traditional structures of substantive law and environmental institutions as a supplement to adaptive legal structures. If given a clear role and sufficiently specific goals, substantive law could instead provide a more defined path and thus more effective long-term environmental protection, as opposed to approaches that may make it difficult to see the aim and purpose of environmental protection.[65]

The significance of new thinking on institutional design and governance for environmental and natural resources law is striking. While scholars, environmentalists and lawyers are all increasingly pushing for this kind of institutional change, an important point is to avoid blindly following the new governance approaches and integrating them into regulation without a thorough analysis of the consequences from a legal perspective. It is important to explore whether the promise of these new approaches will result in more effective environmental protection, as well as whether the relation between goals and the role of law in these new approaches to governance and protection is sufficient. Ultimately, this means to find out whether these new institutional models are sufficient to achieve a goal of effective long-term environmental protection.[66] To some extent, recent case studies on the applicability of legal tools have already started to provide some answers, although not in relation to international or EU law.[67] The transboundary effects of problems also make it even more urgent to find other and more effective problem-solving mechanisms, and thus such mechanisms have to be possible to implement on an international scale – and include nonstate actors.

Pathways for participation by stakeholders and nongovernmental organizations (NGOs) have given nonstate actors significant influence in both environmental treaty negotiations and in the environmental agenda of international bodies, as well as in national decision-making. In some cases, flexible rule-making processes allow for easy and regular amendments, in the light of technical development and advances in scientific and other knowledge. Most regulatory systems are based on multilateral agreements, but soft-law instruments, including codes of conduct, guidelines and recommendations, are also employed. In addition, framework agreements allow for successive negotiations and additional protocols.[68] Regardless, the effectiveness and efficiency of new

[65] Wiersema, A., "A Train without Tracks: Rethinking the Place of Law and Goals in Environmental and Natural Resources Law," *Environmental Law*, Vol. 38, 2008.

[66] Ibid., pp. 1242–1244.

[67] See e.g. Cosens, B. and Gunderson, L. H. (eds.), 2018.

[68] Birnie, P., Boyle, A. and Redgwell, C., 2009, pp. 9–10; Jänicke, M. and Jörgens, H., 2006, pp. 167–168.

environmental legal design also depend strongly on additional measures being taken. It has been held that in order to avoid the decline of the overall level of environmental protection, new modes of legal governance need to be complemented and safeguarded by direct and hierarchical regulation, and effective compliance control, so that so-called traditional environmental regulations are not regarded as obsolete.[69] However, it has also been said that such new forms of rule making with open-ended participation may create a new more effective mode for governance in an uncertain and flexible world order. Moreover, these new structures at their best may contribute to "self-governance under the rule of law."[70]

2.4.4 *New Environmental Law Structures and "New Governance" in the EU*

Adaptive law approaches share a number of characteristics that distinguish them from other more traditional models of legislation. The so-called "new governance" approaches were initially adopted by the EU in 2001 and exhibit some of these new adaptive characteristics.[71] These characteristics also include prerequisites that share many features found in the environmental governance approaches and theories on social ecological resilience. Some of the most important of these characteristics or features are participation, multilevel integration, diversity and decentralization, as well as flexibility and revisability. New governance approaches also tend to accept the necessity of coordination of actions and actors at many levels of scale in a governance system, as well as between government and private actors. New governance mechanisms include structures that bring actors from various levels of governance (local, regional, national, European or even international) together in ways that facilitate dialogue and coordination. New governance can be seen as a way of coping with complex problems under conditions of uncertainty, so the trend of new governance indeed reflects the increasing domination of complex environmental problems.[72]

Many of the new-governance processes are designed to foster collective problem solving through stakeholder participation in different areas of law.

69 Jänicke, M. and Jörgens, H., 2006, pp. 167–168; Kiss, A. and Shelton, D., *International Environmental Law*, 2nd ed., Transnational Publishers, 2000, pp. 22–23.

70 De Búrca G., Keohane R. and Sabel C., "New Modes of Pluralist Global Governance," *New York University Journal of International Law & Politics*, Vol. 45:3, 2013, pp. 723–86.

71 EU White Paper (2001).

72 Scott, J. and Trubek, D. M., "Mind the Gap: Law and New Approaches to Governance in the EU," *European Law Journal*, Vol. 8, No. 1, 2002, pp. 5–6.

In systems of new governance, law creates minimal standards while within the governance system is also room to exceed the standards. Furthermore, traditional rights-based structures are often kept as a safety net available to rights-holders, in case the new governance processes prove ineffective. While law may provide general norms, new governance is seen as a tool to make them concrete. This kind of legislation has also been described as "experimentalist governance."[73] Common examples of how these new governance laws are designed in the EU environmental policy area are the Water Framework Directive, Directive 2008/56/EC establishing a framework for community action in the field of marine environmental policy, the Marine Strategy Framework Directive,[74] and to some extent also the Directive 2014/89/EU on Maritime Spatial Planning.[75] Directive 2011/92/EU on the assessment of the effects of certain public and private projects on the environment (Environmental Impact Assessments), the EIA Directive,[76] could also be counted here. The common feature in these directives is that the law establishes a general norm and an environmental goal to be accomplished, without further specifying how it should be applied in different circumstances.[77] The EU has generally come far in elaborating and trying out new forms of law in environmental governance.

The challenges faced by environmental policy today differ sharply from those of past decades, with regard to both the environmental problems calling for the attention and the strategies available to tackle them. After notable successes in some sub-areas of environmental protection, the focus is now on issues where environmental policy has failed to bring about any significant improvement, even over a substantial period of time. There has been continuous growth in both the regulatory repertoire and the range of actors involved. However, some argue that new forms of legal approaches contribute to a weakening of State authority and democratic legitimacy, and reductions in established institutional problem-solving capacity. At the same time, new

73 Sabel, C. F. and Zeitlin, J., "Experimentalist Governance," in Levi-Faur, D. (ed.), *The Oxford Handbook of Governance*, Oxford University Press, 2012.

74 OJ L 164, pp. 19–40.

75 OJ L 257, pp. 135–145.

76 OJ L 26, pp. 1–21. See also Directive 2014/52/EU amending Directive 2011/92/EU on the assessment of the effects of certain public and private projects on the environment, OJ L 124, p. 1–18.

77 Trubek, D. M. and Trubek, L. G., "New Governance and Legal Regulation: Complementarity, Rivalry, and Transformation," *Columbia Journal of European Law*, Vol. 13, 2006, pp. 11f. See also Scott, J. and Holder, J., "Law and New Environmental Governance in the European Union," in de Búrca, G. and Scott, J., *Law and New Governance in the EU and the US*, Hart Publishing, 2006, pp. 211–242.

policy instruments offer an opportunity to plug deficits in existing environmental policy and help address as-yet unresolved environmental problems.[78]

One of the most significant steps taken in integrating more flexible and ecosystem-focused laws is the concept of *the ecosystem approach*. This idea is taking legal regulation far from traditional and directly controlled regulation into a new territory that also changes the perception of acknowledged principles such as the precautionary principle.

2.5 THE CONCEPT OF ECOSYSTEM APPROACH

Initiatives to create flexible and dynamic legal instruments that develop along with theories on environmental governance and management are increasingly common. One such initiative that has won important acknowledgment in the international field is the concept of ecosystem approach. The concept of ecosystem approach, moreover, is the most concrete regulatory tool that is open to the inclusion of a social-ecological resilience perspective within the legal system. It offers an important and interesting stepping-stone for the study of law and social-ecological resilience.

The origin of this concept refers to a comprehensive science-based approach to the conservation and management of natural resources.[79] However, it is the base for a gradual and perceptible evolution of new normative tools to shape the way the law is applied and interpreted; it has successively become a legal concept. As such, this approach should be implemented and applied at all levels in environmental regulation in the areas where it is required. The ecosystem approach is a concept for legal governance, with a specific focus on ecological prerequisites and environmental governance features. It aims to take into account the multilevel dynamics of regulatory and institutional pluralism typical of modern regulatory structures. The approach taken as a result of applying the concept is in a constant state of evolution as a result of a constant development of its core elements.[80]

While an ecosystem approach is central in environmental management and policy – including approaches related to research on social-ecological resilience – such measures are still rather new in law or legal contexts. The

78 Jänicke, M. and Jörgens, H., 2006, p. 168.

79 Wang, H., "Ecosystem Management and Its Application to Large Marine Ecosystems: Science, Law, and Politics," *Ocean Development and International Law*, Vol. 53, No. 1, 2004, p. 43.

80 Long, R., "Legal Aspects of Ecosystem-Based Marine Management in Europe," in Chircop, A., McConnell, M. L. and Coffen-Smou, S. (eds.), *Ocean Yearbook*, Vol. 26, Hijhoff, 2012, pp. 420ff.

concept draws to large extent on ecosystem adaptive management and governance ideas. The basic principles of the concept correspond to a large extent to the main principles and key features of resilience governance and management strategies; thus resilience theories could provide valuable insight into the interpretation and the implementation of the ecosystem approach in a legal context as well.[81] It is significant that resilience governance features, and explicit references to the research on social-ecological resilience, can be detected in the background documents from the original adoption of the concept of the ecosystem approach.[82] Regarding the general attempts to include adaptive management and ecosystem governance in regulation, there are important obstacles and issues to resolve in order to implement such measures in law. It is somewhat unclear what this approach to environmental regulation entails in concrete legal terms beyond what has been written and stated about legal approaches inspired by adaptive management.[83] There are important questions to solve regarding how this kind of regulation is compatible with fundamental principles of law, especially principles of rule of law. The establishment of the concept of ecosystem approach could be a step toward ecosystem-based legal measures and holistic, dynamic perspectives in environmental regulation. Attempts to transpose this concept are increasingly applied. However, it still remains to define more concretely how it will be expressed and transposed into legal rules and mechanisms, especially in national law.[84] Against the backdrop of the references to resilience and the resilience features as inherent in major parts of the concept, the study of compatibility of law and social-ecological resilience may also be useful in this development of the ecosystem approach as a regulatory mechanism.

81 See e.g. Österblom, H., et al., "Making the Ecosystem Approach Operational – Can Regime Shifts in Ecological- and Governance Systems Facilitate the Transition?," *Marine Policy*, Vol. 34, No. 6, 2010, pp. 1290–1299.

82 For example, note the so-called Malawi Principles, adopted by CBD (2000a), The Malawi Principles, COP Convention on Biological Diversity, May 2000, in Nairobi, Kenya (CBD, COP 5), Decision V/6, para. 4–5, part B.

83 See e.g. Langlet, D. and Rayfuse, R., "Challenges in Implementing the Ecosystem Approach: Lessons Learned," in Langlet, D. and Rayfuse, R. (eds.), *The Ecosystem Approach in Ocean Planning and Governance*, Brill/Nijhoff, 2018; De Lucia, V., "Competing Narratives and Complex Genealogies: The Ecosystem Approach in International Environmental Law," *Journal of Environmental Law*, Vol. 27, 2015, 91–117; Long, R., 2012, pp. 420ff. and pp. 475ff. See also Platjouw, F., *Environmental Law and the Ecosystem Approach: Maintaining Ecological Integrity through Consistency in Law*, Routledge, 2016, chapter 2.1.

84 See e.g. the discussion on ecosystem-based legal mechanisms in Nilsson, A. K. and Bohman, B., "Legal Prerequisites for Ecosystem-Based Management in the Baltic Sea Area: The Example of Eutrophication" *Ambio*, Vol. 44, Suppl. 3, 2015.

2.5.1 *Background, Development and Application*

The concept of the ecosystem approach was formally accepted in 1995 when it was adopted in the international Convention of Biological Diversity[85] (the CBD).[86] Since then, the interpretation and application of the concept have been elaborated and developed in guidelines and principles by primarily the CBD and successively also elsewhere.[87] These elaborations and interpretations in the context of the CBD are also important for the understanding of the concept in other contexts. So far, the CBD guidelines are the only formal explanation for how to interpret and understand the ecosystem approach and must thus be considered an authority. According to the CBD, the ecosystem approach "is a strategy for the integrated management of land, water and living resources that promotes conservation and sustainable use in an equitable way."[88] In addition, the ecosystem approach "requires adaptive management to deal with the complex and dynamic nature of ecosystems and the absence of complete knowledge or understanding of their functioning. Ecosystem processes are often non-linear, and the outcome of such processes often shows time-lags."[89] Additionally, it is stated that "[a]n ecosystem approach is based on the application of appropriate scientific methodologies focused on levels of biological organization which encompass the essential processes, functions and interactions among organisms and their environment. It recognizes that humans, with their cultural diversity, are an integral component of ecosystems."[90]

Seen in the light of these quite general descriptions, the ecosystem approach could be regarded as implementing the environmental law principles with a new approach. These descriptions of the ecosystem approach contain a perspective where another role for the environmental principles can be identified. Since the concept of ecosystem approach manifests adaptive and precautionary approaches in regulation, it is indirectly introducing a new and more adjusted way of applying those principles to complex environmental problems (Section 5.3.4). It lies within the concept of ecosystem approach, for example, to account for uncertainty and change; this is demonstrated in its

85 1760 UNTS 79.
86 CBD (1995), CBD II/8, The Second Meeting of the Conference of the Parties (COP) of the Convention on Biological Diversity, held in Jakarta, Indonesia (CBD COP 2) Decision 8, UNEP/CBD/COP/2/19, p. 12.
87 See Platjouw, F., 2016, chapter 2, for an overview of the legal development of the concept.
88 CBD (2000c), Description of the ecosystem approach, COP Convention on Biological Diversity, May 2000, in Nairobi, Kenya (CBD, COP 5) Decision V/6, para. 4–5, part A, p. 1.
89 Ibid., p. 4.
90 Ibid., p. 2.

statement regarding the absence of complete knowledge and in its promotion of adaptive management, sustainable use and integrated management. This could be seen as an expression of the precautionary principle, since the concept states as a fact that we need to create sustainable structures for management despite lack of full of knowledge, and of course that the design of these structures shall have ecosystem dynamics as a foundation. These aspects of the concept provide, in a way, a new basis for the precautionary principle, as well as for the polluter pays principle, the principle of best available technique, the principle of best environmental practice and not least the principle of sustainable development. Although this is not specifically mentioned in the interpretations of the ecosystem approach or in the guidance given for the environmental principles, such a reading of the elaboration of ecosystem approach is not particularly farfetched.[91] The prerequisites in the description of the ecosystem approach may vary from the original interpretation of how to apply these principles, but the aims of the approach as they are described and the application of the environmental principles are similar. The fact that "an ecosystem approach … recognizes that humans, with their cultural diversity, are an integral component of many ecosystems,"[92] as was cited above, furthermore reflects a certain perspective on nature and ecosystem management that emphasizes perspectives that could be interpreted as reflecting the view held in social-ecological resilience. Hence, the research on social-ecological resilience and law may provide an important contribution to the understanding of this concept and its interpretation.

As stated, the concept of ecosystem approach is elaborated in the CBD guidelines and management principles. The most specific definitions and management principles for the concept of ecosystem approach are found in the so-called Malawi principles.[93] The CBD operational guide and the management principles state a number of principles and focus points for how management is to be pursued and operationalized in accordance with an ecosystem approach.[94] The management principles contain a number of statements that are relevant for how the concept is to be applied, and they focus to a large extent on continuous monitoring in multilevel institutional structures.

91 See also the perspective on this given by Trouwborst, A., "The Precautionary Principle and the Ecosystem Approach in International Law: Differences, Similarities and Linkages," *Review of European Community and International Environmental Law*, Vol. 18(1), 2009; Morgera, E., "The Ecosystem Approach and the Precautionary Principle," in Morgera, E. and Razzaque, J. (eds.), *Biodiversity and Nature Protection Law*, Edward Elgar Publishing, 2017.

92 CBD Ecosystem approach, p. 2.

93 CBD Malawi Principles.

94 CBD (2004), "The Ecosystem Approach – Operational and Implementation Guidelines."

The principles also clarify the objectives and aim of an ecosystem approach, while introducing a number of basic points of departure for management. One such basic point is that ecosystem approach must be pursued through adaptive management in order to foresee and cater to ecosystem changes and events. In addition, management should take into account the uncertainties and potential changes that are inherent in social-ecological systems. A significant statement is also that the conservation of ecosystem structure and functioning should be a priority target of the ecosystem approach in order to maintain ecosystem services. The principles also emphasize that the measures should be implemented at the appropriate spatial and temporal scale. Management should be decentralized to the lowest appropriate level and involve all stakeholders. The varying scales and lag effects that characterize ecosystem processes suggest that objectives for ecosystem management should be set for the long term.[95] These principles are similar in many aspects to the features or criteria for resilience governance and management. A main principle for the application of the ecosystem approach is also that conservation of ecosystem structures and functions should be pursued in order to maintain ecosystem services. This can be compared to the idea of resilience in social-ecological systems, which mainly maintains a focus on the functions of the ecosystems and their connection to life-sustaining feedbacks, in the form of ecosystem services that are particularly essential for social systems.

2.5.2 *Operationalization*

The way in which these different features and principles connected to the ecosystem approach should be operationalized is not specified. Since the implementation of an ecosystem approach should be dynamic and thus based on the specific conditions in each ecosystem concerned, there is no universal method for how to do this. However, it must be possible to identify some specifics in the different functions, features and principles attached to the ecosystem approach, which can somehow be translated into law and legal measures.

Ecosystem management through the implementation of an ecosystem approach should be directly based on relevant contemporary scientific understanding of the ecosystems. In international cooperation, this includes joint scientific research, exchange of information, knowledge and experience, transfer of technology and so forth.[96] The holistic approaches associated with the ecosystem approach have been criticized for containing inherent

95 CBD Malawi Principles; Nilsson, A. K. and Bohman, B., 2015.

96 Wang, H., 2004, at p. 44.

obstacles to proper implementation. These refer mainly to the conflicts between multilevel governance, flexibility and traditional legal principles and the need for institutional stability in relation to the rule of law. This conflict has been reflected in many areas in relation to new legal approaches. In some cases, this new approach has also been criticized because it has been transposed into regulation that is far too complex in its design and in the end may not incorporate the aim of being responsive to the ecosystem.[97]

Another issue brought to light in connection to implementation and the varieties found in interpreting the concept is the actual term chosen for the concept. While the most acknowledged formal term is the ecosystem approach, it is often referred to in other contexts as ecosystem management, integrated ecosystem management, holistic approach, ecosystem-based approach and so on. In addition to that, there might be formal discrepancies between the different terms chosen, these terms also contribute to confusion regarding the implementation and understanding of the concept since they are often discussed and argued for in a similar manner. This may also blur the picture of when it refers to general management approaches and when it actually concerns a legal concept connected to formal and legal requirements.[98]

In the perspective of international law and governance, one aspect of the ecosystem approach is particularly interesting. Since this approach aims to take into account the ecosystem integrity and spatial scales associated with the natural components of the system, management measures will not primarily take into account administrative or jurisdictional boundaries. Basically, the spatial scale of management must extend across different biological units and jurisdictions to encompass an entire ecosystem. In this way, the concept of ecosystem approach also becomes a tool for transboundary law and cooperation across State borders where the ecosystem does not align with jurisdictional boundaries, as in the case of international common-pool resources.[99] Therefore, it has also been argued that in addition to being a scientific and legal issue, implementation of the ecosystem approach in transboundary common-pool resources is to a great extent a political choice. The harmonization of jurisdictional conflicts is mainly of a political nature, and is the main challenge for the ecosystem approach in shared areas. Because of this nature of the concept, an effective application relies on

97 See e.g. Lee, M., "Law and Governance of Water Protection Policy," in Scott, J. (ed.), *Environmental Protection – European Law and Governance*, Oxford University Press, 2009, pp. 36ff.

98 See De Lucia, V., 2015, pp. 100–101.

99 Wang, H., 2004, at p. 44.

collective political will and the mutual cooperation of the States concerned.[100] In addition, the variations of the terms and labels applicable to this concept create issues of great importance for implementation. The concretization of the concept and the potential effect that it might have are contingent upon the particular articulation that the ecosystem approach takes in different legal regimes, and in international law in general.[101]

However, it should still be recognized and emphasized that through the ecosystem approach, new and important perspectives have started to take shape for how to regulate environmental problems. It is a formal ground for new approaches to regulation, and as such it establishes a landmark for any environmental regulation. Indeed, many obstacles remain to achieving the full functional operationalization of this approach. In many cases, however, it still provides the best regulatory frame seen so far, for the kind of environmental regulation that the environmental complexities and governance theories require. The ecosystem approach points particularly to the kind of diversity of problems and sources that are found when observing ecosystems and ecosystem response and emphasizes a holistic approach. In this way, the concept of ecosystem approach has provided a basis for designing ecosystem-based law and regulatory institutional structures in accordance with new environmental management strategies.[102]

2.6 COMPLIANCE AND EFFECTIVENESS

One last point within the general scope of environmental law that may be of relevance when discussing the design of law and social-ecological resilience is the question of compliance and ideas on effectiveness. Legal effectiveness is to different degrees connected to compliance or, at least, to some kind of operationalization. However, depending on the perspective chosen, neither *compliance* nor *effectiveness* is as straightforward of a term as it may seem. In relation to the assessment of law and social-ecological resilience, the point is that the legal structure built on resilience theories, of course, must also be effective in some sense. If the legal design created, is not effective, then there is no point to it. In this context, however, effectiveness may also be measured to some degree by the actual institutional settings and design created. This aspect will be analyzed and discussed further throughout the book (Section 8.2).

100 Ibid., at p. 61.
101 See: De Lucia, V., 2015, at p. 113.
102 See also Long, R., 2012.

Compliance and effectiveness are naturally important issues connected to law and regulatory measures. These issues are also complicated, especially in connection with complex environmental problems as well as in dynamic and complex legal structures, such as new legal approaches, including holistic approaches. Effectiveness in international environmental law is generally a debated issue, and it can be measured with different criteria. In comparison, EU environmental law is a little more directly defined and controlled. Depending on the criteria chosen, effectiveness can have multiple meanings. Definitions of effectiveness can vary in meaning, from solving the problems for which the regime was established, to achieving the goals set out in the constitutive instruments, to altering behavior patterns, to enhancing national compliance with rules in international agreements. The effectiveness of different regulatory techniques is largely determined by the nature and complexity of the problem. Therefore, the possibility to assess effectiveness and compliance varies with both the complexity of the problem and the regulatory technique applied.

Behavioral effectiveness focuses on the role of international environmental law in making States and individuals modify their behavior toward achieving the regime's objective, while problem-solving effectiveness is the degree to which an agreement achieves its objectives or, more generally, solves the environmental problem it addresses. Lawyers tend to concentrate on the issue of legal effectiveness.[103] However, it is difficult to say whether legal effectiveness is possible to assess when regulatory or governance structures are set to resolve a diffuse complex problem, due to the ambiguous, pluralistic and flexible feature they reveal. Effectiveness is also determined by the complexity of actors involved. What works in one case may not work in others. In this respect, considerable advantage has been taken of the flexibility of international law-making processes, and their ability to incorporate new concepts and techniques.[104] Not least, different mechanisms for evaluating results, or the goals, to be accomplished may be altered along the way. Legal effectiveness generally focuses on the issue of compliance – that is, whether outcomes conform to the requirements set out by a legal rule. If an agreement sets forth an obligation of conduct, then it is legally effective to the degree that States act consistently with its requirements. In contrast, if it sets forth obligations to provide a result, then it is legally effective if emissions decline by the required amount. EU law tends to be effective in compliance from this perspective, in comparison to international law.

[103] Bodansky, D., 2010, pp. 253–255.

[104] Birnie, P., Boyle, A. and Redgwell, C., 2009, p. 12.

Diffuse sources, complex and intertwined problems, large-scale ecosystems and perhaps delayed ecological responses to measures taken – these, on the other hand, are aspects that make it difficult to assess effectiveness in relation to the ecosystem status in many more complex environmental scenarios. In addition, many regulatory structures are quite ambiguous as to what they require of the States. Goal-oriented, long-term, framework legislation and other kinds of adaptive and new legal approaches pose a challenge to assessing effectiveness and to the possibilities to evaluate measures taken by States in relation to strict compliance. New environmental law approaches and ecosystem-based measures, which tend to be transposed into complex instruments and measures, are an important part of these complex legal structures that are so difficult to assess. Concepts such as the ecosystem approach and similar regulatory approaches that refer directly to the state and quality of ecosystems set other criteria for effectiveness.

The governance features presented in this study do not actually present strict measurement points for effectiveness or compliance. If effectiveness is not possible to assess with regard to the ecosystem, behavioral effectiveness is an alternative. The study aims to assess prerequisites or potential obstacles found in relation to both legal and problem-solving effectiveness. Understanding how we can estimate effectiveness in this regard is key, and it is intricately interwoven in investigating further the features and functions of law and legal measures in relation to social-ecological resilience governance.

3

Law and Governance

In this chapter, the relationship between law and governance is introduced. There are three aspects that must be clarified first before one can substantially review the main subject of law and social-ecological resilience. The first is the law, its general design, methods, rules of interpretation, objectives and the scope of environmental law, as discussed in the previous chapter. The second is social-ecological resilience, the theoretical framework, resilience governance and its principles or features. Several theories on social-ecological resilience were introduced in the first chapter, and the features for designing governance for social-ecological resilience will be presented in the next. They are the foundation of the study and analysis of legal design. However, when discussing the theories of resilience in this context, the focus is on resilience governance. The third aspect that needs to be clarified before going further with the study is the concept of governance and effective environmental governance. As the review builds on the idea of resilience governance, it is not simply enough to understand the objectives of social-ecological resilience; to discuss the compatibility between law and resilience governance, the role of law for governance must also be addressed. More specifically, the role of law in resilience governance and the specific aspects of resilience governance where law may have a particular role in the governance system must be analyzed. The purpose of this chapter is thus to discuss and clarify the general relationship between the concepts of governance and law.

3.1 THE ROLE OF LAW IN GOVERNANCE

International common-pool resources[1] and the need for cooperation were the main reasons for the rise of international environmental law. Common-pool

[1] A *common-pool resource* is usually defined as a public good that is considered as free to all and shared by all, where users are also generally difficult to exclude or limit; it is also referred to simply as a “common.” See e.g. Ostrom, E., Gardner, R. and Walker, J., *Rules, Games, and Common-Pool*

problems created a need for States to agree on how to govern the commons and the transboundary effects connected to them. These issues are still the main reasons for adopting international environmental agreements.[2] The concept of governance can signify and represent a wide range of ideas. It has been described, inter alia, as a social function centered on efforts to steer societies or human groups away from collectively undesirable outcomes.[3] How commons are best governed by a governance system, and the manifold, sometimes conflicting, theoretical ideas behind it, are central issues in the current study. Environmental governance theories propose strategies, structures, institutions and actions that are meant to respond to different aspects of complexity and uncertainty in efforts to protect the environment from harm, not least resulting from the pressures of human activities.[4] Although the focus of this study is the role of law and institutional structures set out by it, law will mainly be discussed as a tool within or as a basis for a governance system. The understanding of governance as a concept in this study is in line with this established formal definition of global governance:

> Governance is the sum of many ways individuals and institutions, public and private, manage their common affairs. It is a continuing process through which conflicting or diverse interests may be accommodated and co-operative action taken. It includes formal institutions and regimes empowered to enforce compliance, as well as informal arrangements that people and institutions either have agreed to or perceive to be in their interest.[5]
>
> . . . It is a broad, dynamic, complex, process of interactive decision-making that is constantly evolving and responding to changing circumstances.[6]

This description of the concept of governance is thus not equal to governance through government but instead reflects a system where legal institutions are

Resources, University of Michigan Press, 1994, p. 4. See also the elaboration of the concept in Rosenbloom, J., "Defining Nature as a Common Pool Resource," in Hirokawa, K. H. (ed.), *Environmental Law and Contrasting Ideas of Nature – A Constructivist Approach*, Cambridge University Press, 2014, p. 49ff.

2 See e.g. Bodansky, D., Brunnée, J. and Hey, E., 2007a, p. 10f.

3 Delmas, M. A. and Young, O. R., "Introduction: New Perspectives on Governance for Sustainable Development," in Delmas, M. A. and Young, O. R. (eds.), *Governance for the Environment – New Perspectives*, Cambridge University Press, 2009, p. 6.

4 See e.g. what is written on this in Young, O. R., *International Governance – Protecting the Environmental in a Stateless Society*, Cornell University Press, Ithaca and London, 1994, pp. 12ff; Duit, A. and Galaz, V., "Governance and Complexity – Emerging Issues for Governance Theory," *Governance: An International Journal of Policy, Administration and Institutions*, Vol. 21, No. 3, 2008, pp. 311–335.

5 Commission on Global Governance, 1995, p. 2.

6 Commission on Global Governance, 1995, p. 4.

seen as one part of a structural nest with multiple mechanisms, measures and actions. International law and the international community are increasingly less characterized by only strict interactions reflecting and arising between independent sovereign States.[7] Instead, international law is progressively characterized by a general demand for openness, transparency, fairness and mechanisms for accountability. States and international law are thus compelled to interact with a growing number of actors, including international organizations, private companies and NGOs. Due to these developments, it is natural to view law as part of a wider concept.[8]

In addition to the concept of governance described here, *management* is a term that is also common in relation to governance. Both governance and management of the environment are often discussed in terms of adaptive governance and adaptive management. The concept of adaptive management generally implies the response system connected to learning and monitoring. Management in relation to governance generally applies to actions by a single entity – the operationalization of the more general steering measures or strategies indicated by the governance system. Management is seen as the activity of translating visions or strategies into reality.[9] Governance and management could also be compared to the hierarchy or levels found in legal structures. In such comparison to legal structures, the concept of governance is reflected primarily by international law and sometimes by EU law, as a top, general level of steering. Management, on the other hand, could be seen to be at the level of national and local implementation of those international laws and some forms of EU law, when it is more directly applicable to the national and local levels. This does not mean that governance or management is always reflected in the legal system; instead, it aims to present a comparison in terms of scales.[10]

7 See e.g. Jönsson, C. and Tallberg, J., "Transnational Actor Participation in International Institutions: Where, Why, and with What Consequences?," in Jönsson, C. and Tallberg, J. (eds.), *Transnational Actors in Global Governance*, Palgrave Macmillan, 2010, pp. 1ff.

8 For more discussion and review of these aspects of international law and governance, see Toope, S. J., "Emerging Patterns of Governance and International Law," in Byers, M. (ed.), *The Role of Law in International Politics: Essays in International Relations and International Law*, Oxford University Press, 2000; see also Birnie, P., Boyle, A. and Redgwell, C., 2009, pp. 43ff. See also De Búrca, G., Keohane, R. and Sabel, C., 2013.

9 This is well described by Cosens, B. A., "Legitimacy, Adaptation, and Resilience in Ecosystem Management," in *Ecology and Society*, Vol. 18, No. 1, 2013, p. 3; and Boyle, M., Kay, J. and Pond, B., "Monitoring in Support of Policy: An Adaptive Ecosystem Approach," in Munn, T., *Encyclopedia of Global Environmental Change*, Vol. 4, Wiley, 2001, p. 122.

10 The use and understanding of the concepts of governance and management in this study is equal to the terms used in Biggs, R., Schlüter, M. and Schoon, M. L., 2015b, p. 24; Pahl-Wostl, C., "A Conceptual Framework for Analysing Adaptive Capacity and Multi-level Learning

Governance systems in international settings vary substantially with respect to different variables. They may differ in both functional and geographical scope, for example, just as in their membership composition, degree of formalization or administrative structures. One form that a governance system can take in international settings, when applying this understanding of the concept, is as conventions and regional agreements. A governance system can also comprise a number of different institutions tied together to form a larger system. Despite the structure taken, the basis for a governance system will generally be a reflection of how the environmental problem is formulated and framed.[11] The same problem can be framed differently, though, depending on perspectives and choice of scale. Most problems need to be dealt with on different scales in parallel and in coordination (e.g., globally, regionally, nationally and locally). Depending on the scale, different measures or actions may be suitable and applicable. Other examples of the forms that governance systems could take are inter alia through private governance, such as codes of conduct, certification schemes and voluntary markets for emissions permits. This could also be pursued through the civil sector and NGOs. At any rate, different approaches taken by various sectors are often found in combination or in parallel, thus creating a diverse multidimensional or polycentric structure.[12]

The potential effectiveness of governance systems varies and depends both on scale or the complexity of the problem (i.e., the possibilities to trace and follow the reasons for environmental problems) as well as on the discrepancies between the different State Parties sharing an ecosystem in international settings that could involve different perspectives on the problem. These discrepancies also affect the ability to actually steer the participants toward action to address the problem accurately.[13] If it is a regulatory regime that is the basis of the governance system – a regional agreement, for example – effectiveness can also be connected to regulatory features such as the opportunity it offers for multilateral solutions to environmental problems, as well as its application and development of international legal standards.[14] Generally, effective environmental governance may be translated as the governance strategies with the

Processes in Resource Governance Regimes," *Global Environmental Change*, Vol. 19, 2009, pp. 355–356.

11 Young, O. R., 1994, pp. 15–18; see also Birnie, P., Boyle, A. and Redgwell, C., 2009, pp. 43 ff.

12 Delmas, M. A. and Young, O. R., 2009, pp. 6–9.

13 See e.g. Juda, L., "Considerations in Developing a Functional Approach to the Governance of Large Marine Ecosystems," *Ocean Development and International Law*, Vol. 30, No. 2, 1999, p. 91.

14 Birnie, P., Boyle, A. and Redgwell, C., 2009, p. 84.

best effects in terms of mitigating environmental problems, but whether the system also matches the scale of the problem is an additionally relevant factor. When investigating the role of law in governance, these regulatory features need to be scrutinized in relation to the general apprehension of effectiveness and effective approaches or measures in environmental governance. However, the definition of what effectiveness is with regard to international environmental problems is ambiguous and manifold. Therefore, it is often difficult to identify precise, effective measures. Environmental governance systems aim to take the most effective approaches, though, in trying to solve or reduce the harm from environmental problems and the human activities causing them.[15] Additionally, although these aspects of environmental governance have been in focus for a long time, there are still many questions about the compatibility of legal mechanisms with effective dynamic environmental governance and management. Indeed, it is a common opinion that law and regulation generally contradict the effective governance of dynamic environmental problems.[16] It seems especially difficult to identify effective legal mechanisms in relation to complexity and governance for social-ecological resilience.[17]

3.2 EFFECTIVE GOVERNANCE

As stated, effectiveness is generally difficult to assess in relation to complex environmental problems and not least in relation to the different States in a transboundary setting. Effectiveness is understood under these circumstances as the potential to provide for ecosystem-based governance and management. It could generally mean governance strategies with the best effects on mitigating environmental problems. The regulatory approaches applied generally aim to fit the diversity connected to complexity. Thus, instead of fixating on detailed regulation in relation to the varying nature of different problems across regions, a broad approach is applied. This approach aims to find and comprehend specific categories of more generic

[15] Young, O. R., 1994, pp. 140–160.

[16] See e.g. Garmestani, A. S. and Benson, M. H., "A Framework for Resilience-based Governance of Social-Ecological Systems," *Ecology and Society*, Vol. 18, No. 1, 2013, p. 9, in the introduction; Ruhl, J. B., 2006; Ruhl, J. B., 1997; and Natarajan, U. and Khoday, K., "Locating Nature: Making and Unmaking International Law," *Leiden Journal of International Law*, Vol. 27, No. 3, 2014, pp. 573–593.

[17] Young especially identified this as a problem in Young, O. R., "Institutional Dynamics: Resilience, Vulnerability and Adaptation in Environmental and Resource Regimes," *Global Environmental Change*, Vol. 20, No. 3, 2010. See also Garmestani, A. S., et al., "Introduction – Social-Ecological Resilience and Law," in Garmestani, A. S. and Allen, C. R. (eds.), *Social-Ecological Resilience and Law*, Columbia University Press, 2014b.

activities or governance features. These are generic activities or features that can be of value in different scenarios and cases, as opposed to detailed measures that may be only occasionally effective or applicable. The opinion in these circumstances emphasizes that how things are done and who does them (i.e., management) primarily should be decided nationally or locally. However, the general approach is provided through governance strategies, but at this level, more specific measures cannot be pointed out. What is important is that certain necessary functions can be effectively performed; this kind of approach in governance accepts and acknowledges that there is a need for flexibility and space for adaptations in relation to different settings.[18]

As a result, many governance regimes have chosen to focus their evaluation of effectiveness on processes or mechanisms through which it is possible to identify whether institutions more generally affect the behavior of important actors. Other normative indicators of good governance are also accounted for in this regard – for example, procedures that create accountability, stakeholder participation, legitimacy and democracy.[19] Such normative features are also seen as important in a governance system and in terms of overall effectiveness. Still, additional features also need to be identified in order to pinpoint governance actions that could match the complexity and dynamics of ecosystems.[20] It is in this light that identifying features significant for governance and management for social-ecological resilience, as discussed previously, become important.

The knowledge is still limited regarding how governance features matching ecosystem dynamics and social-ecological resilience, integrated into law, can be recognized and developed. It is especially important to further elaborate and develop views on how such flexible adaptive features promoted by theories on

18 See Juda, L., 1999, p. 91.

19 Young, O. R., "Governance for Sustainable Development in a World of Rising Interdependencies," in Delmas, M. A. and Young, O. R. (eds.), *Governance for the Environment – New Perspectives*, Cambridge University Press, Cambridge 2009, pp. 12–39. See also Chambers, W. B., "Towards an Improved Understanding of Legal Effectiveness of International Environmental Treaties," *Georgetown International Environmental Law Review*, Vol. 16, 2003–2004, pp. 501f. The author reviews different perspectives on effectiveness in international environmental law and also lists several components that contribute to effectiveness. Beyond compliance, other features that foster change and support processes initiated by the treaty are listed as part of a broader view of a treaty regime.

20 This is well defined in Juda, L., 1999, where new governance approaches are discussed. In a section where it is pointed out what is necessary for an operationalization of ecosystem governance, it is stated that there is a need to develop "1. An understanding of what functions must be fulfilled to effectuate a working LME [Large Marine Ecosystem] governance system and what basic principles may be used for guidance as those functions are carried out."

resilience governance play out in combination with the other roles of law.[21] Primarily, roles such as compliance control, institutional stability and rule of law need further review.[22] Despite a growing amount of research, much work also remains to identify concrete legal measures that match resilience perspectives. However, many of the so-called new legal approaches have been discussed with regard to environmental governance perspectives. Questions related to flexibility and adaptivity particularly have been discussed, although without specific connections to governance for social-ecological resilience. Instead, adaptive governance has been in focus. However, as noted previously, measures for integrating resilience governance in legal contexts also have been gaining traction in this field of research. Issues on flexibility and adaptivity have been receiving much attention because many consider these issues to especially contrast with what is considered, in this perspective, as traditional legal approaches and, not least, basic legal principles.[23] These contrasting ideas of law and flexible regulatory approaches are generally pictured as opposing and fundamentally different, while, in practice, environmental law measures could probably be defined more along a range of different legal approaches that are often adaptive or flexible at some level. Thus such measures are not necessarily in a contradictory relationship. In practice, different measures and approaches are also applied in parallel and in combination; thus different approaches may be seen instead as complementary to a complex problem.[24]

Theories on resilience in social-ecological systems combine these different issues and offer a transdisciplinary perspective on effective environmental governance, where law should have a prominent role.[25] In order to increase

21 See also Soininen, N. and Platjouw, F. M., "Resilience and Adaptive Capacity of Aquatic Environmental Law in the EU: An Evaluation and Comparison of the WFD, MSFD, and MSPD," in Langlet, D. and Rayfuse, R. (eds.), *The Ecosystem Approach in Ocean Planning and Governance – Perspectives from Europe and Beyond*, Leiden, 2018, pp. 22–26.

22 This is discussed in Ebbesson, J., "The Rule of Law in Governance of Complex Socio-Ecological Changes," *Global Environmental Change*, Vol. 20, No. 3, 2010, pp. 414–422. See also Ebbesson, J. and Hey, E., "Introduction: Where in Law Is Social-Ecological Resilience?," *Ecology and Society*, Vol. 18, No. 3, 25, 2013; Cosens, B. A., 2013.

23 Some examples are Arnold, C. A. and Gunderson, L. H., "Adaptive Law and Resilience," originally printed in *Environmental Law Reporter*, Vol. 43, No. 5, pp. 10426–10443, reprinted with copyright to Environmental Law Institute, Washington, DC, 2013, University of Louisville, Legal Studies Research Paper Series, Paper No. 2104–04; Wiersema, A., 2008; Angelo, M. J., 2007–2008; Jänicke, M. and Jörgens, H., 2006; Trubek, D. and Trubek, L., 2006; Ruhl, J. B., 2006; Scott, J. and Trubek, D. M., 2002, pp. 1–18; Ruhl, J. B., 1997; Profeta, T. H., 1996; Tarlock, A. D., 1994.

24 Sands, P. H., 2007, p. 31.

25 See some reflections in inter alia Green, O. O., et al., 2015a; Garmestani, A. S., Allen, C. R. and Benson, M. H., "Can Law Foster Social-Ecological Resilience?" *Ecology and Society*, 18 (2):37, 2013; Ebbesson, J. and Hey, E., 2013, at p. 2.

our understanding of the role of law in governance for social-ecological resilience, one main point of concern is to identify features and components of resilience governance in law and thus place law in relation to different aspects of governance for social-ecological resilience.

3.3 SOCIAL SYSTEM PREREQUISITES FOR RESILIENCE GOVERNANCE

In trying to grasp the necessary perspective for resilience governance, it is pertinent to understand more of the social system side to social-ecological systems. It is also important to make some clear distinctions between different aspects in this regard. When discussing law and social-ecological resilience one needs to realize that this concept contains different parts that need to be taken into consideration. The first, and perhaps most obvious, is the resilience of ecosystems; the second part is what can be recognized as the resilience of the social systems; and the third part that requires reflection is something referred to here as the resilience of the legal system.[26] The latter must also be considered as an important integrated part of social resilience.

While the preconditions given by ecosystems are rather well explored, less attention has been paid to the way social systems react in this context. Although such issues are gaining increasing interest, most attention is given issues of social justice and fair distribution of resources as an aspect of social resilience. Beyond these issues and those of adaptive management and law, the resilience of legal systems in the perspective of social-ecological systems has been given only a little attention.[27] It is therefore an important aspect to add when discussing social-ecological resilience. Some support can be gained from research made within political science, and as part of more specific case

26 See Adger, W. N., "Social and Ecological Resilience: Are They Related?," *Progress in Human Geography*, 24(3), 2000, pp. 347–364. Adger discusses these distinctions and investigates whether resilience is even a useful term for social systems in this regard. He defines social resilience as the ability of groups or communities to cope with external stresses and disturbances as a result of social, political and environmental change. A conclusion is that resilience in natural systems provides the capacity to cope with surprises and large-scale changes, and that this is precisely what will allow innovation, coping with change, and social learning in social institutions. See also a short discussion on those distinctions in Ebbesson, J. and Hey, E., 2013, and Cosens, B. A., 2013.

27 See inter alia Adger, W. N., 2000; Cosens, B. A., 2013; Ebbesson, J., 2010; Galaz, V., et al., "Analytical Themes: The Problem of Fit among Biophysical Systems, Environmental and Resource Regimes, and Broader Governance Systems: Insights and Emerging Challenges," in Young, O. R., King, L. K. and Schröder, H. (eds.), *Institutions and Environmental Change – Principal Findings, Applications, and Research Frontiers*, MIT Press, 2008.

studies aiming to pinpoint more precise principles or research areas of social-ecological resilience.[28]

Identifying cornerstones for resilience and fundamental features for dynamic, prosperous social systems is crucial for a governance system. It is also important to realize that these factors, in a transdisciplinary theoretical frame, might adhere to another vocabulary and another line of research. Much of the vocabulary and the definitions used for discussing ecological systems were originally defined by ecologists and not by social scientists. Rather than trying to apply a natural-science frame on social systems, it seems more fruitful to focus on and compare purpose, aim and functionality in a systems composition and design, in this case primarily the legal design. In comparison with natural ecological systems, resilience in social systems may be resting on fundamentally different factors, not least in terms of law and legal institutional structures. Social stability and rule of law, for example, are major factors in social resilience, as opposed to flexibility and adaptivity in ecological resilience.[29] However, in terms of vocabulary and line of research, flexibility might also have slightly different meanings.[30] Thus, an important task in defining social system issues in relation to social-ecological resilience is to compare such aims, functions and purposes behind these features and vocabularies, in order to evaluate possible matches as well as mismatches in terms of functions.

Factors that have been suggested as important for resilience in social systems include social stability and resource dependency. While access to resources depends on many different factors such as global and local economy, trade and not least resilient ecosystems, it can also be controlled to some extent by regulation. Social stability also relies on a range of different factors and can be affected by external pressures.[31] Choosing stability as a factor for social resilience is complicated, since stability could also imply stability in negative feedbacks or undemocratic government. It is, however, also a state achieved by democracy and rule of law, when societies are flourishing, have little corruption and so forth. The basis for this kind of stability is established to a large extent by law, especially in a society based on the rule of law and legitimacy.

28 See e.g. Galaz, V., et al., 2008, pp. 147–182; Duit, A. and Galaz, V., 2008, pp. 311–332; Young, O. R., 2010, pp. 378–385. See also Biggs R., Schlüter M. and Schoon M. L. (eds.), 2015a.

29 For example, Craig, R. K., et al., "Stability and Flexibility in the Emergence of Adaptive Water Governance," in Cosens, B. and Gunderson, L. H. (eds.), *Practical Panarchy for Adaptive Water Governance*, Springer International, 2018.

30 See e.g. the reasoning in Duit, A., et al., "Governance, Complexity and Resilience," *Global Environmental Change*, Vol. 20, No. 3, 2010, at p. 365; and Ebbesson, J., 2010.

31 See: Adger, W. N., 2000, pp. 351–356.

Thus, in this perspective, the connection to the legal system for social resilience is also apparent.[32] Furthermore, a link is visible here – to the idea of resilience in law. Law has a number of important principles, values and institutional features that it must sustain, and that sometimes risk colliding with values and features important for social-ecological resilience.

In a parallel to the principle of sustainable development, law also has a role in establishing some level of equity and fairness, in relation to the use of natural resources.[33] While law needs on the one hand to provide for social stability and maintain prerequisites for the rule of law, it must also become more dynamic and flexible with regard to the ecosystem.[34] It is increasingly noted that social-ecological systems need both a stable basis for trust-building with continuity in interactions in social systems and provide for flexible governance of ecological systems.[35] This requires structures that contain prerequisites to follow and adapt to natural and continuous changes, as well as to new knowledge on governance strategies. Law must also change and persist with different kinds of social or external pressures of time, and adjust, not least to new scientific understanding of the environment. In this way, the legal system in itself must also sustain and embrace a large number of factors and still uphold its main fundament and stay within the framework that creates a baseline of stability and a democratic legal system. If governance is to control the development of social-ecological resilience, all these different aspects need to be intertwined and coexist. To find out how to govern this complex interplay, we need to have a clear picture of all parts of such a governance system and their respective characteristics. In order to maintain basic social needs, in parallel to healthy and productive ecological systems, sustained by a stable legal system, it is necessary to learn more about how to establish institutional structures and law that will provide this in a governance system.[36]

It is important to realize and acknowledge that different features, mechanisms and forms of regulation will vary with different scales to fit both in time and especially in spatial terms. Law and governance structures will have

[32] See also: Cosens, B. A., 2013.

[33] See more in Bosselmann, K., 2008, pp. 58ff.; or Barstow Magraw, D. and Hawke, D., "Sustainable Development," in Bodansky, D., Brunnée, J. and Hey, E. (eds.), p. 630f.

[34] See e.g. Ebbesson, J. and Folke, C., "Matching Scales of Law with Social-Ecological Contexts to Promote Resilience," in Garmestani, A. S. and Allen, C. R. (eds.), *Social-Ecological Resilience and Law*, Columbia University Press, 2014, p. 269f.

[35] Duit, A., et al., 2010.

[36] See Adger, W. N., 2000; Young, O. R., "Effectiveness of International Environmental Regimes: Existing Knowledge, Cutting-Edge Themes, and Research Strategies," *PNAS*, 2011, Vol. 108, No. 50, pp. 19853–19860.

different purposes and roles, depending on whether the scale is local, national or regional. The resilience concept implies that the regulations we set up with the aim to manage a social-ecological system have to be able to respond and adjust to dynamic change, as this is the main characteristic for resilience governance structures.[37]

3.4 PLACING LAW IN THE FRAME OF RESILIENCE GOVERNANCE

As was discussed previously, laws and legal institutions are important in structures for governance, where governance is seen as the sum of the many ways that individuals and institutions, public and private, manage their common affairs.[38] In short, environmental governance theories generally propose strategies and actions that are intended to respond to different aspects of environmental complexity and uncertainty in efforts to protect the environment from harm, and not least from the pressures from human activities. Thus, any strategies for mitigating environmental problems need to consider these governance perspectives, including legal strategies.[39] Resilience governance also includes such perspectives; its theories assume the best ways to cope with environmental pressures and solve environmental problems.

While environmental law should always aim to achieve social-ecological resilience, there are a number of possible scenarios where law may have a role that differs from the approach within resilience governance. Under certain circumstances, the contribution of law in achieving or providing space for social-ecological resilience implies a different approach than what may be prescribed within theories on governance. However, there may also be circumstances where law and legal approaches may contribute to resilience governance approaches to a much greater extent than might be expected. An important component in this study is the transformation of the resilience governance theories into applicable concepts for the integration of law and governance theories. The focus will thus be on comparing the functions and intentions of the resilience principles with law and the functions or approaches of legal mechanisms.

Traditionally there has been a distinction between mainly two opposing perspectives on how governance of commons is best pursued. These opposing

[37] See also Ebbesson, J. and Folke, C., 2014.

[38] Commission on Global Governance, 1995, p. 2.

[39] See e.g. what is written on this in Young, O. R., 1994, pp. 12 ff.

perspectives are central to the environmental debate and were originally presented by Garrett Hardin and Elinor Ostrom. Both perspectives presented still influence governance approaches and theories. Hence, they provide an important background to general theoretical perspectives on governance for social-ecological resilience.[40] According to the theory in the tale by Hardin, users of a common resource always have and always will use such a common area and its natural resources primarily for their own gain and best interests – no matter the consequences.[41] As a contrast, Elinor Ostrom's theories emphasize that a will and an understanding of the importance of sustainability and resilience in a system will make people govern it together through self-organization and also manage to organize sustainable use, thus avoiding over-harvesting.[42] While Hardin's ideas in their most strict version are difficult to enforce in transboundary settings due to lack of governmental force, Ostrom's ideas are instead mainly applicable to local or small-scale communities and therefore would not either function in international transboundary settings. However, her theories have influenced the research developments on the governance of commons.[43]

The role of law in the frame of social-ecological resilience is two-sided. On one side, law has its role as regulator and thus sets the boundaries for the use and governance of natural resources and environmental protection in this regard. This means that law must set the prerequisites for such uses with consideration of the ecosystems and insights that the resilience theories bring in this regard. On the other side, law has a significant role to establish and uphold social stability, comparable to social resilience (see Sections 1.2 and 3.3). Hence, law must balance between contributing to ecological resilience and contributing to upholding social resilience. Social stability, or social resilience in this sense, is to a large extent connected to the principles of a society that is based on democratic values and the rule of

40 See e.g. Underdal, A., "Complexity and Challenges of Long-Term Environmental Governance," *Global Environmental Change*, Vol. 20, No. 3, 2010, pp. 386–393.

41 Hardin, G., "The Tragedy of the Commons," *Science*, Vol. 162, No. 3859, 1968, pp. 1243–1248.

42 Most significantly introduced by Ostrom's case studies in Ostrom, E., *Governing the Commons – The Evolution of Institutions for Collective Action*, Cambridge University Press, 1990.

43 See e.g. Armitage, D., "Governance and the Commons in a Multi-Level World," *International Journal of the Commons*, Vol. 2, No. 1, 2008, pp. 14 ff; Cosens, B. and Gunderson, L. H., "An Introduction to Practical Panarchy: Linking Law, Resilience, and Adaptive Water Governance of Regional Scale Social-Ecological Systems," in Cosens, B. and Gunderson, L. H. (eds.), *Practical Panarchy for Adaptive Water Governance – Linking Law to Social-Ecological Resilience*, Springer International, 2018, p 6f.

law (although of course social stability could also rest on less democratic values and structures).

The next chapter provides a review of governance principles or features for social-ecological resilience. These are the fundaments for further study. They are the features of the kind of governance that law is to match and at the same time the features of governance that law is to be measured against.

4

Defining Features for Resilience Governance

So far, the concepts of social-ecological resilience, law and governance have been discussed and presented from a general view. Their general compatibility has been discussed and analyzed. This general view of social-ecological resilience and its associated prerequisites reflect objectives that should influence governance to achieve social-ecological resilience. These objectives should also influence the objectives, functions and delimitations of law in the bigger picture. Although the general picture is important, it does not reveal to any extent how governance for social-ecological resilience should be shaped and realized in practice. As explained previously, however, the point of this study is to discuss and evaluate the role of law in governance for social-ecological resilience with the aim to identify matching components for legal design. The legal components at disposal are those reviewed. In order to find out more specifically which of those that match resilience governance, it is necessary to define more concrete prerequisites and features or principles for effective and appropriate governance approaches. Throughout the study, these components for resilience governance will hereinafter be referred to as *resilience features*.[1]

The choice of terming the different governance components as "features" is to establish a more distinct language for what they actually are. In other studies and contexts, these governance components have sometimes been described or termed as *principles*. The reason for not adhering to the concept of principles when referring to these components is that they are more than just principles; they are a set of functions and principles with certain

1 The themes or categories of importance for governance could also be described as principles or criteria for governance. The choice to call them features is connected to the fact that they are more generic categories – features – or thematic approaches of importance for governance strategies, rather than precise or unconditional concepts like principles or criteria.

characteristics that represent certain features on which the governance system depends on. Choosing the word "feature" is also to signal that they are not fixed and clearly defined but rather seem to be a nest of functions that together form a feature that is typical of resilience governance. Additionally, not calling these governance components principles is also a choice to separate them from the concept of legal principles.

For the context of this book, the meaning of the terms or concepts of "governance" versus "management" must also be addressed. Governance, as presented previously (Section 3.1), is in this study seen as the sum of the many ways that individuals and institutions, public and private, manage their common affairs. Governance theories propose strategies, structures, institutions and actions on an overarching level. Resilience management in this context should be viewed as more instrumental and as representing concrete operationalization and monitoring, while governance is the structure that will provide overall strategies and measures that are meant to provide a platform and tools for management. It is necessary to understand both these dimensions to evaluate appropriate governance approaches.[2] It is worth emphasizing that the view of the terms governance and management presented here reflects the general use of these concepts throughout the book. They primarily reflect the scale on which the control and application of laws or other measures referred to are operating. In relation to resilience governance and management, the focus in this study is mainly on the role, scale and function of measures or other features rather than on the use of the terms within the cited references of social-ecological resilience. It is especially relevant and necessary to keep this in mind when discussing the role of law, since the role of law also varies depending on scale, both in time and space. National and local laws, moreover, will be nested as a part of the overall governance system of international and EU laws.

Identifying resilience features can be done through different methods. A general literature review combining different attempts to formalize or concretize resilience governance presents a number of points of concern for governance. Furthermore, specific features for building resilience have previously been developed within different research studies.[3] Also research studies on

[2] See e.g. Lebel, L., et al., "Governance and the Capacity to Manage Resilience in Regional Social-Ecological Systems," *Ecology and Society*, Vol. 11(1): 19, 2006.

[3] See e.g. Biggs, R., Schlüter, M. and Schoon, M. L. (eds.), 2015a. The seven principles that the authors have identified are, more concretely, Principle 1 – Maintain diversity and redundancy; Principle 2 – Manage connectivity; Principle 3 – Manage slow variables and feedbacks; Principle 4 – Foster complex adaptive systems thinking; Principle 5 – Encourage learning; Principle 6 – Broaden participation; Principle 7 – Promote polycentric governance systems. See also Chapin, F. S., Kofinas, G. P. and Folke, C. (eds.), 2009, generally.

law and resilience have contributed to identifying different features. Altogether, these features take into account inter alia diversity and redundancy, connectivity, slow variables and complexity. They also emphasize learning (i.e., knowledge as a basis for governance), as well as multilevel or multidimensional, polycentric structures[4] and broad participation. Through combining some aspects of these features with a general literature review, the following points have been chosen for the present study. They are deemed to represent important and constructive governance features that may also be of concern in a legal context:[5]

- Flexibility, knowledge-based adaptivity, diversity, redundancy and transformability (*adaptivity, flexibility and transformability*)
- Multilevel governance, cross-scale interactions, diversity and redundant structures and ecosystem match (*multidimensional and polycentric structures*)
- Pathways for participation, with structures for including stakeholders, local and social knowledge (*stakeholders and structures for participation*)
- Controlling and monitoring slow ecological variables and feedbacks, ensuring trust building, including structures for sanctions and institutional fit (*operationalization, monitoring, compliance and trust building*)

4 *Polycentric structures* is a term often used within resilience theories. In this context, the understanding of this term primarily aims at a governance system with multiple, nested, governing authorities at different scales, close to the general comprehension of multilevel governance. Although polycentric structures are also acknowledged within legal research, this is beyond the scope here, since the legal term has a different meaning.

5 In addition to Biggs, R., Schlüter, M. and Schoon, M. L. (eds.), 2015a, the general literature review that these identified features is based on includes e.g. Chapin, F. S., Kofinas, G. P. and Folke, C. (eds.), 2009; Berkes, F., Colding, J. and Folke, C. (eds.), *Navigating Social-Ecological Systems: Building Resilience for Complexity and Change*, Cambridge University Press, 2003; Duit, A. and Galaz, V., 2008; Galaz, V., et al., 2008; Hahn, T., et al., "Trust-Building, Knowledge Generation and Organizational Innovations: The Role of Bridging Organization for Adaptive Comanagment of a Wetland Landscape around Kristianstad, Sweden," *Human Ecology*, Vol. 34, 2006. See also more general literature on the perspectives and origins of social-ecological resilience theories: Folke, C., "Resilience: The Emergence of a Perspective for Social-Ecological Systems Analysis," *Global Environmental Change*, Vol. 16, No. 3, 2006, pp. 253–267; Walker, B. and Salt, D., *Resilience Thinking – Sustaining Ecosystems and People in a Changing World*, Island Press, 2006; Folke, C., Carpenter, S., Elmqvist, T., et al., "Resilience and Sustainable Development: Building Adaptive Capacity in a World of Transformations," *Ambio*, Vol. 31, No. 5, 2002, pp. 437–440; Liu, J., et al., "Complexity of Coupled Human and Natural Systems," *Science*, Vol. 317, No. 5844, 2007, pp. 1513–1516; Folke, C., et al., "Resilience Thinking: Integrating Resilience, Adaptability and Transformability," *Ecology and Society*, Vol. 15, No. 4, 2010, pp. 20–28; Folke, C., Jansson, Å., Rockström, J., et al., "Reconnecting to the Biosphere," *Ambio*, Vol. 40:719, 2011; Carpenter, S., et al., "From Metaphor to Measurement: Resilience of What to What?," *Ecosystems*, Vol. 4, 2001, pp. 765–781.

While these different categories may include a range of different functions and features from a resilience perspective, they will hereinafter primarily be addressed with a shorter summary of their features – provided previously in brackets. The shorter summaries of these features match the legal context better, but the intention is not to disregard any of the included functions or features from the analysis.

Some aspects of these features or criteria may change in significance and focus depending on the perspective taken – that is, whether they are seen from a social system or an ecological system perspective.[6] Given what has been discussed so far, it is also likely that the understanding of these features may change even more if seen from a strictly legal perspective. In some aspects, there are conflicting interests and priorities between the different systems and perspectives. In addition, the interpretation and significance will vary because the same purpose may take another expression in different scientific fields, and not least with regard to the differences in scientific vocabulary. In addition, law does entail some rather specific prerequisites and principles to be acknowledged, which are not taken into account within the general governance perspective. This is not to say that these interests cannot somehow be aligned or even be productive when put into, and seen from, another perspective. Specific prerequisites of law could just as well have room to be activated and play out within these governance structures, but this is also what must be explored further when establishing the compatibility of law with these theories. The following sections present the resilience perspective on the chosen resilience features that the study is built on. They form the basis for the continued study. They are the foundation of the components for a legal design for social-ecological resilience.

4.1 ADAPTIVITY, FLEXIBILITY AND TRANSFORMABILITY

The first resilience feature identified and presented here – adaptivity, flexibility and transformability – responds directly to the idea of adaptive governance. This feature includes the most fundamental components of resilience governance. In this section, adaptivity, flexibility and transformability are described from a general perspective on resilience research, in their role in resilience thinking more generally.

Adaptivity and its connected functions are frequently mentioned in the resilience theories.[7] Adaptivity in this sense is connected to knowledge and

[6] See also Chapin, F. S., Folke, C. and Kofinas, G. P., 2009, p. 8, Box 1.1.

[7] See Folke, C., 2006, pp. 253–267; Folke, C., et al., 2005, pp. 441–473; Folke, C., Chapin, F. S. and Olsson, P., 2009, p. 118.

knowledge-based measures, as well as to a structure for continuous review and adjustments. It entails a demand for functions that enable a change of approach and measures taken as a result of changed knowledge or new scientific findings. Such functions and processes are crucial to complex and unpredictable systems. This should, among other things, entail governance structures and routines for continuous assessments and on-going reviews of measures and effects. Such structures also indirectly create opportunities to learn and then adjust behavior in order to build resilience. They include the capacity of actors in a system to influence resilience. These functions are characterized by and connected to features of transformability and flexibility, as opposed to rigid organizations with slowly changing structures. In this sense, flexibility is a function that is more direct and represents a faster response, in comparison to adaptive functions. Transformability is primarily seen as a result of adaptive and flexible governance approaches and points to the kind of transformation a system may have to undergo to achieve a state of resilience.[8] Functions for adaptivity, flexibility and so-called transformability are significant and create a feature that will enable systems to cope with, or adjust to, unavoidable changes, as these kinds of managing approaches include flexibility and transformability also with regard to unforeseen changes.[9]

In its essence, creating resilience is all about understanding the social-ecological system, its drivers and thresholds to alternative states, and then trying to enhance parts of the system that may make the system stay in the resilient state or move toward a better alternative state. While always involving a range of variables affecting the system, the multiscale social-ecological system is often controlled by only a few interacting variables that are generally slow-moving. These are the most effective variables to focus on in governance based on adaptive change.[10] Changes to be made and measures that should be taken also depend on the scale chosen for framing the problem, as well as the phase in the adaptive cycle where the action is imposed. It is noteworthy that in a large-scale perspective, the changes and activities required generally represent a slow shift and slow variables. A fast response is often connected to activities and changes at a smaller scale or in a faster phase of the adaptive

8 For example, Folke, C., et al., 2010, pp. 20–28.

9 Folke, C., Colding, J. and Berkes, F., "Synthesis: Building Resilience and Adaptive Capacity in Social-Ecological Systems," in Berkes, F., Colding, J. and Folke, C. (eds.), *Navigating Social-Ecological Systems: Building Resilience for Complexity and Change*, Cambridge University Press, 2003, pp. 375ff.; Chapin, F. S., Folke, C. and Kofinas, G. P., 2009, pp. 23ff.; Chapin, F. S., et al., "Resilience-Based Stewardship: Strategies for Navigating Sustainable Pathways in a Changing World," in Chapin, F. S., Kofinas, G. P., Folke, C. (eds.), 2009a, pp. 327ff.

10 See e.g. the description of this found in Walker, B. and Salt, D., 2006, p. 59 and p. 63.

cycle, where spontaneity is of greater value.[11] This is also connected to the feature of operationalization, control and system feedbacks.

4.2 MULTIDIMENSIONAL AND POLYCENTRIC STRUCTURES

There is a general view in resilience research that multilevel and so-called polycentric governance approaches are important in order to match ecological scales and impose a diversity of measures. Cross-scale interaction is directly related to the view of social-ecological systems as consisting of connected adaptive cycles acting on different scales and in different phases of the adaptive cycle. In order to match such a system, governance and management must also act on different scales but still be interconnected, just like the social-ecological system. Diversity is connected to the idea that diversity of measures provides alternative options for response measures and that these options can be applied at different scales, in parallel at different levels of the governance system to create so-called redundancy. Redundancy in multileveled structures thus allows for a multitude of complementary measures at matching ecological scales.[12] This diversity of measures is meant as a response to the diversity of sources and causes of environmental problems and in addition at different levels in a dynamic system.

Multilevel governance is frequently discussed in resilience literature and often referred to in political science, where many of these theories are based. However, it is also suggested that governance should be polycentric. A polycentric governance structure is seen as a concept or structure closely related to multilevel governance. A polycentric order in this setting has been described as "one where many elements are capable of making mutual adjustments for ordering their relationships with one another within a general system of rules where each element acts with independence of other elements."[13] It could be described simply as a governance system with multiple, nested governing authorities at different scales, which is then

[11] Walker, B. and Salt, D., 2006, pp. 88ff.

[12] See inter alia Kotschy, K., et al., "Principle 1 – Maintain Diversity and Redundancy," in Biggs, R., Schlüter, M. and Schoon, M. L. (eds.), 2015, pp. 51ff.; Folke, C., Chapin, F. S. and Olsson, P., 2009, pp. 116ff. See also Low, B., et al., "Redundancy and Diversity: Do They Influence Optimal Management?," in Berkes, F., Colding, J. and Folke, C. (eds.), 2003.

[13] Ostrom, E. and Janssen, M. A., "Multilevel Governance and Resilience of Social Ecological Systems," in Spoor, M. (ed.), *Globalization, Poverty and Conflict*, Kluwer Academic, 2004, p. 255. See also Ostrom, V., "Polycentricity," in McGinnis, M. (ed.), *Polycentricity and Local Public Economies: Readings from the Workshop in Political Theory and Policy Analysis*, University of Michigan Press, 1999, p. 57f.

a description that comes closer to a general comprehension of multilevel governance.[14] It is furthermore stated that

> flexible coping with external pressures and rapid change is enhanced by governance systems that exist at multiple levels with some degree of autonomy, complemented by modest overlaps in authority and capability. Such systems are regarded as effective since they can provide a repertoire of general principles that can be drawn on by resource users at multiple levels to aid in the crafting of new institutions that cope with changing situations.[15]

The aim of diverse measures is to enable institutional match – that is, to ensure that the measures fit and can be applied properly at the different levels of the problem in environmental complex systems. The aim of diversity is furthermore to create redundancy in the system, which means that if measures or other actions taken fail at some level, other activities or measures will still be applicable. This feature is in turn connected to issues of institutional coordination. With multidimensional structures, institutional coordination is crucial for functional governance.[16] Multitude is also important because these kinds of institutional structures have to be implemented differently and at different levels as well. Through such multidimensional structures, the possibility to match the ecosystem is significantly increased. It is important to realize that scale and multileveled or polycentric approaches are not by themselves sufficient for effective governance, but that such institutions must be in line with ecological and biophysical dynamics and scales.[17] In addition, when it comes to institutional fit to the ecosystem and biophysical dynamics, coordination together with adaptive co-management also serves a special purpose in attempting to adjust the measure, and approaches taken in each dimension or institutional level, to the appropriate scale of the problem.[18]

Diverse institutional responses and measures for complex systems and the corresponding multidimensional structures call for institutional coordination. In this regard, institutional coordination means some form of linkages between different institutional regimes in a cross-organizational manner. The purpose is to create prerequisites for the institutional regimes to be in tune with each other as well as with the problem, and it creates more potential

14 Biggs, R., Schlüter, M. and Schoon, M. L., 2015b, p. 22. This description of polycentricity is found among so-called key concepts. Polycentricity is also acknowledged as a principle in its own right: Schoon, M. L, et al., "Principle 7 – Promote a Polycentric Governance System," in Biggs, R., Schlüter, M. and Schoon, M. L. (eds.), 2015, pp. 226ff.

15 Folke, C., et al., 2005, p. 460.

16 See e.g. Galaz, V., et al., 2008, pp. 161ff.

17 Ibid., p. 148, and generally.

18 Ibid., p. 156 and, p. 161.

for taking action at the right scale. A condition for this is that relevant knowledge and data are also fed into these structures, and that relevant processes and actors are identified, in order to achieve an overview of the different dimensions in governance. The diversity of measures and approaches taken must be linked and coordinated, to create an institutional match in relation to the ecosystem. Another important aspect here, again, is participation. The roles of stakeholders and other forms of participatory actors, not least NGOs, are instrumental in keeping ecosystem-based measures in focus and in establishing themselves as glue within the system.[19]

4.3 STAKEHOLDERS AND STRUCTURES FOR PARTICIPATION

Having broad participation by stakeholders or other interest groups, and ensuring that those concerned are involved in the measures taken, are key features in resilience governance and management. This relates to bottom-up approaches in adaptive governance, where self-organization and local knowledge are important factors; it also relates to structural and monitoring issues in multilevel governance. Stakeholders can be a catalyst in this regard for spreading information and knowledge between levels and within dynamic multilevel structures. They will also be important for monitoring procedures in complex and multileveled institutions. Additionally, they will be important in retrieving knowledge and in the cooperation between private actors and institutions (i.e., co-management) and thus preserve important information flows.[20]

One aim with stakeholder participation is that measures should be taken on the appropriate level, thus by the concerned actors themselves in the first instance, and top-down approaches should be avoided. Avoiding top-down approaches is considered to be important since they will undermine the possibilities for appropriate measures to be taken and also hamper legitimacy, and thus the will to perform the agreed-upon measures. Emphasizing the role of stakeholder participation can be seen as a democratic and decentralized approach. The aim to involve the actors directly concerned also includes basing measures on the local knowledge from those groups as well as spreading information. In addition, as mentioned previously, stakeholders at different

19 See inter alia Chapin, F. S., et al., 2009a, p. 328; Folke, C., Chapin, F. S. and Olsson, P., 2009, p. 120f.

20 See e.g. Huitema, D., et al., "Adaptive Water Governance: Assessing the Institutional Prescriptions of Adaptive (Co-)Management from a Governance Perspective and Defining a Research Agenda," *Ecology and Society*, Vol. 14 (1): 26, 2009, p. 30; Folke, C., et al., 2005, pp. 448 ff.

levels are also important in polycentric structures and in co-management. Additionally, participation by the public and NGOs are generally seen as an important feature for assuring transparency, legitimacy and accountability, which have been established as important for governance structure in general. Thus, issues on trust building and effectiveness are also closely tied to issues of participation. Trust, compliance and choice of measures are also directly connected to participation.[21]

Participation could also be seen as a first step in establishing a bridging organization.[22] Such an organizational structure, however, also requires other forms and levels of knowledge, not least scientific knowledge. This is often provided through participation of other categories of stakeholders, such as interest groups and through direct cooperation with scientists themselves. That, however, is an issue more connected to multilevel governance and institutional polycentrism. It is a structure that connects local actors to higher-level organizations and institutions.[23]

4.4 OPERATIONALIZATION, MONITORING, COMPLIANCE AND TRUST BUILDING

A last component in the basic features of resilience governance is an aspect that is somehow wider and less directly instrumental. This feature is here called "operationalization, monitoring, compliance and trust building," although it rather reflects a complicated net of ecosystem functions and governance features. The functions in a stricter resilience perspective are controlling and monitoring slow ecological variables and feedbacks, ensuring trust building, including structures for sanctions and institutional fit. The chosen title of this feature, however, reflects more of the integration of law in this feature. It has been stated before that the essence of creating resilience is about understanding the social-ecological system, its drivers and thresholds to alternative states, and then to enhance parts of the system that may make the system stay in the resilient state or move toward a better alternative state. Social-ecological systems are affected by a multitude of variables that change and interact on a range of time scales. Some of these

[21] Leitch, A. M., et al., "Principle 6 – Broaden Participation," in Biggs R., Schlüter M. and Schoon M. L. (eds.), 2015.

[22] See e.g. Green, O. O., et al., "The Role of Bridging Organizations in Enhancing Ecosystem Services and Facilitating Adaptive Management of Social-Ecological Systems," in Allen, C. R. and Garmestani, A. S. (eds.), *Adaptive Management of Social-Ecological Systems*, Springer Science Dordrecht, 2015b, pp. 110 ff.

[23] See e.g. Hahn, T., et al., 2006, pp. 585ff.

variables are considered to be slow, changing more gradually than those that are considered to be fast.[24]

While a social-ecological system always involves a range of variables affecting the system, a multiscale social-ecological system is often controlled by only a few interacting variables, and these are generally slow-moving.[25] What is considered as slow or fast is not precise; it varies with each type of social-ecological system, but some general factors seem to be established. Slow variables often affect the fast variables, for example, which in turn are often characterized by different kinds of ecosystem services. The reason why governance should focus particularly on the slow variables is because they generally control the fundament of a social-ecological system and thus whether or not a critical threshold is exceeded.[26] Feedback is related to these variables in that they are the result of changes in the controlling variables. The system as a whole is put into motion by changes made in the slow controlling variables, which results in different feedbacks. The feedbacks can be either positive or negative, depending on the kind of change they respond to. However, positive versus negative is not related to good or bad. Whether they are considered good or bad for the system is related to what the system needs to achieve a good resilient state. Feedbacks can be reinforcing a changing trend or they can dampen the effects of change. Sanctions in connection with misbehavior by an actor are an example of a dampening negative feedback; thus a negative feedback does not necessarily entail a negative result. The more the controlling slow variables can be reinforced or adjusted, the better the system will respond to sudden external shocks. Controlling variables set certain bounds on the possible structures of a social-ecological system and determine, to a significant extent, its structure and processes.[27]

The resilience theories also show that reinforcing slow variables at local scale is connected to trust building and knowledge generation. This is because social system trust building and knowledge generation are factors that prepare the system for more abrupt and fast changes.[28] Creating trust between actors and institutions involved in governance and management permeates most of the other prerequisites for resilience governance. It is needed both between

[24] Chapin, F. S., Folke, C. and Kofinas, G. P., 2009, pp. 12ff.

[25] An easily comprehensible description of this is found in Walker, B. and Salt, D., 2006, p. 59 and p. 63.

[26] Walker, B. and Salt, D., 2006, p. 59 and p. 63; Biggs, R., et al., "Principle 3 – Manage Slow Variables and Feedbacks," in Biggs R., Schlüter M. and Schoon M. L. (eds.), 2015, pp. 109f.; Chapin, F. S., Folke, C. and Kofinas, G. P., 2009, pp. 12ff.

[27] Biggs, R., et al., 2015, pp. 109–114.

[28] Hahn, T., et al., 2006.

actors on the same levels and between the different levels, both vertical and horizontal. At a local scale, trust building is dependent to a large extent on participatory actors and NGOs. They contribute to transparency, monitor and create a basis for legitimacy, which is important in trust building.[29] As stated previously, a bridging organization can coordinate and overarch the gaps between different institutions and the actors or networks in governance structures, and thus make the overall structure more efficient. Such an organization is also meant to bridge gaps between both temporal and spatial scales that are present in international environmental governance, where trust on a different level is also important. This is directly connected to problems that might occur in polycentric governance structures.[30]

29 See e.g. Folke, C., et al., 2005, pp. 448ff.
30 Ibid., pp. 460–461.

5

Adaptivity, Flexibility and Transformability

Adaptivity, flexibility and transformability are fundamental features of resilience governance. These features represent the need for governance to match the constant movements of the ecosystem and the environmental effects of pressures on the ecosystem. It is through adaptive and flexible features that transformability can be created. This chapter aims to identify adaptive or flexible mechanisms within law that can match and provide for such features in the governance system. Adaptive or flexible mechanisms within law could be described as legal structures and measures, or other regulatory approaches, that create space for adaptive procedures and flexible responses also within the legal regime. However, it must be noted that law could also create a kind of resistance to flexible changes in the social-ecological system. This could be regarded as one main function connected to the institutional structure and the social resilience that law creates, where stability over time and the potential to anticipate and prevent certain developments are central.[1]

Adaptive legal structures are generally open-ended or framework-based, where they create space for flexibility as a means of change. Adaptive governance and adaptive law are also connected to creating pathways for participation at different institutional levels. Participation is often also an important element for monitoring data and feedback, not least through the participation of NGOs at all scales. With the development of environmental law, the legal principles, new legal structures and different kinds of mechanisms developed. New environmental law structures have been designed to create both flexibility and adaptivity in the aim to respond to environmental variations and the need for continuous review. Thus, legal regulation can also, through these mechanisms, represent the functions of adaptive governance.

[1] See also Cosens, B. A., 2013. Cf. Galaz, V., et al., 2008, pp. 148ff, regarding identifying institutional misfits.

This chapter aims to explore legal mechanisms for adaptivity, flexibility and transformability. This involves reviewing the form such functions can take, the ways that different forms and shapes of adaptivity are linked to other components in the legal systems, and the different roles of law. The kinds of legal mechanisms that could represent such features within law are thus evaluated and assessed in this chapter. Such mechanisms are primarily institutional design, the form of obligations and provisions included in a legal instrument (i.e., whether they are strict, vague or intentionally flexible requirements etc.). Furthermore, the environmental law principles are discussed, as are new regulatory approaches, such as the ecosystem approach, and the effects connected to pluralistic polycentric legal governance. Moreover, review structures and powers invested in a legal instrument are discussed in relation to issues of operationalizing and monitoring, which are crucial questions in relation to flexibility and transformability.

Before exploring and elaborating more on how flexible and adaptive features are reflected in a legal context, the first part of this chapter aims to describe the basic functions and intentions with these features in the resilience theories and in governance. After that, the corresponding functions and legal mechanisms found in law and legal systems are defined and assessed.

5.1 A RESILIENCE PERSPECTIVE ON ADAPTIVITY, FLEXIBILITY AND TRANSFORMABILITY

The very core of social-ecological systems is made up of the dynamics between periods of abrupt and gradual change and the capacity to adapt or transform for persistence. In this context, resilience is the capacity of a social-ecological system to continually change and adapt, yet remain within critical thresholds. Adaptivity represents the capacity to adjust responses to changing external drivers or internal processes, thereby allowing for development along the current path. In some sense, adaptivity could also imply adjustment to changes. Transformability, however, is the capacity to cross thresholds into new development pathways.[2] Transformability, in this sense, is dependent on adaptive functions since such functions will provide updated knowledge. Adaptive governance features provide the knowledge needed to take measures necessary to transform the system also across such system thresholds. Flexibility is connected to adaptivity and transformability, since it is also

[2] Folke, C., et al., 2010, pp. 20–28. See also Chaffin, B. C., et al., "Transformative Environmental Governance," *Annual Review of Environment and Resources*, Vol. 41:1, 2016, pp. 399–423.

a feature that enables changed response or change of measures but on another, faster, scale.[3]

Adaptivity and flexibility may be the most significant features of resilience governance (as discussed in Chapter 4). These features represent characteristics of adaptive governance, which form a base in resilience governance due to the aim of adaptive governance to address or create a fit to environmental complexity.[4] In the sense intended in this context, adaptivity is directly connected to integrating new knowledge and creating knowledge-based measures. It is mainly operationalized through structures where measures and regulations follow an adaptive cycle in which the regulatory measures and approaches are continuously reassessed. Such a structure provides a feedback system, where new knowledge contributes to and changes the system when new experiences and scientific discoveries are made (i.e., transformational change). Hence, it entails flexible functions that enable change of approach and measures as a result of changed knowledge or new scientific findings, as opposed to a static system that sticks only to what was once first set out. What is aimed for and intended with this change is adaptivity that creates change in the connections and feedback that link social-ecological systems. This can be compared to the kind of change that instead concerns social system adaptation to a new order as a result of environmental change that is seen as unavoidable. Such functions and processes are crucial to complex and unpredictable systems. Flexibility can both provide a change of measure and approach in order to achieve the goal set out and change what is to be achieved if new facts create other prerequisites or an alternative picture of what is necessary and reasonable. Hence, a significant aspect of adaptive governance systems is to include flexible structures and routines for continuous assessments and ongoing reviews of actions and measures taken. Then the actors within the system can adjust their measures or behaviors in their efforts to transform the social-ecological system and restore the resilience of the ecosystem in focus.[5] Adaptivity is thus a function characterized by, and connected to, features of flexibility and transformability as described above. Moreover, adaptive structures create a system prepared for both deliberate and active change (i.e., transformation), in order to sustain resilience, but also the kind of adaptivity that is needed in response to a changing world and changing conditions.

[3] See e.g. Chapin, F. S., Folke, C. and Kofinas, G. P., 2009, pp. 20–21; Folke, C., 2006, p. 262.

[4] See inter alia Folke, C., 2006; Folke, C., et al., 2005; Folke, C., Chapin, F. S. and Olsson, P., 2009, p. 118.

[5] Folke, C., et al., 2010.

The knowledge necessary for adaptive governance is closely connected to inter alia participation. It is necessary to create pathways for participation, for both those directly concerned with the matter and for scientific expertise, in order to gather knowledge to feed into the adaptive systems. Local knowledge is the main factor for management (i.e., in a small-scale perspective).[6] In addition, participation is often an important element for monitoring data and feedbacks, not least through the participation of NGOs.[7] However, an adaptive instrument will also require other forms and levels of knowledge, not least scientific knowledge, which is often provided through the participation of other categories of stakeholders, such as interest groups and the direct cooperation with scientists themselves.

5.2 ADAPTIVITY AND FLEXIBILITY IN ENVIRONMENTAL LEGISLATION

International law can provide adaptivity and flexibility in many different ways, both directly and indirectly. It is flexible in itself to some degree, since the States are to implement the agreed-upon contents, and this can be pursued differently depending on different factors bound to the State.[8] A basic foundation in international law is the principle that all States are sovereign and thereby independent when it comes to regulatory authority and political decisions within the State territory. This creates the prerequisites for cooperation and the development of legal instruments.[9] Although some agreements may have compliance control structures that will scrutinize implementation, or at least aim to coordinate implementation with the other States of the agreement, in the end, States still have the sovereign right to decide on their own measures. When a State agrees to be a Party to an agreement, an

6 See e.g. Hahn, T., et al., 2006.

7 See e.g. Folke, C., et al., 2005; Folke, C., Chapin, F. S. and Olsson, P., 2009. See also Ebbesson, J., “Public Participation,” in Bodansky, D., Brunnée, J. and Hey, E. (eds.), 2007a, p. 689.

8 It must be noted here that flexibility in international law is sometimes discussed in terms of escape clauses or other forms of more direct ways for how States can manage the risk of joining an agreement. While this is closely connected the other forms of flexibility and also an important discussion, it primarily relates to compliance and the choice of treaty design. It is not to any great extent related to the idea of flexibility as it is intended within theories of resilience governance and the resilience features and will not be analyzed further in this chapter. See e.g. Helfner, L. R., “Flexibility in International Agreements,” in Dunoff, J. and Pollack, M. A. (eds.), *Interdisciplinary Perspectives on International Law and International Relations – The State of the Art*, Cambridge University Press, 2013.

9 For a general review of the development and status of international environmental law, see e.g. Birnie, P., Boyle, A. and Redgwell, C., 2009, pp. 1–42.

obligation to implement and interpret the agreement in good faith does of course follow. Still, it is a fact that it lies within the margin of discretion that States do this in their own manner, and it is difficult for an international regime to pierce through that veil of sovereignty in order to steer the implementation (Section 2.1). In addition, since international law is a result of negotiations, the contents and requirements stated in an agreement as a rule are vague and thus also in this regard leave space for a variety in interpretation and implementation. Thus, international legal demands are generally quite flexible in themselves.[10]

EU law is mostly implemented with State discretion as well, and this thus also leaves a gap between different States in the ways of implementing a directive. As a contrast to international law, however, EU directives are usually at least a little more precise to their contents, and EU regulations are definitely more precise.[11] Most importantly, the supranational structure of the EU provides a more direct review of implementation than what is generally possible under international law (Section 2.2.1).[12] In comparison with international law agreements, which must first be accepted and ratified by each State before it becomes binding, the supranational structure of the EU legal order entails that the laws adopted become binding on the Member States without prior approval or ratification. It is already indirectly accepted with the transfer of competence made when becoming a Member State. In this way, the individual Member States have abandoned the ability to block legislation adopted by the EU, although the Member States do vote on new legislation.[13] Seen in this perspective, the laws set out in EU directives have different effects on the States. However, legislation by the EU takes different forms, depending on the issue area in focus and the competence given by the Treaty in that policy area (Section 2.2). The main forms of legislative instruments are regulations, directives and decisions.[14] Regulations are the most direct and

[10] On the ambiguity of international agreements, see e.g. Chayes, A. and Chayes, A. H., *The New Sovereignty: Compliance with International Regulatory Agreements*, Harvard University Press, 1995, pp. 10f.; Gehring, T., 2007, pp. 469–471. See also Boyle, A., “Some Reflections on the Relationship of Treaties and Soft Law,” in Gowlland-Debbas, V. (ed.), *Multilateral Treaty-Making – The Current Status of Challenges to and Reforms Needed in the International Legislative Process* (part of the series Nijhoff Law Specials, Vol. 47), Kluwer Law International, 2000, pp. 31f.

[11] See more detailed description in Craig, P. and de Búrca, G., 2011, pp. 104ff.

[12] See Langlet, D. and Mahmoudi, S., 2016, pp. 134ff.

[13] According to Article 192 TFEU, it is only legislation that is supported by consensus, or a qualified majority of Member States representing a qualified majority of the EU citizens that can be adopted.

[14] TFEU Article 288.

detailed form of legislation in the EU. They are binding in their entirety and are directly applicable within all Member States. Directives differ from regulations in that they are only binding with regard to what is to be achieved; they leave the choices of methods, measures or regulatory mechanisms to the Member States. Directives thus need to be implemented and are not directly applicable. The third alternative, decisions, are just like regulations in that they are binding in their entirety but are only binding on those to whom the decision is addressed.[15] Implementation under EU law is thus not as flexible as under international law. However, it is increasingly common in EU environmental law to adopt framework directives with very loose and flexible design (Section 2.4.4).[16] Framework directives set up an environmental or ecological goal, the goal decided on is to be monitored and reported on, but besides that, this form of legislation leaves much space for States to further adopt measures to achieve those goals.

The extent of success with these kinds of new regulatory approaches is partly related to the extent to which they are able to reflect the intentions and functions implied in the resilience governance structures. The governance system is only effective if all components are integrated and combined. Adaptive features in a legal system also risk becoming a leeway away from strict obligations if they are not governed and monitored in a well-designed system. The effectiveness of these features is also related to the extent to which these regulatory features in addition and in parallel can fulfill the other fundamental functions and roles of law with relevance for social system resilience (Section 3.3).

5.3 IDENTIFYING LEGAL FEATURES OF ADAPTIVITY AND FLEXIBILITY

Transformability is connected to the aim to improve social-ecological systems, by creating forceful and effective measures for change (see the discussion on slow variables in Chapter 8).[17] To create this kind of transformation, as noted previously, governance systems must be adaptable to new knowledge about the social-ecological system they are designed to govern. A governance system has to respond to both fast and slow changes as well as to the threat of critical threshold values. The governance perspective also implies a further focus on

15 See more detailed description in Craig, P. and de Búrca, G., 2011, pp. 104ff.

16 See also Trubek, D. M. and Trubek, L. G., 2006, pp. 11f.

17 Biggs, R., et al., "Principle 3 – Manage Slow Variables and Feedbacks," in Biggs, R., Schlüter, M. and Schoon M. L. (eds.), *Principles for Building Resilience: Sustaining Ecosystem Services in Social-Ecological Systems*, Cambridge University Press, 2015.

the social dimensions of social-ecological systems and the mechanisms that are prerequisites for effective adaptive governance and ecosystem-based management. This includes inter alia areas of building adaptive capacity to deal with uncertainty and surprise, including external drivers, and supporting flexible institutions and social networks in multilevel governance systems.[18]

As discussed in Chapter 4, parallels between concepts might not be directly translatable when approaching questions of social-ecological systems. This is also the case regarding questions of what is significant for flexible and adaptive governance in ecological systems. Moreover, issues connected to temporal or spatial scales and their implications for adaptive governance in legal regulation must be regarded in the perspective of a transition or translation of governance features into legal mechanisms. In this way, we also find new conceptual frames for continued evaluations and research on these matters. One important issue to sort out, therefore, is how to link aspects of adaptivity and flexibility to features such as liability and accountability and other functions inherent in law which lie beyond environmental governance, and to explore the compatibility of these concepts.[19]

International law is rarely applied directly. The idea of international law is for it to be transposed or implemented, as discussed previously. International agreements must be translated into national legislation in each State Party. This means that each State that is a Party to an agreement creates its own national laws that reflect the intent and substance of the agreement, so that the agreement comes into action. The level of flexibility is then reflected inter alia in the capacity given to the States in determining just how to do this. Given the nature of international agreements, flexibility in terms of international law could probably be defined by different aspects.[20] Open-structure laws and framework agreements contain significant flexibility for State Parties to choose their own way of implementation and implementation measures – that is, making their own choice of instruments and measures in relation to the national preferences and the actions concerned. The flexibility here is visible at the point where the process of implementation is to be defined. Another aspect of flexibility is thus as a contrast, seen when States are free to continuously choose and adjust the instruments and measures by which to implement

18 See e.g. Folke, C., 2006; Folke, C., Jansson, Å., Rockström, J., et al., 2011.

19 See also Cosens, B. A., 2013; Ebbesson, J., 2010, pp. 414–422; Adger, N., W., 2000, pp. 347–364; Duit, A., et al., 2010, pp. 363–368.

20 See e.g. Redgwell, C., "Multilateral Environmental Treaty-Making," in Gowlland-Debbas, V. (ed.), *Multilateral Treaty-Making – The Current Status of Challenges to and Reforms Needed in the International Legislative Process* (part of the series Nijhoff Law Specials, Vol. 47), Kluwer Law International, 2000, pp. 89–107.

the agreement. This requires a structure that allows for the continuous change of measures according to local environmental circumstances and the nature of the problem, and thus makes changes as a response to unforeseen developments in the prerequisites. It also necessitates flexibility on a lower scale, primarily to provide space for flexibility in the national legal system. Flexibility in this regard is then potentially restricted by prerequisites given in the national legal system.[21] An open-structure legal framework could still be formed around a substance agreement, while open-structure laws, with requirements on continuous review of measures and implementation, would probably characterize more of a procedural system and procedural obligations. This could also be a goal-oriented framework, where the target goal is what is being evaluated. In frameworks where the main obligation is to take measures to achieve a certain environmental goal, this has inter alia become characteristic for EU environmental law, particularly in the area of marine and water protection. The use of the word *open* in the sense in which it is applied here reflects a kind of regulatory structure that is not locked to one single solution (i.e., one way of implementation). Instead, it is connected with the intention of flexibility and openness to what the State determines to be a suitable instrument or measure.[22]

The most prominent example of a framework directive is the Water Framework Directive. The overall goal of the Water Framework Directive is good ecological and chemical status.[23] The main purpose of the Water Framework Directive is to protect the quality of waters on the landward side of the baseline. The different types of waters and their classification in relation to the overarching environmental goal are defined and categorized in the directive.[24] The directive also sets out a timetable for arranging a national institutional structure for regularly assessing the water status in different areas

21 See e.g. Nilsson, A. K. and Bohman, B., 2015; Cosens, B. and Gunderson, L. H., "Adaptive Water Governance: Summary and Synthesis," in Cosens, B. and Gunderson, L. H. (eds.), *Practical Panarchy for Adaptive Water Governance*, Springer International, 2018, pp. 316–317, and Craig, R. K., et al., 2018.

22 See also Gehring, T., 2007, pp. 476–483; Ebbesson, J., *Compatibility of International and National Environmental Law*, Iustus Förlag AB, 1996, pp. 83–99; Bodansky, D., 2010, pp. 57ff.

23 The Water Framework Directive Art 1, defines as its purpose the protection of inland surface waters, transitional waters, coastal waters and groundwaters. In order to achieve this, ecological objectives are set out in Article 4. A general requirement for ecological protection, and a general minimum chemical standard, was introduced to cover all surface waters in relation to the ecological objectives. Two elements of "good ecological status" and "good chemical status" were then defined. These are elaborated in Annex V of the Water Framework Proposal, in terms of the quality of the biological community, hydrological characteristics and chemical characteristics.

24 The Water Framework Directive, Articles 1 and 2 (and Article 4).

and for taking measures to achieve the goal. These instructions in the directive are very detailed, but beyond that, the Member States have a wide national freedom in how to take measures.

In summary, the role of environmental law and environmental legal regulations could be narrowed down to the task of providing incentives for actors who cause environmental deterioration, to change their behavior to a more environmentally sustainable one. In the perspective of adaptive and flexible governance, this entails measures corresponding to this. There are many ways to accomplish this, and some are more flexible than others. Examples range from what is usually discussed in terms of command-and-control approaches that often entail bans or targets, to incentive-based systems that usually include economic incentives, to less structured approaches based on information systems. These different kinds of regulations also contain specific features, and they can be applied alone or in combination.[25]

Adaptivity in international environmental law could also be a function resulting from flexibility at the national level, as described previously. However, adaptivity in an international legal structure could also take other forms. A typical example would be an international structure that provides for continuous evaluations, assessment and other kinds of procedures – for example, procedures that entail a continuous update on knowledge, science and new possible measures, which could then be incorporated into institutional structures and substantial contents. This structure would have a secondary effect for the State Parties as the new knowledge is incorporated. Such structure is typical of how many international agreements work. Another, or additional, mechanism for such knowledge-based adaptive international structures would be a mechanism for transferring knowledge and information to States and other stakeholders. Thus, in addition to incorporating the new knowledge into the international regime and its content, and affecting the State implementation, this structure can also transfer knowledge directly to the relevant authorities and other stakeholders through different institutional pathways, thus contributing to the general knowledge and acceptance of the problems as well as enabling capacity building.

These are just some general ideas and pictures, but of course, adaptive international legal structures could be, and are, arranged in many different ways. In addition to these interpretations of the direct function of flexibility and adaptivity, there are many different kinds of regulatory measures and principles that also accomplish flexibility in international agreements. The principles and structures developed as part of environmental law can generally

[25] Bodansky, D., 2010, p. 84; Stewart, R. B., 2007, p. 148ff. See also Sands, P., Peel, J., Fabra, A. and MacKenzie, R., 2012, pp. 121ff.

be seen on some level as adaptive and flexible in themselves. In the next section, the different functions defined here are reviewed and evaluated more specifically with regard to legal structures, approaches and measures.

5.3.1 *Institutional Design and the Form of General Provisions*

One way of making international agreements flexible in different ways and to different degrees is related to their design, or procedural structure.[26] Many international and regional environmental agreements adopted in the years after the Stockholm Conference show signs of new kinds of institutional structures. These new kinds of institutions include a different approach to institutional collaboration between States, in comparison to previous institutions. They are both more informal and more flexible, and are often innovative in relation to norm creation and compliance. More traditional forms of institutional structures were generally governed by an International Governmental Organization (IGO) and adopted more detailed measures. One significant substantial function with the modern and less formal agreements is that they have decision-making power to amend the convention in a less formal way than the procedure under an IGO.[27]

Since many of the environmental law agreements are adopted after the Stockholm Conference, most of the most significant are such autonomous agreements. Due to their institutional structures, they have also developed over time, adopting protocols to address new issues within their applicable scope.[28] A way to more deliberately create space for adaptivity and the adoption of protocols in an agreement is also to create so-called framework agreements. This is usually a binding agreement for cooperation where the general provisions do not go into much detail. The intention is instead to continuously fill the framework by adopting protocols or other forms of Annexes with more

[26] On the interrelationship between form and substance in the design of international agreements see: Raustiala, K., "Form and Substance in International Agreements," *American Journal of International Law*, Vol. 99, No. 3, 2005.

[27] Churchill, R. R. and Ulfstein, G., 2000, p. 625, and p. 628. See also e.g. Gehring, T., 2007, pp. 473, and pp. 474–475; Ulfstein, G., 2007, pp. 880ff.

[28] Churchill, R. R. and Ulfstein, G., 2000, p 624, lists the treaties they deem fall within this category and that includes *The 1973 Convention on International Trade in Endangered Species of Wild Fauna and Flora (CITES), the Convention on the Conservation of Migratory Species of Wild Animals, of 1979 (the Bonn Convention), the 1985 Convention for the Protection of the Ozone Layer; the 1992 United Nations Framework Convention on Climate Change (the Climate Change Convention), the 1992 Convention on Biological Diversity (the Biodiversity Convention) and the 1998 Convention on the Prior Informed Consent Procedure for Certain Hazardous Chemicals and Pesticides in International Trade (the Prior Informed Consent Convention)*. Some of these have one or more protocols.

specified requirements. However, once adopted, such Annexes must be ratified before they become binding on the States.[29] Many environmental agreements adopted after the 1970s include a less complicated order for decision-making, also in these institutional structures. This less complicated design entails inter alia that amendments can be adopted without the formal and time-consuming routines that otherwise prevail.[30] Adding protocols to a framework agreement requires a gathering of all the Parties, in a Conference or Meeting of the Parties (COP or MOP). The new provisions have to be negotiated and adopted in a manner similar to the one used in the original agreement negotiations. This is still less formal than under an IGO, however, and the reason for creating framework structures is that although Parties to a convention have the will and intention to cooperate, it may be difficult to agree directly on certain measures. With a framework agreement, the intention to cooperate can be established as a first step, and then with time the development of obligations and the form of cooperation can be developed. This type of structure is also often connected to a lack of scientific facts or scientific uncertainty at the time of adopting the actual agreement, but as science advances more and better requirements can be added. Another reason, especially in the case of environmental agreements, is that the agreement intends to create an adaptive approach where provisions can be adopted continuously. Amendments can be adopted as a result of new knowledge and scientific findings on the problem or because the prerequisites and the nature of the problem are in constant flux, and then these amendments can be made without a lengthy procedure.[31] The Vienna Convention for the Protection of the Ozone Layer,[32] which adopted the Montreal Protocol on Substances that Deplete the Ozone Layer[33] (the Montreal Protocol) to reduce emissions of ozone-depleting substances and the Convention on Long-Range Transboundary Air-Pollution (LRTAP) are presented as successful examples of agreements adopting amendments to develop the provisions in an adaptive way in relation to the problem in focus.

In addition to an adaptive structure, the provisions (i.e., the form of provisions or obligations) also determine the level of flexibility of a legal instrument. This is also connected to the structure and design of the instrument. As stated previously, flexibility is then often reflected in the margin of discretion given to the Parties in interpreting the requirements, as well as in how to implement them. As stated, many open-structure laws and framework

29 See e.g. Birnie, P., Boyle, A. and Redgwell, C., 2009, p. 85 and pp. 86ff; Gehring, T., 2007, p. 477f.

30 See also Churchill, R. and Ulfstein, G., 2000, p. 637.

31 See Gehring, T., 2007, pp. 478f. See also Churchill, R. R. and Ulfstein, G., 2000, pp. 636–637.

32 1513 UNTS 323.

33 1522 UNTS 3.

agreements contain flexibility for State Parties to choose their own method of implementation and implementation measures – that is, making their own choice of instruments and measures in relation to the national preferences and the actions concerned. This can be due to the more or less intentional room for flexibility; see, for example, the discussion on vagueness noted previously in this chapter. In some cases, this kind of instrument is also goal-oriented and thus only requires States to work toward a goal. It is important here to make a remark concerning the difference between having a wider margin of discretion and having a goal to achieve, and thus a requirement to work toward a common target, from a structure that lacks any common design or controls.

5.3.2 *Principles*

The general environmental law principles are perhaps the most apparent way to incorporate flexible, and in some regards adaptive, features in an international environmental agreement, as introduced in Section 2.4.1. These principles, such as the precautionary principle, the polluter pays principle, the principles on the use of best available technique and the best environmental practices, have ambiguous legal status. It is argued that they are developed from a reluctance to take strict measures, but they have generally been developed also as a response to the need for proactivity and precaution in relation to the environment.[34] These principles add an important element to the environmental laws, as they are adaptive and flexible. The interpretation of the environmental law principles changes with the continuous change in the environment, as well as developments in technical, scientific or other forms of knowledge. To some extent, this shift to an acceptance of general principles, with no exact definition, also changes the approaches, measures and methods adopted in environmental law.[35] The principles are constructed to respond to, and develop with, changing environmental and regulatory circumstances. Through application of the precautionary principle, for example, certain activities could be stopped if new knowledge implies that the given action could be harmful; this could be described as an adaptive feature. This applies even if the activity was previously under regulatory sanction, so it also integrates a flexible approach. The principles of best available techniques and the best environmental practices show typical adaptive features in that their

34 See inter alia Beyerlin, U., 2007, pp. 446f.; Sands, P., et al., 2012, pp. 187ff.; Birnie, P., Boyle, A. and Redgwell, C., 2009, pp. 152ff.; de Sadeleer, N., 2002, pp. 258ff.

35 de Sadeleer, N., 2002, p. 371.

requirements and level of strictness will change with technical development and knowledge regarding environmental practices in different areas.

5.3.3 *New Governance Approaches*

As a basis for adaptive law, framework structures have become an important feature of EU environmental regulations, as mentioned previously. This is also a response to new governance approaches.[36] Since EU directives are to be applied and thus must be applicable in all the EU Member States, an approach has been developed in which the details of the requirements are adopted locally in order to create a better match and can be adjusted to the local or regional circumstances. In particular, the Water Framework Directive has been attracting a lot of attention, as it was the first environmental framework directive of its kind. The Marine Strategy Framework Directive has followed the Water Framework Directive in this approach. Besides creating a better match to different environmental circumstances throughout the EU, the framework structure has also become a way to include an ecosystem approach (see Sections 2.4.4 and 2.5). The main feature of the ecosystem approach in these directives rests on requirements for water quality that are to be estimated and agreed on locally, thus making the status and specific problems of each area the basis for legal measures.[37] The flexible and adaptive features in the concept of ecosystem approach are each elaborated further in the next section, since to a large extent the approach is a legal mechanism in its own right.

5.3.4 *Ecosystem Approach*

The concept of ecosystem approach is probably the newest and least developed part of the flexible and adaptive features in environmental law. It is a concept that reflects parallels to features of resilience governance in comparison with other legal mechanisms and approaches (Section 2.5).

The concept of ecosystem approach has the potential to further the preventive and precautionary approaches taken as a result of the introduction of the environmental law principles. With its focus on the status of the ecosystem and emphasis on adaptive and pluralistic measures, the concept could be a tool

36 EU White Paper (2001).

37 Scott, J. and Trubek, D. M., 2002, pp. 1–18; Trubek, D. M. and Trubek, L. G., 2006; Jänicke, M. and Jörgens, H., 2006. See also Green, O. O., et al., "EU Water Governance: Striking the Right Balance Between Regulatory Flexibility and Enforcement?" *Ecology and Society*, Vol. 18(2):10, 2013.

that further merges the social and ecological systems in legal governance. It has opened up for a new field for flexibility of measures that combines both general environmental governance and legal regulation.[38]

The ecosystem approach brings light to an issue of flexibility in international environmental and legal governance, and this issue needs to be acknowledged. The ecosystem approach not only aims to make the status of the ecosystem the focus of protective and preventive measures; it also entails and invokes an adaptive approach to legal governance. This means that different measures are to be implemented at different levels of governance. The implementation of an ecosystem approach thus adjusts the whole realm of environmental regulation, as it takes its departure in environmental or ecological status.

5.3.5 *Polycentric Legal Governance*

An increasing amount of international or regional environmental agreements are continuously being adopted (see Chapter 5). These agreements thus coexist and, sometimes, regulate the same problem or different aspects of the same problem. In addition, regional organizations like the EU co-govern with different kinds of international regimes.[39] Some scholars and experts argue that this is a problem, since a conflict of interests and of authority could arise. It could also be considered, however, as a way in which another form of flexibility and adaptivity is constituted. Parallel regulatory instruments provide a multitude of measures and provide further solutions to the related problems (Chapter 6).[40]

The environmental problems in focus are often highly complex and persistent environmental problems. The problems are connected to a range of human activities and need to be solved through a complex range of measures. These complex structures could thus contribute to environmental recovery since the multitude of sources calls for a multitude of possible measures. In this sense, flexibility in the governance system can also add flexibility in

38 See e.g. CBD Malawi Principles; Österblom, H., et al., 2010; Long, R., 2012; Trouwborst, A., 2009, pp. 26–37.

39 See e.g. van Leeuwen, J., van Hoof, L. and van Tatenhove, J., "Institutional Ambiguity in Implementing the European Union Marine Strategy Framework Directive," *Marine Policy*, Vol. 36, 2012.

40 Sands, P., et al., 2012, p. 95f.; Gehring, T., 2007, p. 475f. See also Oberthür, S. and Gehring, T., "Conceptual Foundations of Institutional Interaction," in Oberthür, S. and Gehring, T. (eds.), *Institutional Interaction in Global Environmental Governance: Synergy and Conflict among International and EU Policies*, MIT Press, Cambridge, 2006.

activities and measures, because there is also no single, fundamental or immediate all-encompassing solution.[41]

5.3.6 *Review Structure and Powers*

It is not only the substantial contents that are important in a legal agreement. Its institutional construction (i.e., structure and powers) is also of great significance for the results. It has to be recognized that international agreements are composed of complementary features. The institutional arrangements of an agreement are also crucial to its effectiveness.[42] In addition to the formulation of specific requirements, then, what also matters is the possibility provided in an agreement to pursue monitoring and act on non-compliance, and the structures set out for developing, updating and adapting the provisions to changing prerequisites (Chapter 8). If requirements are vague or too flexible, then reporting requirements or other forms of monitoring can compensate for this.[43] This means that if the pressure on States provided by substantive requirements is low due to vagueness, then the pressure to ensure a satisfactory implementation could be compensated to some extent by an effective reporting or monitoring requirement. This could be provided if the administrative organization has the competence to extract and evaluate information on implementation measures in regard to each State Party. This kind of evaluation would not have to trigger a dispute settlement in cases of non-compliance. However, a compliance organ that could open up for a general dialogue with the State concerned regarding its measures and compliance, would be an effective tool as has been shown in other environmental agreements.[44]

5.4 SUMMARY AND CONCLUSIONS

As has been shown throughout this chapter, there are a number of ways in which legal systems can be adaptive and provide for flexibility and transformability. In research on adaptive governance, adaptivity is often presented as

[41] On the effects and effectivity of regime interaction, see Oberthür, S. and Gehring, T., "Comparative Empirical Analysis and Ideal Types of Institutional Interaction," in Oberthür, S. and Gehring, T. (eds.), 2006. See also Gehring, T., 2007, p. 475.

[42] See e.g. Chambers, W. B., 2004, pp. 525–527. The author emphasizes the role of "robustness" for the effectiveness of international environmental law – that is, built in treaty mechanisms that allow it to learn and adapt by incorporating new provisions that strengthen its internal ability to solve the problems it has be created to address.

[43] See e.g. Raustiala, K., 2005, pp. 581–614; and Churchill, R. R. and Ulfstein, G., 2000, pp. 628–631.

[44] Chayes, A. and Chayes, A. H, 1995, pp. 1–28 and pp. 184–197; Gehring, T., 2007, p. 485ff.

a form of local self-organization without any pressures or regulations posed from the outside. They possess structures that are flexible to adapt to changed prerequisites at any time. Legal systems are somewhat inert in comparison. This resistance in the legal system is important, however, for a legal system to sustain and preserve its basic functions – inter alia to provide for legitimacy and the rule of law. The basic functions in the core of law need some level of institutional stability (Section 3.3).

While international environmental agreements have to be adaptive to changes, both in knowledge and in preconditions provided for regulation, they also have to foster or take into account some level of stability. This implies stability in the sense that what has been agreed upon is a long-term goal, which could also contribute to trust and may enhance the willingness to cooperate and, as a consequence, to invest in measures. Thus, in this sense, it is important that flexibility does not apply to what the States are to accomplish, but merely how to accomplish a common goal. On the other hand, it is possible to imagine that the notion of what is to be achieved also could alter with new knowledge or other prerequisites. In a long-term environmental agreement, it is not unlikely that the main environmental concerns will vary over time, but that is also a shift that will come slowly and thus the States concerned will have the opportunity to communicate and adapt. It is an important task of international law to create trust and stability as a precondition for compliance. When reviewing adaptive and flexible structures and features of environmental law, it is important to keep in mind that one function connected to these concepts is transformability. The transformative action is connected to actual change in results and in relation to slow variables of the system (Section 4.1 and Chapter 8). In regard to the goal that is sought, transformability is the capacity to cross thresholds and turn the social-ecological system into new development pathways. In law, transformability will thus most likely come first when the Parties to an agreement actually comply with and enforce agreed-upon measures (cf. Chapter 8).

It is still a fact that legal systems can have at least similar functions to the adaptivity and flexibility constituted in self-organizing communities. Laws and legal systems do not provide a directly corresponding function of such self-governance. One main important purpose of law is to direct human behaviors and actions through rules. This is usually accomplished by a system where control of requirements is also possible in some way. To the extent that a feature of control can be pushed toward a clear monitoring of the environment or ecosystem instead of controlling behavior and actions, the possibilities for flexibility within a legal regime are also extended. That is, control can instead be performed by measurements and monitoring of environmental change. Another alternative way of providing extended space for flexibility is self-reporting of actions and measures. Such control systems open for the possibilities to have both adaptive and flexible features in an agreement, and still control binding requirements. This requires, however, the ability to establish exactly which measures are necessary and that the effects of such measures are possible to monitor.

It has to be noted, however, that rules can of course be binding without comprehensive control or a monitoring system. Whether such rules are flexible or not still depends on their design. However, the advantage of legal regulations and their role in environmental adaptive governance must be regarded as this potential to provide binding requirements. Binding requirements are what can actually force or enforce more effective environmental governance than what would have been accomplished on just a voluntary basis. The binding force of law, to a large extent but not entirely, is what divides it from other forms of governance.

Effectiveness is also linked to the issue of the spatial scale of the governance approach. As mentioned previously, most examples from research on resilience and adaptive governance point to a local or national scale. In such cases, the governance actions or measures and their results are often directly linked. This link between cause and effect provides the actors concerned with incentives to act. This scale of action furthermore generally implies that the numbers of stakeholders are limited and thus no formal system is needed for control or monitoring measures. However, when it comes to common resources on the international level, the prerequisites for stakeholder involvement and monitoring change, as do the incentives for action and measures. For a majority of those actions affecting a large-scale common resource, the stakeholders are not as directly dependent on or connected to it as in the case of small-scale systems. The incentives to take action are thus affected. A general theory is that a stakeholder will generally not make the effort to invoke strict measures if it cannot be sure that the other stakeholders are acting in the same way, since a one-sided action will not make much difference in the overall situation. This aspect of the situation also refers once again back to other advantages of legal regulation in this case. A legal agreement with a mechanism for controlling actions provides a stakeholder, or Party, with the insurance that the others are making equal contributions. This is especially true if measures are also costly.[45]

[45] See e.g. Mitchell, R. B., "Compliance Theory – Compliance, Effectiveness, and Behaviour Change in International Environmental Law," in Bodansky, D., Brunneé, J. and Hey, E. (eds.), *The Oxford Handbook of International Environmental Law*, Oxford University Press, 2007, pp. 904ff.

Another important issue regarding different levels of regulation involves the temporal scale. Inertia within the legal system is primarily present at the international level. Generally, the speed of change and the level of flexibility are connected to the level of a governance system. Flexibility and adaptivity can be relatively fast on the national levels, as the governing actions are more directly connected to the ecosystem, and because control functions are more directly applied. The need for fast reactions, however, is also greater at this level of governance. On the other hand, there might also be more legislative obstacles to flexibility in national legislation.[46] In the international field, adaptivity is related to the development of new knowledge, which is generated at a slower pace. Given that the international regulations have these functions of creating open structures for flexibility at the local levels, the actions and approaches taken by the international institutions do not have to be adapted as often.

To conclude, there seems to be great potential for the first component of legal design for resilience governance. Both EU law and international environmental law already include many adaptive and flexible features. There are also many legal mechanisms that are deliberately designed to include these features within legal structures. The effectiveness and operationalization of these mechanisms, however, depend on the combination with the other components or features for resilience governance.

46 See e.g. Nilsson, A. K. and Bohman, B., 2015, pp. 376–378. The article inter alia explains how the duties on public authorities based on the Marine Strategy Framework Directive and the Water Framework Directive are not necessarily combined with competences to intervene in ongoing lawful activities.

6

Multidimensional and Polycentric Structures

In the resilience theories, multilevel, cross-scale and polycentric governance approaches are generally regarded as important because they represent a governance system that could match ecological dynamic structures and scales as well as provide for a diversity of measures.[1] In a perspective of law, this raises questions regarding both how parallel regulatory regimes are structured and intertwined, and the extent to which legal regulatory approaches are able to match ecosystem scales. Furthermore, issues regarding authority, review and implementation of measures in such overlapping, polycentric regulations need to be reviewed and discussed. This also relates to questions of institutional or regulatory coordination.

Multilevel and polycentric governance in a broader sense are complicated concepts to define, but they are generally displayed in how societies are governed. Multilevel governance is generally seen as the concept of governance consisting of organization and governance at different dynamic levels, including nested, intertwined contacts and cooperation among a number of different kinds of actors and organizations.[2] This is a view that could be seen as providing a conceptual tool for the dispersion of governance, decision-making

[1] The term "polycentric" is only intended to reflect the use of this term within resilience research and not the general research on polycentric law. See Section 4 and n. 4. Polycentrism has been discussed in legal research; however, this research does not match the ideas of polycentric governance as it is discussed in research on social-ecological resilience, which is the perception that guides this study. Thus polycentric law in a strict legal perspective will not be discussed. The description of polycentricity used here and throughout the study is found in Biggs R., Schlüter M. and Schoon M. L., 2015a, p. 22, where so-called key concepts are defined, including polycentricity. Polycentricity is also acknowledged as a principle of its own in this review: Schoon, M. L., et al., 2015, pp. 226ff. See also Ostrom, E. and Janssen, M. A., 2004, p. 255; Ostrom, V., 1999, p. 59.

[2] For a more detailed discussion on the concept of multilevel governance, see e.g. Piattoni, S., "Multi-Level Governance: A Historical and Conceptual Analysis," *Journal Of European Integration*, Vol. 31, No. 2, 2009.

and management action, which represents how most societies are governed. The concept is mostly used and applied in a nonspecific sense in resilience research, and in the context of this study, it will be used in general terms. Cross-scale interaction within resilience governance is directly related to the view of social-ecological systems as a range in connected adaptive cycles acting on different scales and in different phases of the current adaptive cycle. The idea here is that in order to match such scales, a governance and management system must act in a coordinated, interconnected way on different scales – just like the social-ecological system.[3]

Diversity in these kinds of structures is a result of these dynamics and is often connected to an idea that a multitude of parallel measures provides alternative options for response; that these measures can be applied on different scales and in parallel at different levels in the governance system to create redundancy. Redundancy in multileveled structures thus allows a multitude of complementary measures on matching ecological scales. To some extent, this is also connected to a general idea within resilience research: appropriate measures are found if actors involved are given a possibility to experiment and try out what is and is not effective.[4] This diversity of measures is meant to be a response to the diversity of sources and causes of environmental problems and, in addition, at different levels in a dynamic system.[5]

All of the issues discussed previously must also be connected to questions of institutional coordination. In multidimensional governance structures, institutional coordination is crucial from a practical perspective. It is even more necessary in terms of legal structures. In addition, when it comes to institutional fit and matching scales of the ecosystem and biophysical dynamics, coordination together with adaptive co-management is claimed to serve a special purpose in attempting to adjust the measures and approaches taken in each dimension or on each institutional level to the appropriate scale of the problem. This adjustment results from the fact that actors in each part, or level, of the system will be more likely to have the ability to see the needs and particular circumstances for the application of measures in that specific part of the system.[6]

While multilevel governance is the concept most frequently used, it is often also seen as being parallel to polycentric structures, which is the case in resilience theories. Polycentric governance can in brief be described as a governance system with multiple, nested, governing authorities at different scales, which is

3 See e.g. Kotschy, K., et al., 2015, pp. 51ff; Folke, C., Chapin, F. S. and Olsson, P., 2009, pp. 116ff.; Folke, C., Colding, J. and Berkes, F., 2003. See also Low, B., et al., 2003.

4 See e.g. Folke, C., et al., 2005.

5 See e.g. Galaz, V., et al., 2008, pp. 155–156.

6 Galaz, V., et al., 2008, pp. 155–156, and pp. 160–163.

a description that comes close to a general comprehension of multilevel governance. One could also add a horizontal perspective in comparison to multilevel governance, which tends to suggest more of a hierarchal or vertical multiplicity. It also comes close to nested regulatory structures in an international setting. As noted earlier, the legal system is by nature similar to resilience structures in this regard. Law is developed, structured, designed, adopted and implemented at many different scales and levels in parallel, in different legal regimes, and is often governed by separate authorities or administrative organizations. Law is constituted by nested systems and measures that function in parallel on different levels, at different geographical and temporal scales. The chosen geographical scale will affect the system design and the kind of measures and mechanisms chosen to fulfill the aims of the current institutional structure.[7]

This chapter presents a review and discussion on the existence and potential consequences of multilevel and polycentric governance approaches and structures in international and EU law. This general review includes an assessment of what effect such approaches and structures may have from a legal point of view. In addition, the ecosystem approach, as a factor in such governance, will also be evaluated with regard to whether it contributes to a more nuanced structure with ecosystem-based regulatory structures; this will be evaluated primarily in terms of scale and ecosystem match. Furthermore, the question is assessed of whether overlapping and multilevel governance also provide a solid basis for a diversity of measures in legal contexts, as well as how this governance can be coordinated and the consequences of such regulation. Moreover, it is evaluated the extent to which such ideas and concepts in law, can be seen to reflect the same purposes as they have in resilience research.

6.1 MULTIDIMENSIONAL LEGAL STRUCTURES AND OVERLAPPING LEGISLATION

International law – global and regional – imposes obligations that States have to uphold and reflect in relation to the other States. The monitoring of compliance with these obligations is handled individually and differently in each separate regime or treaty body. At the same time, international law also gives rise to national laws with rights and duties on a national or even local

7 See Kim, R. E., 2013, pp. 980–991. See also Kim, R. E., "The Emergent Network Structure of the Multilateral Environmental Agreement System," *Global Environmental Change*, Vol. 23, 2013. See also Kim, R. E. and Mackey, B., "International Environmental Law as a Complex Adaptive System," *International Environmental Agreements: Politics, Law and Economics*, Springer, Vol. 14(1), 2014, pp. 5–24. The author compares the features of international environmental law with complex adaptive systems.

level, through transposition and implementation. These national laws, together with the preexisting web of national laws, are in turn monitored at different levels in the national system. In addition, regional organizations such as the EU also have law-creating structures and functions that impose a separate legal regime with consequences on all regulatory levels. EU laws are also implemented in parallel and partly in an overlapping fashion, to both national and international legal systems. This is a visualization of how law by nature also can be said to be multidimensional and cross-scale with parallel obligations and authorities.[8] In addition, the legal system is intertwined in a global governance system with other actors that interact with States and contribute to both rule making and implementation in different ways (see Chapter 7), thus creating additional complexity.

The majority of the EU legislation is binding on a national level in the EU Member States, thus creating an additional layer to the nest of national laws.[9] With regard to the EU, the Member States also have separate reporting and compliance responsibilities. In some instances and as yet another dimension, EU law may be intertwined with or include links to the conventions to which the EU is also a Party. To mention a few, the EU is, for example, Party to the CBD and its protocols, the UNFCCC, the Paris Agreement adopted under the UNFCCC, the 1982 United Nations Convention of the Law of the Sea[10] (LOSC), the Convention on the Protection of the Marine Environment of the Baltic Sea Area[11] (the Helsinki Convention) and all other European regional seas Convention, the 1979 Convention on Long-Range Transboundary Air Pollution[12] (LRTAP), the Basel Convention on the Control of Transboundary Movements of Hazardous Wastes and Their Disposal[13] (the Basel Convention) and many more.[14]

In cases where the EU is Party to a convention, another level of law also arises since the convention provision becomes binding on all the EU Member States in the EU legal regime.[15] In short, the legal systems are in themselves

8 See also the distinction between multidimensional and multi-layered that are explained in Hey, E., "Multi-Dimensional Public Governance Arrangements for the Protection of Transboundary Aquatic Environment in the European Union – The Changing Interplay between European and Public International Law," *International Organizations Law Review*, Vol. 6, 2009, pp. 193–194.

9 Article 288 TFEU states the binding force of different legal acts of the EU.

10 1833 UNTS 3.

11 1507 UNTS 167.

12 1302 UNTS 217.

13 1673 UNTS 126.

14 For a complete compilation see the EU Treaties Office Database of the European External Action Service, see http://ec.europa.eu/world/agreements/default.home.do.

15 Article 216(2) TFEU. On this dual relationship between the EU directives in relation to international agreements, see also Hey, E., 2009, pp. 200–202.

multilevel, polycentric and intertwined, thus creating a platform for a diversity of measures. However, how this actually turns out – what the consequences are and to what extent they really lead to the application of multiple measures, with a match to the ecological scale, and whether such measures will achieve the effects intended in the theories on resilience governance – depends on how the States cooperate and incorporate these different regime requirements, along with the actions taken to create ecosystem match.

The intertwined legal structural processes that drive development toward a more polycentric and diverse system cannot and should not be stopped or rewound, but the overall situation and basis for this development do raise a lot of questions that must be dealt with and indeed some problems that must be addressed. It has been pointed out that power gaps and power dynamics in polycentric structures are important to analyze and understand, since that also affects the effectiveness of the governance structure.[16] There has been a debate regarding this diversity in the international legal system, both in the international community and the world of research on international law. The focus in the debate has been on the effects of this development of incoherent, fragmented and pluralistic or polycentric systems of law. The risk of overlapping and parallel laws is for example that the rules could contradict each other, or that conflicts in the applicability of laws will arise.[17] A related and central question in international environmental governance is where to place responsibility. When it comes to scale and different levels of authority in international governance and law, where should the responsibility for different environmental problems be placed? Moreover, the question of what fragmentation means for environmental regimes has been heavily debated.[18]

16 Morrison, T. H., et al., "The Black Box of Power in Polycentric Environmental Governance," *Global Environmental Change*, Vol. 57, 2019.

17 See e.g. Hafner, G., "Risks Ensuing from Fragmentation of International Law," in UN ILC 2000, Yearbook of the International Law Commission 2000, Vol. 2 (Part 2): Report of the Commission to the General Assembly, Document A/55/10; Report of the International Law Commission on the Work of Its Fifty-Second Session, p. 144 and p. 147; UN ILC Report 2006, "Fragmentation of International Law: Difficulties Arising from Diversification and Expansion of International Law," Report of the Study Group of the International Law Commission, Finalized by Martti Koskenniemi, International Law Commission, Fifty-Eighth Session, Geneva 2006, United Nations, General Assembly, Document: A/CN.4/L.682 13 April 2006, pp. 8ff.; Koskenniemi, M. and Leino, P., "Fragmentation of International Law? Postmodern Anxieties," *Leiden Journal of International Law*, Vol. 15, No. 3, 2002.

18 Dunoff, J. L., "Levels of Environmental Governance," in Bodansky, D., Brunnée, J. and Hey, E. (eds.), *The Oxford Handbook of International Environmental Law*, Oxford University Press, 2007, pp. 86–88, and pp. 98–106; Biermann, F., et al.,"The Fragmentation of Global Governance Architectures: A Framework for Analysis," *Global Environmental Politics*, Vol. 9, No. 4, 2009, pp. 14–21.

As stated earlier in this chapter, the ideas and concepts of cross-scale interactions, multilevel structures, diversity and redundancy, as they are developed in the research on social-ecological resilience, will be assessed and evaluated in relation to law and regulatory structures. The purpose of this chapter is to explore these perspectives of dynamic and cross-scale interactions in relation to regulatory aspects of governance.[19] Hence, the goal is not to discuss these issues from a straightforward multilevel governance perspective. In line with the main aim of the overall study, the role of legal structures in the governance system will be evaluated. The aim is to assess how and to what extent law represents or contributes to the kinds of dynamic and diverse structures connected with multilevel governance and polycentric governance structures. In addition, the goal is also to assess the consequences this may have from a legal perspective.

Law may on the one hand exhibit multilevel and polycentric structures similar to those promoted in resilience governance theories. However, on the other hand, it presents a risk of creating an excessive diversity and multitude of measures in relation to what is cost-effective and possible to administrate in a purposeful manner. These aspects of polycentric legal structures could create obstacles for effective regulation.[20] A diversity of laws and requirements at different levels of the legal structures may make implementation and compliance control more difficult. At the same time, such structures create a basis for new regulatory situations, solutions and approaches.

These new regulatory situations, solutions and approaches also need further evaluation. At the center of all this is the goal of enabling institutional match – that is, ensuring that the measures taken fit the environmental problems and the ecological scales. Regulatory approaches must also reflect this correspondence, and this is why it is valuable to explore these structures further from this perspective. In addition, institutional structures must be implemented or structured differently at different levels. The institutions created must be in line with ecological scale and biophysical dynamics.[21]

19 While law is generally a nonhierarchal system with independent layers and structures with dynamic interactions and connections, it still occurs that these different regulatory layers are referred to as levels of regulation. This is not necessarily to imply any order of authority of one over the other. It is rather a use of words that corresponds to the concept of multilevel governance, which is generally neither referring to nor reflecting any mutual hierarchal relationships. Sometimes there is a hierarchal structure where, for example, a State Party is bound to follow obligations set out in a binding treaty. These kinds of legal relationships are, however, not what is primarily intended with the use of the term *regulatory levels* in this context.

20 See also a similar discussion by Schoon, M. L., et al., 2015, p. 236.

21 See e.g. Galaz, V., et al., 2008, p. 148, and generally.

6.2 ALLOCATION OF AUTHORITY AND COMPETING APPLICABILITY

The proliferation of law and legal structures described previously as an intensified increase in the number of international agreements across the world is sometimes discussed in terms of a fragmentation of international law. Such fragmentation of the system appears also if an overall perspective of the international legal system is chosen. Fragmentation is then perceptible as incoherence in the system, manifested by the different areas of law that have emerged in this expansion. These areas of law have successively established their own fields of law, such as environmental law, or the law of the sea, with the LOSC, as opposed to being part of a general international law.[22] Fragmentation was a frequently debated issue at the turn of the millennium, at the time when this development was at its peak.[23] While the potential problems of fragmentation remain, the pace of adopting new agreements has slowed. According to some scholars, fragmentation causes problems, as it creates obstacles to a coherent and clearly hierarchal system, in the sense of how law is traditionally built.[24] The legal system rests on clear authority – often a court – that has the competence to interpret the law and produce jurisprudence. This is also applicable to the traditional view of international law, where such a system also creates a control system for proper implementation by the States. With increased fragmentation, however, the system becomes diverse. The different areas of international law create their own regimes with specific norms and guiding principles, as well as specified courts that interpret only certain agreements. In the end, this implies that there are multiple authorities which can interpret agreements and come to contradictory conclusions regarding their application. When agreements are adopted, the Parties may also choose from a range of different organizations or courts for dispute settlement. The critics are referring to the risks of an initial erosion of general international law, a risk of conflicting jurisprudence causing further incoherence and confusion among Parties concerned, also emanating in forum-shopping for dispute settlement and loss of legal security. Those opposing this view by the critics seem to view fragmentation mainly as a technical problem, to be solved inter alia through coordination.[25] This also seems to be

22 UN ILC Report 2006, para 8, p. 9.

23 See e.g. UN ILC Report 2006; Hafner, G., 2000; Koskenniemi, M. and Leino, P., 2002; Hafner, G., 2004.

24 On the background to these conflicting views see Dupuy, P-M., "A Doctrinal Debate in the Globalisation Era: On the Fragmentation of International Law," *European Journal of Legal Studies*, Vol. 1, No. 1, 2007, pp. 25–41.

25 UN ILC Report 2006, para 9, p. 9. See also Koskenniemi, M. and Leino, P., 2002, p. 575f.; Charney, J. I., "The Impact on the International Legal System of the Growth of International

the prevailing point of view, and a resulting conclusion is that the law is designed to handle these kinds of conflicts, and moreover if coordination is successful, then it is not a problem for law to have multidimensional legal structures (Section 6.5).

A similar development can be identified at another scale in specific areas of law. Partly as a result of the increase in adopting new international agreements, an agreement in a particular area of law could constitute a separate rule-complex or regulatory regime. This is seen, for example, when different multilateral or regional environmental agreements are emerging in parallel as a complex system of treaties. However, rather than describing this development as fragmentation, another description would be to regard this as multidimensional regulatory structures. This is a system where treaties sometimes overlap and sometimes refer to other treaties, creating a complex net of legislation, which is inconsistent with and indifferent to preexisting rules and regimes.[26] These kinds of structures and developments could be regarded in different aspects as reflecting those features in resilience governance that are often described as polycentric and multilevel governance. Given the conclusion in Chapter 5 regarding flexible goal-centered obligations, these structures could even create incentives for further force to compel States concerned to take relevant measures, rather than creating a problem.

In addition to the general multidimensional development that has occurred mainly as a result of increased activity in treaty-making within the frame of international law, the legal regime of the EU has emerged in parallel. The EU establishes a legal system of its own. At the same time, the EU is often a Party to international agreements. EU environmental laws must be adhered to in addition to the international laws and, at the same time, are often a result of EU implementation of international environmental laws (Section 5.3.5). This adds to the complexity and fragmentation of the legal system at a regional level. The EU as a legal regime is also somewhat pluralistic and complex in itself, since it is composed of different policy areas and legal bases that create the ground for any legislative act.[27] Although the EU has also established principles for how these different policy areas are to be coordinated in order to avoid conflicting rules, these policies still appear to be in conflict in many different areas. Such conflicts arise not least with regard to the marine and

Courts and Tribunals," *NYU Journal of International Law and Politics*, Vol. 31, 1999; Young, M. A., "Regime Interaction in Creating, Implementing and Enforcing International Law," in Young, M. A. (ed.), *Regime Interaction in International Law: Facing Fragmentation*, Cambridge University Press, 2012. See also Saunders, C., 2012, pp. 72–73 and generally.

26 See e.g. Kim, R. E., 2013; and Mitchell, R. B., 2003, pp. 430–439.

27 See e.g. Langlet, D. and Mahmoudi, S., 2016, pp. 95ff.

environmental policies that often have opposing interests with respect to both trade policies and agricultural policies.[28]

6.2.1 *The Example of the MOX Plant Case*

Some general guidance for how the different parallel regulatory instruments are to be applied can be found in a case regarding localization of a nuclear facility in the waters between the United Kingdom and Ireland. The case concerns a conflict between Ireland and the United Kingdom (the UK) regarding the MOX Plant nuclear facility (the MOX Plant Case).[29] This case arose from a conflict, dating back to 1993, about the construction and operation of the MOX Plant at Sellafield in the Irish Sea. The plant was designed to recycle the plutonium produced during the reprocessing of nuclear fuel (i.e., MOX). Ireland contested this project from the beginning of the planning and requested access to information from the UK about the plant in order to protect the marine environment of the Irish Sea.[30]

The LOSC, the 1992 Convention for the Protection of the Marine Environment of the North-East Atlantic[31] (OSPAR Convention), and EU legislation were all legal instruments applicable to this situation; hence cases arose in different forums in parallel. Cases were brought in three different institutional procedures: an Arbitral Tribunal set up under Annex VII of the LOSC, a compulsory dispute settlement procedure under the OSPAR Convention and under EU law in the EU Court.[32] All three procedures addressed the same issues but, in the end, would assess these using different rules. As a result, the question was thus posed as to which of these regimes should be determinative. Furthermore, because the UK objected to the jurisdiction of the LOSC Arbitral Tribunal, the LOSC Tribunal had to make a statement and evaluation regarding its jurisdiction in the matter.[33]

28 Cf. Young, M. A., 2012, p. 93, on lack of policy coordination at domestic level.

29 Dispute Concerning Access to Information under Article 9 of the OSPAR Convention, Final Award (Ireland v. the United Kingdom) (2 July 2003) Permanent Court of Arbitration, ILM Vol. 42 (2003) p. 1118.

30 Dispute Concerning Access to Information under Article 9 of the OSPAR Convention (2003), pp. 1124–1130, paras. 15–45.

31 2354 UNTS 67.

32 International Tribunal for the Law of the Sea (ITLOS): The MOX Plant Case (*Ireland v. United Kingdom*), Request for Provisional Measures, Order (3 December 2001), International Legal Materials, Vol. 41, No. 2, 2002, p. 412, paras. 40–43. See also UN ILC Report 2006, para. 10, p. 12.

33 International Tribunal for the Law of the Sea (ITLOS): The MOX Plant Case, 2002, p. 412, paras. 44–45.

The LOSC Arbitral Tribunal then stated that "even if the OSPAR Convention, the EC Treaty and the Euratom treaty contain rights of obligations similar or identical with the rights set out in [the LOSC], the rights and obligations under these agreements have a separate existence from those under [the LOSC]."[34]

In short, all three legal regimes were applicable in parallel. The LOSC Arbitral Tribunal also held that the application of the same rules in the different legal regimes did not rule out the others, even if the obligations are similar or even identical. Even with the same rules, the intent and translation might be different due to differences in context, objective, practice and so forth. The LOSC Arbitral tribunal also recognized that the meaning of legal rules and principles is dependent on the context in which they are applied.[35] The regulatory situation reflected in the MOX Plant Case makes for a reliable example for evaluating a legal situation with mixed and parallel regulation at the levels of both the EU and the international legal system. It is important to understand the foundation for how these rules are to be interpreted in themselves, as long as no deviation from such interpretation or application is imposed by the legal instrument.

6.3 ECOSYSTEM FIT

One important issue to address in relation to multilevel and polycentric governance is the question of how to assess institutional levels in relation to the ecosystem and environmental problems. In regulatory structures, this issue involves a question of the suitable level or levels for regulation to fit the problem at hand.[36] It follows from the general principles of international law that each State is sovereign; each State decides on its own legal action, regardless of the magnitude or particularities of the problem. However, as a contrast, the foundation and the rise of international environmental law are built on the insight that some issues are best dealt with in cooperation on a transboundary scale, based on a common interest to protect the environment and common resources (Section 3.1).[37] Furthermore, it can be concluded that this development of international law includes the acknowledgment that

34 Ibid. p. 413, para. 50.

35 Ibid. p. 413, paras. 51–52. See also Shany, Y., "The First MOX Plant Award: The Need to Harmonize Competing Environmental Regimes and Dispute Settlement Procedures," *Leiden Journal of International Law*, Vol. 17, No. 4, 2004, pp. 815–827.

36 See e.g. Dunoff, J. L., 2007, pp. 86ff.

37 See e.g. Bodansky, D., 2010, pp. 18ff. on the evolution of international environmental law and the attitudes developed among States and other actors.

action in one sovereign State can cause environmental harm to other States and that this is not internationally accepted (Sections 2.1 and 2.4.1).[38]

A similar phenomenon of acknowledging that some environmental problems are best dealt with in cooperation is found when reviewing the EU legal regime. A general principle of EU law is the principle of subsidiarity, meaning that all measures or regulations shall be decided on locally and nationally to the extent possible.[39] Only when a problem cannot be solved in a satisfactory way by means of national law is the EU to regulate the issue. This of course is given that the EU has been provided the competence by the Member States, and that the competence is shared and not exclusive to the EU – in which case the Member States are no longer permitted to legislate on the issue in question. However, the competence to enact environmental legislation is generally shared between the EU and the Member States (Section 2.2).[40] It is also an issue area where questions of different approaches or levels of regulation often emerge in relation to the problem at hand. It can thus be concluded that if an environmental problem is addressed within the EU legal regime, it has been considered by the EU and its Member States to be of such nature as to be better addressed on a regional rather than national level.[41]

In creating ecosystem match in the sense discussed here, the EU environmental laws are rather well developed. First of all, since the subsidiarity principle applies, only such problems that are best approached at Union level will be regulated.[42] This means, at least at some level, that the problems are approached at a level that matches the ecosystem best. Moreover, many directives in EU environmental law include provisions that are rather general and often goal-based, which set environmental objectives (Section 2.4.4),

38 About the evolution of international environmental law and the attitudes developed among States and other actors, see Bodansky, D., 2010, pp. 18 ff. See also Principle 2 of the 1992 UN Declaration on Environment and Development and the corresponding Principle 21 of the 1972 Declaration on the Human Environment.

39 Article 5(3) EUT. See also the Protocol (No. 2) on the Application of the Principles of Subsidiarity and Proportionality, EUT C 83/206, 2010.

40 Article 4(2)(e), TFEU.

41 See also Langlet, D. and Mahmoudi, S., 2016, pp. 46–48.

42 Article 5(3) TEU: "Under the principle of subsidiarity, in areas which do not fall within its exclusive competence, the Union shall act only if and in so far as the objectives of the proposed action cannot be sufficiently achieved by the Member States, either at central level or at regional and local level, but can rather, by reason of the scale or effects of the proposed action, be better achieved at Union level." In summary, the principle of subsidiarity aims to ensure that decisions are taken as closely as possible to the citizens and to verify that action at EU level is justified in light of the possibilities available at national, regional or local level. The EU is not to take action in any area (except in the areas that fall within its exclusive competence), unless actions/measures will be more effective if taken on EU-level in comparison to action taken at national, regional or local level.

especially in relation to protection of nature. This provides space for each Member State to implement or apply the measures meant to achieve the set goal in a way adjusted to the specific circumstances in that State. Such margin for the State can also follow from the fact that directives are always only binding to their intention, leaving to the Member States to decide on implementation. The effects of having polycentric structures can be illustrated by looking at the CBD and the EU nature directives. In the EU regime, the CBD is implemented, at least in part, through Directive 92/43/EEC on the conservation of natural habitats and of wild fauna and flora[43] (the Habitats Directive) and Directive 2009/147/EC on the conservation of wild birds[44] (the Birds Directive). Although not as flexible as a framework directive, the Habitats and Bird directives gives rather broad directions to the States on how to select sites to protect under within the Natura 2000 network. The aim of the Natura 2000 network is to ensure the long-term survival of the most valuable and threatened species and habitats in the EU, in line with the objectives of the CBD. These species and habitats are listed under the Habitats and Bird Directives. Despite the fact that the listing and general structure for protection of species and habitats in the Habitats Directive is rather complicated, the directive still leaves room for ecosystem fit.[45] First, it is identified at the level of the Union what habitats and species must have different degrees of protection, but it is left to each Member State to take action to implement this protection within their own territory, as applicable. In the end, the directive aims for each Member State to make their own assessments. A general objective in the Habitats Directive is "favourable conservation status" (Section 2.4.2).[46] At the same time, there is a rather strict coordination between the EU and the Member States in that these directives include lists with species and nature types that more specifically must be protected. What kind of nature or biotopes and species that are protected in each Member State then also depends on what species or habitats that can be found in each State. In addition to this rather ambitious legislation that all Members States implement under fairly strict control by the EU Commission, Member States may also have additional national systems for protecting biological diversity since the EU Competence is shared. Hence, it also creates diversity of measures in practice. In Sweden, for example, the Natura 2000 network of protection is only one of a number of forms of nature protection that also in part is reflecting Sweden's

[43] OJ L 206, p. 7–50.
[44] OJ L 20, p. 7–25.
[45] See further on the structure of the Habitats Directive in Langlet, D. and Mahmoudi, S., 2016, pp. 354ff.
[46] Habitats Directive, Article 2(2).

obligations under the CBD beside that imposed by the EU. The national protection measures have somewhat different focus and objectives, thus establishing diversity in nature protection nationally. A similar pattern for protection of natural resources can be seen in many other areas in the EU. For example, the marine and water protection and in some ways also the regulation on climate change show such tendencies.

A general complaint regarding legal regulation of environmental problems is often that the regulation is not sufficiently adjusted to fit the problem and thus is not sufficiently flexible (Section 2.4).[47] It is often mentioned that top-down legislative approaches regulate problems that appear mainly on a local level, although these problems also primarily should be handled at this local level. This is a point often made in relation to the research on adaptive governance. It follows that if only high-level, top-down regulation is created and applied, it will be difficult to match the regulation to small-scale local problems. This implies that measures taken to address the problems are not implemented at the right scale. Instead, there is a risk that a gap is created between the sources or causes of the problem – the object of regulation – and the institutional settings or authorities that are to control and regulate these activities. There are a number of ways to design legal structures to overcome such problems. One main reason that legislation is adopted on a broad scale or at the top level to regulate a particular problem is that the problem appears on this higher level as well. It is not an efficient approach to address problems that also appear on a large scale – only at a local level. Instead, most environmental problems have to be approached on several levels in parallel. One purpose of the ecosystem approach is to bridge these kinds of gaps, since the approach requires matching the right scale with a multilevel governance approach.[48] This is also the basis for the EU legal regime and the subsidiarity principle. With the development of environmental law, however, the trends in environmental governance have been toward a centralized authority for environmental regulation – nationally, regionally and internationally.[49] These laws still create an intricate, multilevel network in combination, but one that is just a little less diverse and dynamic. The increased focus on solving problems internationally has also led to an increasing number of international and regional regulations that often overlap and are applicable in parallel with each other – as described in the previous example. This web of legislative instruments or regimes is now the natural order of legal regulatory structures,

47 See e.g. Garmestani, A. S., Allen, C. R. and Cabezas, H., 2008.
48 See CBD Ecosystem approach (2000c), especially paras. 2 and 3.
49 Dunoff, J. L., 2007, pp. 86 ff.

thus creating pluralistic and polycentric systems.[50] The general approach to environmental treaty-making has created a "maze" or an "evolving structure of a web" of international agreements. Studies show that the many hundreds of existing multilateral environmental agreements have "self-organized into an interlocking system with a complex network structure."[51]

In general, solving the same environmental problem requires legal measures at different levels in parallel. Regardless of the primary scale chosen to address a problem, capturing it with governance measures and regulation will demand a wide and more diverse approach. The concept of ecosystem approach – as is also suggested in the theories of social-ecological resilience – emphasizes that multilevel governance is essential for creating institutional fit.[52] This, in a resilience governance perspective, implies much more than just regulatory levels and diversity. Other aspects – such as, participation – will be discussed in the next chapter. The focus here is on the basic foundations and prerequisites for multilevel and polycentric regulatory structures and how to coordinate redundancy. Having multiple legal regimes and overlapping regulations and requirements creates synergistic effects but also involves complications, contradictions and the risk of blurring the legal situation. This blur could make implementation difficult, contradictory and widely different between countries. This situation could also result in a higher level of noncompliance. However, this scenario cannot be discussed in general terms; it is necessary to assess the application of law separately in every given case and evaluate the effects of the intertwined legal systems in each given situation.[53]

6.3.1 *The Role of the Ecosystem Approach in Multidimensional Legal Structures*

Multidimensional governance implies that measures should be taken in parallel at different levels and scales of regulation, and create cross-scale interactions. This also seems to be the general state of the art in the

50 See also Biermann, F., et al., 2009, pp. 24–32.

51 Kim, R. E., 2013, pp. 980–991. The study in the article "reveals and characterizes the evolving structure of the web of international treaty law. The structure was approximated using 1001 cross-references among 747 multilateral environmental agreements concluded from 1857–2012."

52 See e.g. CBD Malawi Principles, especially principle 7.

53 Hafner, G., "Pros and Cons Ensuing from Fragmentation of International Law," *Michigan Journal of International Law*, Vol. 25, 2004, pp. 854–860. Regarding causes and potentially negative effects or complications, see also Biermann, F., et al., 2009 on the conditions for positive effects.

international or transboundary legal system, which is shifting toward increasingly fragmented or multidimensional structures. However, according to the resilience theories, the intention or purpose of such an order of governance is to match ecological dynamics. Thus, the increased diversity and cross-scale regulations require an assessment and adjustment to the scale of the ecosystem if they are to be effective from an environmental and, for instance, resilience governance point of view. Beyond the fact that transboundary cooperation in itself implies that this is the most suitable level for governance (i.e., that the problem for example is transboundary), there is nothing beyond this in transboundary regulatory structures to guarantee that the levels of regulation match ecological scales. The concept of ecosystem approach can be regarded as a regulatory mechanism that aims to introduce a better match in this regard. The question is whether the application of the concept of ecosystem approach will also play out in this way.

In the description of the concept as it was originally developed within the realm of the CBD, it is stated that "an ecosystem approach is based on the application of appropriate scientific methodologies focused on levels of biological organization which encompass the essential processes, functions and interactions among organisms and their environment. It recognizes that humans, with their cultural diversity, are an integral component of ecosystems."[54]

It is stated in the CBD that what is presented as a focus on processes, functions and interactions is to be regarded as consistent with the definition of an ecosystem.[55] It is also stated that this definition does not specify any particular spatial unit or scale. Instead, the scale of analysis and action should be determined by the problem being addressed.[56] In practice, this presents a great challenge and must include structures and coordination that can bridge both transboundary divides as well as traditional economic or administrative borders. It requires assessments and coordination at all levels and in between different regulatory instruments. One major challenge is adjustments to make different ecosystem perspectives meet in a consistent way, as perspectives on a very local scale may be fundamentally different from the larger-scale perspectives. Indeed,

54 CBD SBSTTA (2000), Subsidiary Body on Scientific, Technical and Technological Advice (SBSTTA), Fifth Meeting, Montreal January 2000, Item 4.2.1 of the provisional agenda; Ecosystem Approach: Further Conceptual Elaboration, Document: UNEP/CBD/SBSTTA/5/11, 23 October 1999, at p. 5, para A7.

55 Definition is found in CBD Article 2: a dynamic complex of plant, animal and microorganism communities and their nonliving environment interacting as a functional unit.

56 CBD SBSTTA (2000), at p. 5, para A8.

enforcing a transboundary large-scale ecosystem approach on the national level will require a transfer also of incentives that can motivate the implementation of a larger-scale approach. This aspect is often framed as legitimacy and trust building, when seen as part of international law. Centralized top-down legislation, it is implied, does not offer the necessary flexibility needed for an adaptive approach to the ecosystem. Moreover, top-down approaches are considered blind to local incentives.[57] Hence, although the ecosystem approach as a regulatory concept includes crucial perspectives to achieve institutional fit for what can be described as ecosystem match, the real challenge is to combine top-down approaches with the local perspective. While flexibility is an important factor in this regard, giving States the possibility to adjust implementation at least with some regard to the specific circumstances, other factors such as participation and information sharing will be important as well.[58] In the end, some form of monitoring and control measures may also be significant if local incentives are not sufficiently strong.

One significant legislative approach connected to the ecosystem approach is environmental quality standards (EQS). This approach is, for example, rather successfully used in water and marine legal management in the EU.[59] EQS also has its challenges and can only be applied to some types of problems. Nevertheless, it reflects how a large-scale, top-down legislation can still transform into a legislative structure that in the end is rather well adjusted to the ecosystem and creates a legislative fit on several levels. Additionally, the example provided previously of the EU's implementation of the CBD into a detailed but still a nationally adjusted EU system for nature protection also provides a way to create an ecosystem fit on many parallel levels. Both these examples are also now in action, thus creating norms and boundaries for exploitation. Hence, norms on how to balance different interests in relation to the ecosystem – given that the protective norms are sufficient to safeguard ecosystem values and take into account the operational space needed in

57 Bodansky, D., 2010, p. 145; Stewart, R. B., 2007, p. 163; Farber, D. A., "Politics and Procedure in Environmental Law," *Journal of Law, Economics and Organization*, Vol. 8, 1992, pp. 59–60. See also Wiener, J. B., "On the Political Economy of Global Environmental Regulation," *The Georgetown Law Journal*, Vol. 87, 1999; and Barrett, S., 2003, generally.

58 See e.g. Bodansky, D., 2010, pp. 127–128; Ebbesson, J., "Public Participation," in Bodansky, D., Brunnée, J. and Hey, E. (eds.), *The Oxford Handbook of International Environmental Law*, Oxford University Press, 2007a, note 330, pp. 686–692.

59 See e.g. Lee, M., 2009 and Long, R., "The Marine Strategy Framework Directive: A New European Approach to the Regulation of the Marine Environment, Marine Natural Resources and Marine Ecological Services," *Journal of Energy and Natural Resource Law*, Vol. 29, No. 1, 2011.

relation to environmental complexity. The ecosystem approach and EQS generally also entails an adaptive review system that can be important in relation to complexity and sudden changes.[60]

Centralized regulations are usually seen as less adaptive to the specific geographical or other circumstances related to the problem. However, if the problem is not entirely local, then incentives for action may have to be introduced through legislation on a higher level. Furthermore, because central regional or international legislation is also to be implemented on a national or local scale, there will still be room for local adjustments. In most cases, though, the sources of pollution are complex, diversified and most often local, so implementation of measures must be done on a matching local scale. This is also an example of why multilevel governance and cross-scale interactions are seen as inevitable and rather elementary in legal regulation. Action is taken on different scales in parallel as a result of regional cooperation on regulatory agreements, and this is often initiated by the need to regulate environmental problems in different ways or from different perspectives.

6.4 OVERLAPPING REQUIREMENTS

Multilevel and polycentric governance entails that measures should be taken in parallel at different levels and scales of regulation. It is therefore relevant to scrutinize further the international and EU legal systems to find the extent to which parallel and multilevel regulatory measures are applied, along with the consequences this could have for the legal system. In addition to providing institutional adjustment to the scale of the ecosystem and the environmental problem at hand, such regulation would allow for a multitude of complementary or even overlapping measures. This kind of regulatory structure would also mean that a number of different organizations, or institutions, are responsible for controlling and regulating the same issue. The extent of their authority then becomes important to define, not just in relation to a convention Party but also in relation to other organizations. Thus the authority and coordination of different legal instruments and their administrative arrangements must also be investigated in more detail. These issues are the focus of this section.

As explained previously, the international legal system has developed to large extent in a dynamic way, resembling the ideas behind polycentric

60 Bohman, B., "The Ecosystem Approach as a Basis for Managerial Compliance: An Example from the Regulatory Development in the Baltic Sea Region," in Langlet, D. and Rayfuse, R. (eds.), *The Ecosystem Approach in Ocean Planning and Governance – Perspectives from Europe and Beyond*, Brill/Nijhoff, 2018c, pp. 80–116.

governance, with a multitude of legal regimes, agreements and institutional organizations, focusing in many cases in parallel on regulating the same problem. It has long been a recognized phenomenon in international legal research and the international community that international law creates a fragmented system of different agreements.[61] The system of international law has expanded dramatically since the establishment of the UN in the late 1940s. The international law complex has in recent decades particularly emerged in this way by a continuously increasing number of international agreements.[62] The question then is what consequences this entails and how this number of agreements may affect the implementation and application of laws under different circumstances. Another question is whether these features in the legal system also match those in resilience thinking and the aims identified within resilience governance – such as fostering complementary measures and adding a wide range of measures to complex problems with many sources, as a way to find effective solutions. As has been stated in the introduction of this study, it is important to realize that it is the functions behind these features and formal concepts that are interesting to compare.

Effectiveness and compliance are central issues when it comes to multidimensional legal structures and governance (see also Section 8.2). Effective implementation of coexisting multiple legal regimes and the multitude of requirements resulting from such systems is linked to the governance structure as a whole. That is, effective implementation is connected to a system, including its compliance mechanisms. The level of coordination between both the different regimes and the different measures required within different regimes are equally important parts of such system. This is also linked to issues on clarity and transparency.[63] Whether the prescribed measures are obligations of conduct or obligations of results is also of significance.[64] If the measures required are detailed in terms of requiring a behavioral change by the Parties concerned, too many such requirements might be difficult and costly for States to implement and keep track of, and perhaps even contradictory if they are not clearly synergistic.[65]

61 See e.g. UN ILC Report 2006, pp. 8 ff.; Kim, R. E., 2013; Koskenniemi, M. and Leino, 2002; Hafner, G., 2004; Biermann, F., et al., 2009.

62 See inter alia UN ILC Report 2006, pp. 8ff. See also Kim, R. E., 2013.

63 See e.g. Dunoff, J. L., 2007, p. 99, where it is emphasized that systematic coordination within polycentric regulatory governance is useful for supporting implementation – at least with regard to global instruments.

64 See Bodansky, D., 2010, p. 76, for a concise explanation of the different distinctions.

65 Cf. Dunoff, J. L., 2007, p. 99; Biermann, F., et al., 2009, pp. 19–21.

A State Party is obligated toward each separate organization to enforce given requirements. If requirements by separate organizations, or institutions, are overlapping or synergistic, the State concerned can apply the same actions to implement a multitude of requirements. If requirements are not overlapping and synergistic, implementing a large number of requirements in parallel could be burdensome.[66] If measures are goal specific and require obligations only in terms of certain environmental results, increased pressure from parallel institutional obligations to implement measures may foster and promote the required results. This is to be expected because such a scenario does not mean that different or conflicting measures need to be adopted. In this way, it also strengthens incentives for adaptive and flexible regulatory instruments (Chapter 5). However, it is only likely to be effective to the extent that it is possible to evaluate such environmental recovery and track this to the specific States concerned.[67] Most States enter international agreements with the intention to comply, but then what is expected for compliance must be clear and the goal must be within reach (see also Section 8.2).[68]

It is generally considered that international law contains elements of rational choice theories (Section 8.2.2.1). Rational choice is connected to theories of international relations; it is founded on the idea that States calculate on their incentives to act and only take into account that which is in their best interest, for example, when they are to agree or implement particular agreements.[69] Based on this assumption about States' behavior, it is held that multiple environmental regimes could trigger a race to the bottom if an issue is not strictly regulated.[70] Furthermore, attention has been directed toward policy gaps, incoherent decision-making structures, and the lack of meaningful coordination. Actors have increasingly emphasized that the sheer proliferation of institutions, issues and agreements is placing severe stress on the legal system. This, it is implied, creates a number of obstacles to an effective legal system.

66 See also Saunders, C., "International Regimes and Domestic Arrangements: A View from Inside Out," in Young, M. A. (ed.), *Regime Interaction in International Law: Facing Fragmentation*, Cambridge University Press, 2012.

67 See e.g. Mitchell, R. B., 2007, pp. 896 ff.; Biermann, F., et al., 2009, p. 25; Mitchell, R. B., 2003, pp. 444ff.

68 Mitchell, R. B., 2007, pp. 904–910. See also e.g. Chayes, A. and Chayes, A. H., "On Compliance," *International Organization*, Vol. 47, No. 2, 1993, pp. 175–205.

69 This theory is closely connected to game theory and the traditional concept of the prisoner's dilemma. It is also connected to the kind of reasoning that Hardin illustrated in his story of the Tragedy of Commons in Hardin, G., 1968.

70 See e.g. Bodansky, D., 2010, pp. 110–112; Mitchell, R. B., 2007, p. 901f.; Barrett, S., *Environment and Statecraft: Strategy for Environmental Treaty Making*, Oxford University Press, 2003, pp. 49–84.; Guzman, A. T., *How International Law Works: A Rational Choice Theory*, Oxford University Press, 2008, chapter 2.

Examples of such obstacles range from difficulties for Parties to participate meaningfully in all of the activities due to limited resources, to the inability to tackle problems coherently and comprehensively as a result of legal fragmentation. This problem once again raises the question of the appropriate level and way to regulate as well as whether the aim of the resilience governance approach is reflected in the same structures in the legal system. Some scholars point to a more centralized approach, but there is no simple answer.[71] From an environmental point of view, these factors must also be viewed in relation to ecological dynamics and the concept of ecosystem approach.

6.5 REDUNDANCY AND COORDINATION OF LEGAL INSTRUMENTS

Multidimensional legal structures like those described in this chapter provide for potential diversity in measures. This diversity may not correspond exactly to what is intended with diversity in resilience governance, but it still provides prerequisites for such diversity in governance structures. The diversity in resilience governance aims to create redundancy – that is, a range of measures aiming to achieve the same result and where one could replace or complement another, if necessary. They could also be complementary in that they would apply to the system at different scales. As stated previously, diversity in these kinds of structures is a result of the connection to ecological dynamics. The purpose of diversity is often connected to an idea that a multitude of parallel measures provides alternative options for response and that these measures can be applied at different scales in parallel, or at different levels in the governance system to create redundancy. Redundancy in multilevel structures thus allows for a multitude of complementary measures at matching ecological scales. This redundancy or diversity of measures could also act as a response to the diversity of sources and causes of environmental problems and their occurrence at different levels in a dynamic system.[72]

Law directs only human activities and not the environment itself; it is not direct as in the case of operational management actions. Thus, redundancy and diversity in legal structures will function differently than redundancy in actual operational management, where actions are more in connection with the actual sources. Furthermore, each legal requirement in a redundant legal structure is binding in its own regime. The obligation to implement requirements within each separate instrument thus stands separately in relation to

[71] Dunoff, J. L., 2007, pp. 98–99.

[72] Galaz, V., et al., 2008, p. 154; Kotschy, K., et al., 2015, pp. 52ff.

each regulatory regime, even though the aim of different regulatory instruments might be the same. A redundant function in the legal structures is connected to the fact that measures taken in accordance with requirements in one of these instruments could also be accounted for under the other regulatory instruments, if the goal or aim is equivalent. Thus, an important factor of redundancy in international legal obligations is that States tend to account for the same national measure as the implementation of parallel but similar obligations. This means that redundancy in international legal obligations does not necessarily mean redundant or parallel measures in national legislation. This is natural since generally implementation will be less costly and easier to manage effectively when the different regulatory instruments are coordinated and coherent so that the same implementation measures can be accounted for both regimes. This would especially benefit States that are both Parties to an international agreement and Member States of the EU, when EU is a Party to the same agreement. However, this fact does not mean that redundancy in international or EU law does not have any effect. In some instances, it could still entail a diversity of measures on the national or local level. Most significantly, international and EU law redundancy will increase the pressure on States to take effective measures.

Coordination and combination of the different requirements could also affect what signifies compliance and the interpretation of the provisions of the respective regulation.[73] Moreover, coordination is important for the ecosystem approach and in the implementation process. This coordination is not only an issue of national implementation but must also take place between States that are Parties to an agreement and thus bound by the same obligations. Through such coordination and coherence, the prerequisites for enforcement are being established. In addition, the coordination among States on the goals set up in international regimes may also be the key for effective implementation. If the goals are also ecosystem specific, such coordination will also be key for achieving an ecosystem approach or ecosystem-based regulation. Hence, coordination is crucial, for both legal and potential ecological effectiveness through the ecosystem approach.[74]

[73] See also Juda, L., "The EU and the Marine Strategy Framework Directive: Continuing the Development of the European Ocean Use Management," *Ocean Development and International Law*, Vol. 41, 2010, pp. 39ff.

[74] See e.g. Platjouw, F. M., "Dimensions of Transboundary Legal Coherence Needed to Foster Ecosystem-Based Governance in the Arctic," *Marine Policy*, Vol. 110, 2019, pp. 7–9. The paper presents the effects of coherence and coordination, but much of the same goals of coherence could be achieved by what is here discussed as coordination.

An example from marine governance in the EU is the Marine Strategy Framework Directive and its connection to international law. As mentioned, the Marine Strategy Framework Directive is a goal-oriented framework directive that acknowledges the ecosystem approach and leaves a wide space of flexibility to Member State implementation. The goal of the Marine Strategy Framework Directive is good environmental status in the marine waters, measured according to a range of different ecological factors in each marine region. A first important step in the implementation of the Marine Strategy Framework Directive is that all Member States concerned within the same marine regions must agree on a common assessment. They must also decide on common ecological indicators for such an assessment. This work in itself triggers important coordination and cooperation that may increase the level of implementation by the States. According to the Marine Strategy Framework Directive, the international organizational structures in the marine region are to contribute to achieving good environmental status. The international structures intended are the regional convention structures. This is important since the regional conventions – as opposed to the EU directives – cover the marine regions as a whole, including non-EU States. The reason behind this is that good environmental status can only be achieved with the support of regional organizations and their activities in the frame of marine conventions.[75] However, it also establishes a parallel obligation for those Member States that are Parties to both the convention and Members of the EU. The EU Commission has confirmed that the Marine Strategy Framework Directive has triggered new developments in regional seas conventions and the mutual benefits that this provides. The regional seas organizations, as in the case of Baltic Marine Environment Protection Commission – Helsinki Commission (HELCOM), have provided reports on the state of their seas to feed into the initial assessments to be done by the individual Member States. Generally, the regional conventions have also developed new regional-level indicators, targets and methods and have agreed to the work for improved regional coordination.[76] In addition to the work pursued directly in the realm of the EU or HELCOM, other projects are being hosted by, and in

75 See e.g. Bohman, B. and Langlet, D., "Float or Sinker for Europe's Seas? The Role of Law in Marine Governance," in Gilek, M. and Kern, K. (eds.), *Governing Europe's Marine Environment: Europeanization of Regional Seas or Regionalization of EU Policies?* Ashgate, 2015, s. 53–73; Bohman, B., "Regulating Eutrophication: Flexible Legal Approaches and Environmental Governance in the Baltic Sea Area," in Ringbom, H. (ed.), *Regulatory Gaps in Baltic Sea Governance – Selected Issues*, MARE Publications Series, Springer Cham, 2018b.

76 EU COM Report (2014), Report from the Commission to the Council and the European Parliament, "The First Phase of Implementation of the Marine Strategy Framework Directive (2008/56/EC) – The European Commission's Assessment and Guidance," Brussels, 20.2.2014 COM(2014) 97 final, p. 5.

cooperation with, actors that are not tied to these organizations but that are supporting different efforts to coordinate and provide basic information to these processes.[77] Thus diversity and redundancy have somewhat different function and application in legal structures than in the general resilience governance. Still, they may well contribute to increased effectiveness and ecosystem fit.

6.6 SUMMARY AND CONCLUSIONS

This chapter provided a review of the legal aspects of cross-scale interaction, polycentric structures, multilevel governance approaches, diversity and redundancy. As stated, cross-scale interaction, polycentric structures and multilevel governance approaches, as presented in resilience research, imply that measures should be taken in parallel at different levels and scales of regulation. Such structures represent a governance approach that could match ecological dynamic structures and scales and provide for diversity in measures. This kind of regulatory structure entails adjustment of regulation to the scale of the ecosystem and the framing of the environmental problem. Furthermore, such regulation allows a multitude of complementary measures. A diversity of measures could represent an appropriate response to the diversity of sources and causes of environmental problems. An important aim with diverse measures is the increased possibility to match the measures to different aspects or levels of the problem. In addition, diversity in measures creates possibilities and incentives for redundancy.

First, it can be concluded that these kinds of structures for governance are clearly present in legal systems. The international law system has developed – on its own terms – in a pluralistic and nested way, thus creating a complex, multidimensional system similar to what is usually described in resilience terms. Such a system also creates a natural platform for a diversity of measures. Still, the effects this will have on enforcing stricter measures or accomplishing the diversity of measures aimed for in resilience governance theories also depend on successful coordination and redundancy. Through coordination, the prerequisites for compliance and enforcement are also established.

To conclude, it is obvious that legal structures and law are generally both multidimensional and polycentric. International law expands continuously in many different areas in parallel. Sometimes agreements adopted are bilateral or regional, sometimes they are multilateral or global – and sometimes they

77 Bohman, B., "Lessons from the Regulatory Approaches to Combat Eutrophication in the Baltic Sea," *Marine Policy*, Vol. 98, 2018c.

overlap to some extent. It creates a nest of agreements, obligations and treaty regimes. In addition, many other actors are often involved in the implementation process. Altogether, this creates a complex picture. It has been debated whether this creates fragmentation in international law and whether this makes the control of and implementation of the different obligations difficult. On the contrary, it seems that this has not become a serious problem – instead, it seems like the fragmented or polycentric system sometimes makes international law better adjusted for ecosystem fit and for complexity.

In parallel to this polycentric system of international law is the EU, with its diverse range of legislation. EU obligations add to the complexity of the international legal system for EU Member States – not least since the EU is also sometimes a Party to international agreements. EU laws are also implemented in parallel and partly in an overlapping fashion, to both national and international legal systems. For States that are EU Member States, this creates multiple obligations to a diversity of requirements relating to parallel and overlapping laws. There are obvious issues of authority and coordination that must be overcome to make implementation effective for the States. Still, while having overlapping obligations may not create the kind of diversity or redundancy of measures as intended in resilience governance, it seems to create increased incentives for effective implementation. Coordination is key here, though. Coordination is also key for ecosystem fit.

Multidimensional legal structures are not in themselves creating ecosystem match, as aimed for in the resilience theories. However, it is important to keep in mind that both EU law and international laws on the environment will not be adopted unless the problems are deemed best solved on a regional or international level. Moreover, even when the problem is framed at an international scale, the implementation is often connected to the specific ecosystem in each State, thus creating some level of ecosystem fit. New regulatory approaches and coordination can also help create an ecosystem fit in the implementation at different levels. While multidimensional legal structures create the potential for a more dynamic regulatory approach, they are not always focused as such on the environmental or ecological perspective. Thus, the adoption of the ecosystem approach becomes important as a legal mechanism for adjusting measures to the appropriate ecological scale and implementing ecosystem-based measures. This ecosystem perspective on regulation, or the ecosystem approach, exerts a force on the relevant States to go further in identifying measures in relation to the problem from a broader perspective. Stakeholder participation, as will be analyzed in the next chapter, is also crucial in this process.

The second Resilience Feature of Multidimensional and Polycentric Legal Structures seems to some extent already be implemented in all legal structures, just as a result of how law generally is structured. However, increasing focus on the ecosystem fit and EQS effectiveness will depend on strict structures for coordination and compliance. Still, although slightly differently than aimed for in resilience governance, multidimensional legal structures could contribute to such governance goals. With new regulatory approaches, including the ecosystem approach, and with stricter control, these structures could well contribute to diversity and effectiveness in legal structures for resilience.

7

Stakeholders and Structures for Participation

The previous chapters emphasized the importance of participation from different perspectives. In resilience theories, stakeholder participation, or the involvement of other interest groups, is a key feature of resilience governance and management. Participation is important for bottom-up approaches in adaptive governance, where self-organization and local knowledge are important factors. Different kinds of participation are also important for structural and monitoring issues in multilevel governance. Stakeholders in this context (e.g., NGOs) are in this sense important both in terms of transferring knowledge and information in multidimensional governance structures and for bridging structural or institutional gaps.

Law generally includes many different pathways for participation. However, participation in legal structures has to some extent another purpose than participation in resilience governance. Additionally, the term *stakeholder* is complicated in a legal context due to its wide applicability. For efficiency reasons, law generally has incentives to narrow down the number of actors that can participate. Moreover, the concept of stakeholders includes many different groups, where some may have opposing interests; thus it is not clear exactly what their role and effects of their participation are within such structures.

This chapter aims to present and discuss the wide spectrum of important features and functions provided by stakeholder participation in resilience research. These features and functions will be compared to similar features and functions in international and EU environmental law. The intention is to identify the ways in which law may also provide them and whether they are based on the same prerequisites. The aim is furthermore to discuss the role of participation in law and legal structures, as well as the role of law in creating structures for participation. One part of that aim is to define and review more formalized pathways for participation, in contrast to other, sometimes wider and less regulated forms of participation. While the latter forms might be more in line with participation presented in social-ecological resilience research, it may not be directly comparable because of the different contexts.

The chapter outline is as follows. After this introduction, the concept of stakeholder participation, as it is perceived within the research on social-ecological resilience, is presented and discussed. The following section describes the different forms of participation and pathways for participation in international and EU law, with a discussion and comparison to the concept of stakeholder participation. That section is followed by a section presenting other forms and channels of participation.

The review of participation as set out in this chapter will focus specifically on different concepts of participation – that is, how participation is formally defined within law. Furthermore, pathways for participation, along with how participation is provided in legal structures at international, regional and, in part, national levels, will be reviewed. The review includes a comparison of the role and functions connected to participation within law with the functions of participation in governance for social-ecological resilience. In addition, the role and function of participation in law associated with creating democracy, legitimacy and institutional ecosystem fit or ecosystem approach will also be included in the focus of this chapter. Generally, participation fosters values such as democracy and legitimacy, then of course it is also indirectly reflected by the extent to which participation is formally provided for in legal structures.

7.1 DIFFERENT FORMS AND ROLES OF PARTICIPATION

Multilevel governance, together with general theories on governance for social-ecological resilience, stipulates the inclusion of stakeholder participation (cf. Chapter 6). Stakeholder participation in governance and law is about assuring that those concerned are involved in decision-making and in measures taken. Participation in this sense can be seen both as an instrument to ensure legitimacy and as a means to value and make use of social inherited knowledge to enhance the decisions taken. Stakeholder participation in these terms is connected to core aspects of adaptive management and especially adaptive co-management.[1] Co-management and management

[1] The difference between adaptive management and adaptive co-management is that co-management to a larger extent claims to address and include institutional and epistemological aspects, multi-stakeholder processes and the sharing of power in natural resource management; see Folke, C., et al., 2005, pp. 448–449. Adaptive co-management typically can be described as

guided by the collective memory of experiences is also one important aspect of flexibility and adaptive capacity in the system, especially at a local level or for connecting different levels of management and governance.[2] Because of these factors, stakeholder participation is a key feature in theories on governance and management for social-ecological resilience. It relates to the ideas of adaptive governance, social knowledge and self-organization, as well as a multilevel approach.[3] Theories on self-organization is an important aspect of resilience thinking along with the multilevel or polycentric approach. Since the origin of the theories can be traced back to small-scale case studies, the ability to self-organize at this small-scale level is considered as key for adaptive and sustainable management. These theories are also linked to governance theories proposed primarily by Elinor Ostrom on collective action in governing common-pool resources, where self-organization is considered a key feature.[4] Theories, which have influenced the resilience governance theories (Section 3.4). The role of stakeholder participation for such theories, is connected to the idea that measures should be imposed directly, on the appropriate level, by the actors most directly concerned in a democratic and decentralized approach. The main aim with this resilience feature is thus to base measures on local knowledge and avoid top-down approaches. Such approaches are considered to ultimately undermine the

part of governance where private actors cooperate with the public (i.e., the State or other governing actors) in a problem-solving and information sharing process.

See a review on adaptive co-management in Plummer, R., "The Adaptive Co-Management Process: An Initial Synthesis of Representative Models and Influential Variables," *Ecology and Society*, Vol. 14(2), 2009, p. 24. This is a frequent means of cooperation and operationalization in international law and is also common in the EU policy and governance structures, and can then be seen as equal to so-called *public-private partnerships*. (See Jönsson, C. and Tallberg, J., "Transnational Actor Participation in International Institutions: Where, Why, and with What Consequences?," at p. 4ff; see also Tallberg, J., "Transnational Access to International Institutions: Three Approaches," both are chapters in Jönsson, C. and Tallberg, J. (eds.), *Transnational Actors in Global Governance*, Palgrave Macmillan, 2010.)

The structures or processes included in co-management will not be further investigated or developed here but they are important to take note of, since they are an important side to adaptive governance features. They are, however, also signifying a function more connected to multilevel governance and institutional polycentricism, as it is a structure that connects local actors to higher-level organizations and institutions.

2 Folke, C., Carpenter, S., Elmqvist, T., et al., "Resilience and Sustainable Development: Building Adaptive Capacity in a World of Transformations," *Scientific Background Paper on Resilience for the Process of the World Summit on Sustainable Development on behalf of the Environmental Advisory Council to the Swedish Government*, Edita Norstedts Tryckeri AB, Stockholm 2002a, pp. 45–46.

3 See e.g. Folke, C., et al., 2005, pp. 445ff.

4 See e.g. Ostrom, E., *Governing the Commons – The Evolution of Institutions for Collective Action*, Cambridge University Press, 1990.

possibilities of appropriate measures being taken, as well as the will to perform the measures agreed upon.

Stakeholder participation is also an important feature in international environmental law. Although the appropriateness of the term stakeholder in this context can be debated, the essence of the term is that someone has an interest in the issues at stake. Sometimes such stakeholders are in legal terms instead presented as actors, NGOs or the public and the like with similar intents. Thus, participation or actor involvement occurs in many different ways in legal structures as well, through both formal and informal channels. In recent decades, international law, national legal regimes and the EU have increasingly supported and included mechanisms and structures for different kinds of actor involvement.[5] In this light, participation is acknowledged as a means to inter alia balance international multilateral and multileveled norms with local action, in a democratic spirit. Some emphasize that such participation or involvement contributes to increased legitimacy in international law.[6] The aspects reflected also correspond to what has been stated in the general international elaborations of the concept of ecosystem approach in the CBD. The guiding principles developed for the implementation of the ecosystem approach emphasize stakeholder participation and exchange of knowledge and information.[7]

Stakeholder participation is a rather broad concept, however. It includes a large span of actors or groups of actors concerned by a certain issue.[8] This is also true for how the concept is applied and discussed in research on social-ecological resilience – stakeholder participation includes a range of actors that represent a wide diversity of interests and incentives for being involved. It

[5] See e.g. Charnovitz, S., "Two Centuries of Participation: NGOs and International Governance," *Michigan Journal of International Law*, Vol. 18, No. 2, 1997, pp. 183–286; Ambrus, M., Arts, K., Hey, E. and Raulus, H., "The Role of Experts in International and European Decision-Making Processes: Setting the Scene," in Ambrus, M., Arts, K., Hey, E. and Raulus, H. (eds.), *The Role of "Experts" in International and European Decision-Making Processes: Advisors, Decision Makers or Irrelevant Actors?*, Cambridge University Press, 2014; Ebbesson, J., 2007a, p. 681–702.

[6] Ebbesson, J., 2007a, p. 686ff.; Schrefler, L., "Reflections on the Different Roles of Expertise in Regulatory Policy Making," in Ambrus, M., Arts, K., Hey, E. and Raulus, H. (eds.), *The Role of "Experts" in International and European Decision-Making Processes: Advisors, Decision Makers or Irrelevant Actors?*, Cambridge University Press, 2014. See also, for example, the conclusions of Andresen, S., "The Role of Scientific Expertise in Multilateral Environmental Agreements: Influence and Effectiveness," in Ambrus, M., Arts, K., Hey, E. and Raulus, H. (eds.), *The Role of "Experts" in International and European Decision-Making Processes: Advisors, Decision Makers or Irrelevant Actors?*, Cambridge University Press, 2014.

[7] CBD Malawi Principles, 1, 2, 7 and 11.

[8] See e.g. Phillips, R., Freeman, R. E. and Wicks, A. C., "What Stakeholder Theory Is Not," *Business Ethics Quarterly*, Vol. 13, No. 4, 2003, p. 479.

includes both private and public actors, from individuals or local groups with experience in local resource and ecosystem management – groups otherwise often referred to as civil society – to NGOs and NGO networks, scientists or other experts, and not least interest groups from different industrial or economic sectors and corporations.[9] The breadth of the concept complicates the analysis of the potential benefits of participation. This analysis requires a discussion on the significance of the definition and more narrow delimited aspects of the concept, to identify the parameters that can be compared and accounted for.

Because stakeholder participation is such a broad concept, the review here is subject to certain delimitations. Some aspects of these delimitations are discussed in the following sections, because they are of relevance for the current exploration and comparison of concepts. However, it must be emphasized that it is the focus on the concept of participation within theories on social-ecological resilience that is also leading the focus of the review. This means that some aspects often connected with participation in a legal perspective are not included here, or are dealt with only briefly. Some of these aspects are issues of standing, access to justice, and the right to appeal.

7.2 STAKEHOLDER PARTICIPATION AS A FEATURE IN SOCIAL-ECOLOGICAL RESILIENCE GOVERNANCE

As stated, the concept of stakeholder participation in social-ecological resilience is primarily about assuring that those concerned and closely connected to the environment at different, but primarily local levels are involved in the management measures taken. The benefit is to be able to base measures on local knowledge and to avoid top-down approaches that could otherwise undermine the possibilities for appropriate measures as well as the will to perform the measures agreed upon. Stakeholder participation is also a consequence or feature inherent in a multilevel approach in governance and management – a governance approach that necessitates action at different levels in the system. Moreover, the many significant functions and purposes to which the stakeholders in management for social-ecological resilience are claimed to contribute are discussed here, in terms of both larger and more local scales. One function frequently emphasized is the issue of institutional fit and the matching of management systems with the biophysical, or ecological, systems, so that temporal and spatial processes are synchronized. This is of course also connected to the functions of a multilevel approach but is

9 Folke, C., Carpenter, S., Elmqvist, T., et al., 2002a, n. 850, pp. 45–46.

taken further with stakeholder participation on the appropriate level of management. Although the existence of organizational linkages among institutions with relatively autonomous but interdependent actors is not the only factor that contributes to enabling institutional fit, it is claimed that these linkages are crucial in avoiding fragmented and sectorial approaches to ecosystem management.[10]

On a larger scale, governance processes – such as those that are the object of decision processes in international and EU law – actors and knowledge exchange must also be active on top levels. This is because the overall goal of legislation is generally set in relation to the larger scales of ecosystem dynamics. Local or lower-scale management is not sufficient to deal with all aspects of the problem, which is an obvious reason why actions are coordinated at these higher levels in the first place. This fact has been acknowledged in research on social-ecological resilience. Adaptive governance of social-ecological resilience requires the capacity to deal with the broader environmental perspective in preparation for uncertainty and surprise. Adaptive management focuses on understanding ecosystem dynamics and feeding ecological knowledge into management and governance organizations. One instrument to accomplish this for a broader or higher-level approach in this context comprises the organizations that act as bridges for adaptive management by local actors or communities with the other scales of management organizations (Section 4.3).[11] This builds upon the collaboration of a diverse set of stakeholders and managing measures at different levels, from local levels to municipalities to regional and national organizations, and also to international bodies.[12] If seen as a composed network, from local, municipal and national laws to regional (European) and international laws, the legal system may reveal the same kind of bridging function through its general structures and pathways for participation.

It has been pointed out that organizations and stakeholders serving as bridges between levels of management are no guarantee of either more democratic decision-making or of avoiding top-down approaches; they can just as well come to play a role in the implementation of top-down policies.[13] This is an important point that cannot be disregarded in relation to legal

[10] Galaz, V., et al., 2008, pp. 163–164; Folke, C., et al., 2005, pp. 448–449.

[11] Folke, C., et al., 2005, pp. 460–461.

[12] Ibid., pp. 448–449.

[13] Galaz, V., et al., 2008, pp. 163–164. See also: Agné, H., Dellmuth, L. M. and Tallberg, J., "Does Stakeholder Involvement Foster Democratic Legitimacy in International Organizations? An Empirical Assessment of a Normative Theory," *The Review of International Organizations*, Vol. 10, No. 4, 2015, pp. 465–488.

bridging features. To a large extent, the legal structures create prerequisites for the implementation of laws that have often been determined on levels that are higher than those where the laws are enforced. When participation is enabled, the participatory role is to scrutinize and question such laws and their implementation. In this way, bridging functions could still work as a buffer. This is especially the case with international and EU laws. One example referred to in the resilience literature is a case where a change in EU agricultural subsidies of cattle grazing became a factor that caused disruption in the national system and thus led to irreversible change.[14] Such events demonstrate the importance of having structures for communication and decision-making that involve participants from different levels and who represent different ecological knowledge, so the knowledge and local interests can be taken into account, and severe, negative consequences following from legal decisions at international or EU levels can be avoided; this is where the role of law as a bridging and boundary organization becomes obvious.[15]

Other legal structures or instruments are intentionally designed to be implemented with local and other forms of participatory influence, like some of the different EU environmental framework directives. Even if the legal act is established and adopted at the institutional level of the EU, there are still opportunities for participants to influence its measures with respect to implementation.[16] There are processes and participatory pathways in these legal structures that are indeed meant to have democratic functions and promote democratic mechanisms. There are also structures where laws are decided on an appropriate level for those concerned. Decisions are made through democratic processes with access for participation; this is a fundamental feature in a system based on the rule of law. In an increasingly complex and internationally globalized world, however, it is still a fact that many decisions – especially regarding the environment – are drafted and decided on at other levels and by other people than those directly concerned or obliged to realize these decisions. This is also the reason why it is important

14 The example here was taken from a water governance project in Kristianstad in the south of Sweden (Kristianstad Vattenrike), discussed in Folke, C., et al., 2005, p. 459.

15 Cf. Schout, A. and Sleifer, J., "Expertise at the Crossroads of National and International Policy Making: A Public Management Perspective," in Ambrus, M., Arts, K., Hey, E. and Raulus, H. (eds.), *The Role of "Experts" in International and European Decision-Making Processes: Advisors, Decision Makers or Irrelevant Actors?*, Cambridge University Press, 2014.

16 See e.g. van Leeuwen, J., et al., "Implementing the Marine Strategy Framework Directive: A Policy Perspective on Regulatory, Institutional and Stakeholder Impediments to Effective Implementation," *Marine Policy*, Vol. 50, Part B, 2014, p. 329; Newig, J., Pahl-Wostl, C. and Sigel, K., "The Role of Public Participation in Managing Uncertainty in the Implementation of the Water Framework Directive," *European Environment*, Vol. 15, No. 6, 2005, pp. 333–343.

to have structures as an instrument to connect these different levels of management. However, the fact that stakeholder participation is such a broad concept makes it difficult to state any general conclusion regarding these actors' contribution to the processes, because the actors involved may be difficult to pinpoint and define.

Other consequences or democratic features connected to stakeholder participation, which are mentioned in social-ecological resilience research, are legitimacy and accountability.[17] Legitimacy, as mentioned earlier, is claimed to follow from participation and involvement of stakeholders, and is also important in legal systems and the rule of law. It is furthermore stressed in resilience theories that stakeholder participation will increase effectiveness in a governance system, mainly due to the higher level of legitimacy. It is also implied that stakeholder participation – in the sense presented in resilience research – promotes a more effective approach in the governance or management actions taken at different levels.[18] However, whether increased legitimacy, accountability and effectiveness actually are the results within a legal system is debated. Wide stakeholder participation within law has in itself been questioned in terms of legitimacy due to factors of representation and follow-up. Representation is poorly assessed or controlled, and thus law does not necessarily reflect a fair representation of actors and interests; another issue is representation dominated by actors with considerable economic resources. The question of follow-up refers to the extent to which the results of actions taken by stakeholders are evaluated with regard to the general goal – that is, in those situations where stakeholders have an independent task to perform.[19]

Stakeholder participation can be seen in many perspectives but appears to provide many very important features in resilience management. The role of stakeholders ranges from feeding local knowledge into systems of adaptive governance, to serving as contributors to institutional fit and organizational structures for bridging, to providing legitimacy, accountability and effectiveness to the governance system. All of these features are important, and to a large extent, this general overview demonstrates that the same kinds of features or roles are possible to distinguish in law and legal structures. In

[17] Folke, C., et al., 2005, p. 449.

[18] Folke, C., et al., 2005, pp. 448–449.

[19] See, for example, the discussions raised on this theme by Bodansky, D., "Legitimacy in International Law and International Relations," in Dunoff, J. L. and Pollack, M. A. (eds.), *Interdisciplinary Perspectives on International Law and International Relations – The State of the Art*, Cambridge University Press, 2012, pp. 321–341; Bäckstrand, K., "Multi-Stakeholder Partnerships for Sustainable Development: Rethinking Legitimacy, Accountability and Effectiveness," *European Environment*, Vol. 16, No. 5, 2006, pp. 290–306.

addition to providing general institutional structures, law often provides different pathways for participation; hence the benefits of participation are reflected. The next section takes a closer look at different channels and more formal pathways for participation found in law.

7.3 PERSPECTIVES ON PARTICIPATION IN INTERNATIONAL AND EU LAW

This section aims to provide a general picture of participation as part of the legal system in terms of its role or function in the context of legal structures, as well as different related tasks or features. The aim is to provide different perspectives on how participation is manifested within legal structures and why participation is more than just the direct instrumental features tied to it. These perspectives can also show that the role and significance of participation in law and social-ecological resilience governance are similar, but that they differ in some respects as well.

First, however, the concept of stakeholder is discussed here. As noted, the notion of stakeholders as a concept is very broad and not always considered useful in a legal setting. The actors often targeted in resilience research are those traditionally cooperating for their own livelihood based on their own direct dependence on the ecosystem services. On higher decision-making levels, these actors are often actors with various business or corporate interests. In addition to the general public and NGOs, corporate economic actors are in some ways key actors in legal decision-making.[20] Even pure lobbying organizations could be included in the category of stakeholders in this context. The concept of stakeholders does generally not exclude any such corporate organizations, as opposed to the concept of the general public.[21] An assumption is that the incentives for such corporate or lobbying organizations to cooperate and exert impact on a decision process regarding management measures may be different from the incentives for such actors that are generally lacking a direct economic incentive. Examples of the latter are actors that are only strictly concerned by the matter in question or general nonprofit actors, such as NGOs. Furthermore, some scholars hold that since there is no specific definition of stakeholders, or requirements for such participation, there is also no supervision or fair distribution of participatory rights in regard to economic

[20] See e.g. Abbot, C. and Lee, M., "Economic Actors in EU Environmental Law," *Yearbook of European Law*, Vol. 34, No. 1, 2015, pp. 1–34.

[21] Ebbesson, J., 2007a, p. 685, means that the concept of *the public* in law and legal discourse generally includes all actors outside the governmental administration but usually then with exception of the *private corporate sector.*

or other resources.[22] It thus needs to be acknowledged that the definitions, requirements or boundaries set with regard to participating actors or groups have consequences – in terms of both general aspects of stakeholder influence and issues of legitimacy and accountability. In a more extended perspective, the actors involved in decision-making, or influencing the choices made in law-making, may also influence, for example, such aspects as distribution and access to natural resources and ecosystem services. The questions of access to resources in this respect, then, are increasingly crucial for sustainable development and social resilience.

In recent decades both international law and national legal regimes have increasingly supported and included mechanisms and structures for different kinds of stakeholder involvement. The EU has also in recent years increased focus on participation and legitimacy issues.[23] Despite the difficulties in defining the concept of stakeholder participation, it is also frequently referred to as a feature when discussing participation in legal processes. It must definitely be regarded generally as part of the role of law to provide structures for stakeholder participation that enable functions such as those presented above, or even incorporate them in different ways. However, it is beyond the role – or even the means – of law to control and evaluate the functions and values that general stakeholder participation may provide. General stakeholder participation is important in overall governance and referred to frequently in discussions about international or EU law. Since the concept of stakeholders is so broad it is difficult to define, and thus even more difficult to evaluate as such. In addition, because of the concept's broadness, few formal pathways for general stakeholder participation exists; such formal pathways for participation are more often provided for a smaller circle of actors, such as those included in the concept of the public or the general public. In this study, formal pathways for participation mean lawfully established or prescribed channels for participation in the institutional structure.

7.3.1 *Formal Pathways to Participation and Definition of Public Participation*

Formal participation in legal institutions and processes is usually open to somewhat more specific or narrow groups of participants, which are thus included through formal access channels. This participation is generally termed as public participation and focuses on a smaller circle of involved

[22] Bäckstrand, K., 2006.

[23] EU White Paper (2001).

parties than those represented by the concept of stakeholders. The actors included in the concept of the public vary, but usually the term encompasses the general public (all actors that are nongovernmental), including NGOs and civil society, but generally with the exception of the corporate sector.[24]

The concept of public participation is thus significantly distinct from the broad concept of stakeholders. Public participation generally does not include actors with private economic interests or corporate actors such as industrial and business organizations; rather, it aims to provide access for civil society and nonprofit organizations. One reason that the group of concerned actors is limited within the legal system is that the concept of public participation often entails rights for those included, such as the rights of access to information and access to justice. In order for a State to provide such rights, those concerned must somehow be possible to identify. Limits must also be set in order to create a system where it makes sense to provide such rights. However, providing access to information and access to justice are primarily State-level responsibilities and thus will not be discussed in depth here. Access will be reviewed only to the extent that it is connected to the actual possibility to participate in decision-making.

Although the public is a more limited concept, it should not be automatically regarded as a narrow group. This is also true when it comes to the definition of NGOs. The general meaning of NGO is an organization separated from State interests or State involvement. However, the concept of NGOs provides room for a wider definition that can include a wide variety of organizations ranging from local to global in status. Although not traditionally considered an NGO, the public concept could even include business organizations. An important distinction is however that this concept generally concerns nonprofit organizations. A significant aspect of the definition of NGOs, as it is intended here, is that NGOs are considered representatives of some element of civil society.[25]

7.3.2 *Participation as a Means of Legitimacy*

The structures and pathways for participation in law have significant impact on issues of legitimacy. There are different forms of legitimacy and the

[24] Ebbesson, J., 2007a, p. 685.

[25] See the elaborations of the NGO definition in Charnovitz, S., 1996–1997, pp. 185–188. See also the distinctions between the concepts of *the Public* and NGO in Ebbesson, J., 2007a. See also Spiro, P. J., "Non-Governmental Organizations and Civil Society," in Bodansky, D., Brunnée, J. and Hey, E. (eds.), *The Oxford Handbook of International Environmental Law*, Oxford University Press, 2007, p. 772.

concept of legitimacy can thus be described, defined and interpreted from different perspectives.[26] In recent times, issues of legitimacy have been used as a justificatory of changes and transformations of legal orders, as well as a reason for their maintenance and dissolution.[27] The legitimacy feature discussed in resilience research, as described previously, seems closest to democratic legitimacy, as it is based on reasoning regarding the involvement of stakeholders. Democratic legitimacy is represented by democratic features, such as accountability and transparency, as well as access to participation, deliberation, and fairness.[28] The issue of legitimacy and democratic features has also been an issue dealt with by the EU. Since being highly institutionalized, it has become evident that increasing democratic and participatory features are necessary to create increased legitimacy both for the institutions and decisions.[29]

Legitimacy is important for compliance with international law. Some reasons for State compliance with international law could be due to pressure, the fact that the State has at some level agreed to the intent or provisions of an agreement and thus respects the outcomes and statements produced by its treaty body, and, as mentioned, legitimacy.[30] As NGOs and other stakeholders have gained more influence in international environmental law processes, these processes have come to change. Change has also occurred because international environmental law also increasingly affects private actors, civil society and business. Thus stakeholders' attitude toward decisions taken becomes likewise important as the States', and they can be considered to have a legitimate claim to influence such decisions that affect them.[31] Therefore international environmental law to a large

[26] See e.g. Bernstein, S., "Legitimacy in Global Environmental Governance," *Journal of International Law and International Relations*, Vol. 1(1–2), 2005, pp. 139ff.; Bodansky, D., 2012, pp. 321ff; Bodansky, D., "Legitimacy," in Bodansky, D., Brunnée, J. and Hey, E. (eds.), *The Oxford Handbook of International Environmental Law*, Oxford University Press, 2007, pp. 704ff.; Thomas, C. A., "The Uses and Abuses of Legitimacy in International Law," *Oxford Journal of Legal Studies*, Vol. 34, No. 4, 2014, pp. 729–758.

[27] Thomas, C. A., 2014, p.758.

[28] Bernstein, S., 2005, p. 147.

[29] Bodansky, D., "The Legitimacy of International Governance: A Coming Challenge for International Environmental Law?," *The American Journal of International Law*, Vol. 93, No. 3, 1999, p. 597. See also EU White Paper (2001).

[30] Bodansky, D., 2007, pp. 706–708. See also Franck, T. M., "Legitimacy in the International System," *American Journal of International Law*, Vol. 82, No. 4, 1988, pp. 705–759, on the role of legitimacy for compliance.

[31] Bodansky, D., 2007, p. 714. See also Raustiala, K., "The 'Participatory Revolution' in International Environmental Law," *Harvard Environmental Law Review*, Vol. 21, 1997b, pp. 556–558.

extent includes such features of democratic legitimacy, based on extended pathways for participation.[32]

The issue of legitimacy also has strong and significant practical implications for the future development of international environmental law. In addition to being a potential basis for compliance, legitimacy is also the basis of willingness by States to accept institutions or treaty bodies to include mechanisms with authority to review compliance, make binding decisions and take action based on its findings.[33] The growing complexity of international environmental problems has initiated a process toward international institutions with greater legislative, administrative and adjudicatory powers. In addition, there is a growing need for legal institutions that include mechanisms for flexible response to new problems and information through the development, implementation and enforcement of international norms. The success of this kind of development depends to a large extent on these regimes being accepted as legitimate.[34] They rely on participation. A clear parallel can be made here to the ideas of participation in resilience research. When it comes to international environmental law and the creation of flexible and more authoritative systems that can make decisions independently, without depending on consensus among States, a new or broader attitude toward compliance and legitimacy is necessary. One idea is that this demands genuine legitimacy based on other factors that can create trust in the system and between Parties. One significant factor, then, is increased participation by the public, NGOs and different kinds of stakeholders, providing accountability as well as expertise and knowledge that will create a sound basis for such decisions.[35]

7.3.3 *Participation in International Environmental Law*

Participation of nonstate actors in international law started to expand in the 1970s, with the Stockholm Conference being an important trigger. Participation in international law is represented mostly by NGOs, but also different kinds of scientists and experts. Most pathways for participation are open primarily to NGOs. This development in NGO participation resulted in important impressions in international environmental law in the decades after the 1970s. As a result, NGOs were increasingly provided access to participate actively and make formal statements in sessions of a number of international

[32] Bernstein, S., 2005, p. 151.
[33] Bodansky, D., 2007, pp. 709–710.
[34] Ibid., p. 706.
[35] Ibid., pp. 718–721.

negotiations, and this way, NGOs had an important role in the development of new agreements.[36] The impact of NGOs is visible in many agreements from the 1970s and onward, as provisions have increasingly included possibilities for NGO and public participation at different levels in the treaty regimes.[37] However, the NGO influence was not limited to participation and making formal statements in meetings. It was also expressed through external actions – through both planned protests and physical actions and in challenging the different treaty provisions legally through raising legal disputes.[38] These are forms of participation that are not directly provided for by the international legal regimes but which still have had a significant impact.

With the Rio Conference in 1992, however, a whole new era of NGO involvement in international environmental law began. NGOs gained further access to international organizations and had greater influence in negotiations. While the number of governments participating in the Rio Conference was 178 compared to 113 governments participating at the Stockholm Conference, the number of NGOs involved at the Rio Conference was over 650, compared to 225 at Stockholm. One of the reasons for this changed attitude toward NGOs and public involvement was that the spread of democratic norms had raised general expectations about transparency and increased opportunities for public participation.[39] The presence of NGOs at these conferences also had an important impact because of their ability to pressure governments to enter into agreements.

The Rio Conference adopted important policy statements regarding the role of NGOs in the international community, not least through the United Nations Environment and Development Agenda[40] (Agenda 21).[41] Another result or effect of the expansion of NGO participation may also be that NGOs have increasingly become free actors directly in international bodies.[42] An important outcome of the conference was a statement in the 1992 Rio Declaration, Principle 10, that resembled the description of

36 Charnovitz, S., 1996–1997, pp. 261–263.

37 Raustiala, K., "States, NGOs, and International Environmental Institutions," *International Studies Quarterly*, Vol. 41, No. 4, 1997a, p. 722.

38 Charnovitz, S., 1996–1997, pp. 264–265.

39 Ibid., p. 266.

40 1992 United Nations Environment and Development Agenda, "Agenda 21," adopted at the 1992 UN Rio Conference on Environmental and Development, U.N. GAOR, 46th Sess., Agenda Item 21, UN Doc A/Conf.151/26 (1992) U.N.

41 Charnovitz, S., 1996–1997, p. 265; see also the United Nations Environment and Development Agenda, "Agenda 21," adopted at the 1992 UN Rio Conference on Environmental and Development, Section 3.

42 See e.g. Raustiala, K., 1997a.

participation in resilience theories. This principle mainly refers to participation in national law, but emphasizes the importance of participation at all relevant levels:

> Environmental issues are best handled with participation of all concerned citizens, at the relevant level. At the national level, each individual shall have appropriate access to information concerning the environment that is held by public authorities, including information on hazardous materials and activities in their communities, and the opportunity to participate in decision-making processes. States shall facilitate and encourage public awareness and participation by making information widely available. Effective access to judicial and administrative proceedings, including redress and remedy, shall be provided.[43]

It was also in parallel with the Rio Conference that the CBD was adopted. Only a few years later in the same spirit of acknowledging the role of stakeholders, the concept of ecosystem approach and the Malawi principles were adopted (Section 2.5).[44] The Malawi principles on how to implement an ecosystem approach clearly establish the important role of stakeholders and participation for ecosystem management.[45] This perspective should thus also be reflected in all regulatory instruments that embrace the ecosystem approach. The guiding Malawi principles state, for example, that different sectors of society view ecosystems in terms of their own economic, cultural and societal needs. As a consequence, indigenous peoples and other local communities concerned are important stakeholders also in a legal context, and their rights and interests should be recognized.[46] Another guiding principle states that decentralized systems may lead to greater efficiency, effectiveness and equity. Thus management should involve all stakeholders and balance local interests with the greater public interest.[47] This principle is also evident in the theories on stakeholder participation for resilience management, described previously. Available guidance on the ecosystem approach also mentions that management should be bounded by spatial and temporal scales that are appropriate to the objectives; these boundaries should be defined

43 The Rio Declaration, principle 10.

44 The Convention on Biological Diversity was finally adopted on May 21, 1992, in Nairobi, Kenya. See Doc No. UNEP/Bio.Div/CONF/1/Add. It was later opened for signature during the Rio Conference in June 1992. The ecosystem approach was adopted at the second meeting in 1995; see COP 2 Decision II/8.

45 See primarily CBD Malawi Principles, Principles 2, 11 and 12, drafted in 1998, and adopted in 2000.

46 CBD Malawi principles, Principle 1.

47 CBD Malawi principles, Principle 2.

operationally by users, managers, scientists, and indigenous and local peoples.[48] As a final example of how these aspects of management are reflected in the general elaboration of the ecosystem approach, it is also stated that information from all sources is critical to arriving at effective ecosystem management strategies.[49]

The trend of public participation and involving NGOs in international law, international bodies and meetings continued in the new millennium. The United Nations 2002 Johannesburg Declaration on Sustainable Development[50] (the Johannesburg Declaration) included two important statements in this regard. The first one acknowledges indigenous peoples and shows strong connections to the CBD and its perspective on the ecosystem approach. Although stakeholder participation in resilience research is not specifically mentioned, the declaration is similar to how the concept can be understood: "We reaffirm the vital role of the indigenous peoples in sustainable development."[51] As presented previously, the Malawi principles state inter alia that different sectors of society view ecosystems in terms of their own economic, cultural and societal needs. A consequence is that indigenous peoples and other local communities concerned are important stakeholders and their rights and interests should be recognized.[52]

The second statement made in the Johannesburg Declaration emphasizes even more than previous statements the importance of broad participation at all levels, and expressly connects participation to sustainable development: "We recognize that sustainable development requires a long-term perspective and broad-based participation in policy formulation, decision-making and implementation at all levels. As social partners, we will continue to work for stable partnerships with all major groups, respecting the independent, important roles of each of them."[53] This statement from the Johannesburg Declaration mentions the importance of so-called partnerships. At the Johannesburg conference, the initiation of multi-stakeholder involvement through public-private networks was a central issue. This form of stakeholder network cooperation could be seen as "post-sovereign."[54] The reason for the post-sovereign perspective is that it is a form of governance regime that can be

48 CBD Malawi principles, Principle 7.
49 CBD Malawi principles, Principle 11.
50 UN Doc No. A/CONF.199/20, Res. 2.
51 The United Nations 2002 Johannesburg Declaration on Sustainable Development (The Johannesburg Declaration), UN Doc No. A/CONF.199/20, Principle 25.
52 CBD Malawi principles, Principle 1.
53 The Johannesburg Declaration, Principle 26.
54 Bäckstrand, K., 2006, p. 290.

seen to go beyond the traditional State-centric international system. These networks of stakeholders may well respond to the systems found in resilience theories on stakeholder participation and bridging organizations (Section 4.3 and Section 7.2). To some extent, these networks are also seen as complementary to traditional systems, while others find them to be more or less a threat to international law.[55] However, issues of representation and transparency with regard to this wide multi-stakeholder concept are especially relevant with regard to such networks or partnerships.[56]

In 2012 at the United Nations Conference on Sustainable Development (the Rio +20 Conference), the importance of participation was once again emphasized.[57] In the outcome of the conference, it was also stated: "We encourage action at regional, national, sub-national, and local levels to promote access to information, public participation, and access to justice in environmental matters, as appropriate."[58] There are no general obligations to provide access or pathways for public participation on an international level. Instead, this is provided individually by international regimes, usually arranged in different ways depending on the agreement. It is more common that NGOs take part as observers, rather than as fully accepted participants. Furthermore, it is common that NGOs are permitted to access public meetings of a convention but not closed sessions. This is of course a dilemma when it comes to influence, since it is primarily in closed sessions that more difficult issues and decisions are dealt with. It should be noted, though, that some convention regimes give NGOs much more formal space to intervene in different forms. One way this can be done is to permit access to provide information, make statements and review working documents. Another way is to allow NGOs to take part in the secretariat's preparatory work.[59]

A crucial point in discussing participation is the existence of different kinds of participation at different levels of law. As shown, participation can be structured in different ways. The first kind of influence provided for participation was through indirect involvement of NGOs. Gradually, due to the pressure exercised, pathways to formal participation were opened up in meetings and negotiations, although with varying extents of openness and

55 See e.g. Bäckstrand, K., 2006, p. 291, where public-private partnership is a debated alternative to the1992 Climate Convention and Kyoto protocol Clean Development Mechanism.

56 Bäckstrand, K., 2006.

57 The Future We Want, outcome document of the United Nations Conference on Sustainable Development, in Rio de Janeiro, June 2012, UN Doc No. A/RES/66/288, Section II C., emphasizing a number of actions for engaging major groups and stakeholders.

58 The Future We Want, Section IV E, Institutional Framework for Sustainable Development, para. 99.

59 See Bodansky, D., 2010, p. 129.

participatory rights. The multi-stakeholder networks and public-private partnerships launched by the Johannesburg Conference, however significant, represent a different kind of participation with specific characteristics and conditions, which is beyond the scope of this chapter. One intention with this type of participation is to encourage innovation, including voluntary measures, in the corporate sector. In the case of Johannesburg, this involvement also included multi-stakeholder dialogues in the preparatory process of the conference.[60] This type of participation thus goes beyond general forms and is an example of the kind of stakeholder involvement that cannot be easily reviewed with respect to the role of law and the terms set with regard to direct participatory rights. Other, and more emphasized, procedures for participation focus on providing access for the public to participate in national decision-making.

The different kinds of procedures for participation have mainly been limited and decided on by States and are set in relation to the traditional State-centric system of international law founded on cooperation between sovereign States. Increasingly, however, NGOs have been given space also to act on their own in the international community, and they have found ways to do so that go partly beyond the traditional system, as shown by the example of partnerships with stakeholder networks.[61] The influence the participating actors have, the extent to which they actually pressure States toward actions, as well as the extent to which they have formal or informal power to intervene, attend meetings, speak at meetings or submit and receive documents and so forth are of course crucial in the discussion of these actors' role in law, as well as discussion of their connection to legitimacy, accountability and effectiveness.[62]

7.3.4 *Participation in EU Environmental Law*

Stakeholder involvement and participation by the public in decision-making processes is also a general feature within the EU. The emergence of such features came a little later, however, than in international law. A general call for more open institutions, participation by the general public, increased accountability and effectiveness of applied policies was published in 2001 in a white paper on European governance.[63] The aspects of governance presented in the white paper were those recognized as new governance. The call

60 Bernstein, S., 2005, p. 149.
61 Raustiala, K., 1997a.
62 This is also acknowledged by Charnovitz, S., 1996–1997, p. 268, in terms of "penetration" and "influence."
63 EU White Paper (2001).

for inter alia greater participation by stakeholders and the general public in this case was not emphasized with specific concern for the environment; instead, the white paper focused on the problems experienced by the EU with regard to European citizens' increasing distrust in its institutions and politics. The EU has a much more institutionalized system, as opposed to general international law, and thus other opportunities for creating features of participation and transparency. Nevertheless, the EU was experiencing significant democratic deficiencies.[64]

Some of the principles for good governance presented in the white paper are especially relevant and interesting in this context. Openness is the first principle presented, it says that EU institutions should work in a more open manner. More specifically, the EU Commission together with the Member States should actively communicate what the EU does and the decisions the Commission makes. The second principle presented was on participation. Stating that the quality, relevance and effectiveness of EU policies depend on ensuring wide participation throughout the whole process of decision-making and implementation. Another important principle in this context is effectiveness. A number of features describe this principle, such as focus on effective and timely policies. What is significant in this context, however, is the white paper's statement that effectiveness is also related to and dependent on the implementation of EU policies in a proportionate manner, as well as on decision-making at the most appropriate level. This last statement is also closely connected to the general EU principles on proportionality and subsidiarity – principles that could be seen as invoking the governance and stakeholder concepts discussed in resilience thinking, in terms of mechanisms for institutional fit and connecting to temporal and spatial scales. However, the white paper claims that all of the good governance principles reinforce these EU principles.[65]

There are also a number of proposals for change included in the EU Commission White Paper on Governance. One of those is to create methods or pathways to integrate improved involvement in the policy- and decision-making pursued in the EU. The aim is to create increased transparency as well as to transfer responsibility to the public at local and national levels, so citizens can be involved in the creation of policies. With reference to the foundations of democracy, the white paper states that citizens must have access to reliable information and the opportunity to scrutinize the policy process, in addition to more active communication with the public by the EU institutions and

64 Ibid., p. 1ff.

65 Ibid., pp. 7–8. See also Schout, A. and Sleifer, J., 2014, pp. 365–368.

Member States. It is mentioned that this should involve national and local levels of participation through networks, grassroots organizations, and national, regional and local authorities.[66] It is also proposed that in attempts to create better and less complex policies and other regulatory instruments, the EU should improve the quality, effectiveness and simplicity of regulatory acts. It is stated that effective decision-making also requires the combination of different forms of policy or legislation (i.e., to combine various forms of policy or regulatory instruments). Furthermore, it is emphasized that legislation is often only one instrument in a broader set of tools to accomplish a goal, implying that there are also non-binding instruments or tools, for which stakeholder or public involvement is also crucial. Some of the more concrete proposals or examples of flexible instruments include framework directives and co-regulation. Framework directives depend to a large extent on regional, national, local involvement, just as much as they depend on scientific and stakeholder involvement in the development of their detailed provisions. This is especially relevant in EU environmental law, which includes a range of different framework directives, as discussed above. A framework directive could be claimed to be an instrument that supports increased stakeholder participation at different levels. Co-regulation is stated as a framework that combines binding legislative or regulatory actions with measures taken by the actors who are most concerned, based on their practical experience.[67] This seems like an approach to regulatory measures that at least comes close to resilience thinking on co-management, but with additional elements of binding obligations, and that definitely opens up for wide stakeholder participation.

Additionally, this approach to regulation and governance in the EU has made private nonstate actors or stakeholders the key resources in many regulatory processes. Some EU laws go far in providing for and taking support from nonstate (and non-EU) actors in the legislation and formulation of rules etc., especially in environmental regulation. For example, such stakeholders provide information, cooperate in standard-setting and play a significant part in the enforcement of certain legal acts. Many stakeholders take part in such regulation within the EU, and although the concept of the public includes environmental NGOs and actors as well, many of these stakeholders are corporate economic actors, including industries. The inclusion of these actors can have great benefits. However, it also raises concerns about legitimacy and the outcome of such regulation.[68]

[66] Ibid., pp. 8–9.
[67] Ibid., pp. 16–17.
[68] Abbot, C. and Lee, M., 2015, pp. 1–14.

One such legal act where corporate actors have important influence in both the elaboration and implementation of regulation of the regulatory process is in the EU directive that regulate industrial emissions, the Directive 2010/75/EU on industrial emissions (i.e., integrated pollution prevention and control; the Industrial Emissions Directive).[69] Also, the Water Framework Directive has some of these features. Under the Industrial Emissions Directive, corporate actors collaborate with each other and with a range of other private and public actors to generate some of the central norms or standards that are underpinning the application of the directive. The actors who themselves are being controlled by the directive are the majority of the actors taking part in the development of the key norms under the directive. Again, though, this is common in EU environmental governance; it demonstrates similarities with the structures of the Water Framework Directive.[70] For the Water Framework Directive, a specific Common Implementation Strategy[71] was adopted to enable effective implementation of the Water Framework Directive. This implementation strategy provides for a network of experts to create the basis for implementation by collecting different kinds of information and data.[72] This, however, includes also scientific experts that can assess and evaluate the biological objectives and indicators that the whole directive is based on. It may be controversial to include actors with, for example, economic interests or just have structures that create norms through nontraditional and nonauthoritative channels. Still, many of these actors are crucial for creating ecosystem fit.[73]

Populating the regulatory space with economic actors can potentially enhance the legitimacy and accountability of decision-making. As mentioned, regulation and law making have traditionally been a task reserved for States. However, with the complex governance system and competence transferred to the EU, regulatory activities are also more complex and pursued at different levels by different actors, parallel to Member State activities in the EU and in implementation. Therefore, in this system, different forms of stakeholder participation become increasingly important as contributors to the regulatory process. One reason for this, for example, is that industry has access to updated information and expertise that is crucial in making well-based and well-informed regulatory decisions. The

69 OJ L 334, p. 17–119.
70 Ibid., pp. 4ff.
71 EU WFD CIS, Common Implementation Strategy for the Water Framework Directive (2000/60/EC), "Carrying Forward the Common Implementation Strategy for the Water Framework Directive: Progress and Work Programme for 2003 and 2004," as agreed by the Water Directors 17 June 2003.
72 Lee, M., 2009, pp. 46ff.
73 See e.g. Bohman, B., 2018c, pp. 8–9.

inclusion of industry's information and expertise may thus improve the quality of regulatory decisions. The intent or outcome may also be successful implementation, because the actors targeted by the regulation have also been active in forming it. This may in turn reduce the need for extensive monitoring and enforcement efforts. The State or the EU is unlikely to know as much about an industrial operation as the industry itself, especially as it often concerns highly technical and rapidly changing areas; thus a regulatory disconnect is a concern if industry does not take part in providing data and information. This is an aspect that may be of more concern in the EU, in comparison to international law, since EU regulatory acts are generally more detailed. This involvement could also create significant conflicts or problems, especially in terms of legitimacy and accountability. It is difficult to guarantee objectivity in the information brought to the process, due to the interests held by many of the actors. Even if they strive to be objective, it is difficult to assess correctness, and even if the circumstances under which these regulatory decisions are made may have positive effects on enforcement, still other actors may object –for example, environmental NGOs, in the case of environmental regulation. Still, their impact is important and cannot be disregarded. There are examples of environmental regulation in some areas, which were extremely ineffective when regulated solely through the public sector. However, mechanisms to limit potential drawbacks and legitimacy issues created by these decision processes may be found in other forms of participation. Aiming for a wider circle of stakeholders and increased transparency must be a goal. In that case, examples of important issues are the formal participatory pathways and the possibilities to appeal such regulatory decisions in the EU institutional structure.[74]

7.4 THE ROLE OF PARTICIPATION IN INTERNATIONAL ENVIRONMENTAL LAW

The role of NGOs in international law is significant.[75] How and to what extent NGOs act and affect international law and international negotiations can, however, vary. The role of NGOs in international law is also generally different than the participation intended in resilience governance, although the functions that result from such participatory elements might still be similar in

[74] Abbot, C. and Lee, M., 2015, pp. 1–14.

[75] As a result of the international developments with regard to participation, more than 2500 NGOs have consultative status in the UN, and considerably more NGOs are active on national level, according to Bodansky. Although these are not all environmentally oriented, it still gives a picture of the extent of NGO involvement and stakeholder participation on these levels. Bodansky, D., 2010, pp. 123.

the end. The role and influence they have in international negotiations and other work of international agreements do vary from issue to issue, as well as with the features and focus of each NGO.[76] Just as the size, composition and focus of NGOs vary. These developments in the past decades have made NGOs international actors, giving them a central position in international decision-making. This has been especially noticeable in international environmental law since this area of law is also relatively new and is continuously expanding. Thus the structures of international environmental law are not as steady and rigorous as other sectors of international law. This has meant that the environmental law institutions and agreements adopted in the past decades have reflected this change in the international scene through a large range of mechanisms provided for NGO participation.[77]

Although much focus has been on the formal forms for participation provided by States, there are also other ways to exert pressure on negotiations and wield influence in the international community. Different theoretical approaches have been applied in the examination of these forms of participation. An important division seems to be between the traditional State-centered perspective, where NGOs mainly act through States, and the perspective of NGOs as independent actors in international institutions or simply as free agents in the international scene.[78]

Beyond working through States, large NGOs also work informally with international bodies and institutions to promote policies or standards. It is an important point to note that NGOs, especially if member based, often represent interests of stakeholders outside the States.[79] Furthermore, NGOs work as free agents, disconnected from the legal sphere; an example is when they pressure corporations to agree to standards or specific certifications through the threat of shaming campaigns and encouragement of public boycotts and the like.[80] This pressure can be significant. In its form, it comes close to public-private partnerships rather than direct participation, and will thus not be explored further here. What can generally be stated regarding NGOs is that they have a narrower agenda and thus are more eager to devote

[76] Bodansky, D., 2010, pp. 123–125. See also Raustiala, K., 1997b, pp. 558–571, and pp. 584–586.

[77] Spiro, P. J., 2007, p. 771. See also Raustiala, K., 1997a.

[78] Spiro, P. J., 2007, pp. 770 ff.; the author calls this different perspective the traditional liberal theory opposed to stakeholder theory and post-national theories. These categories are also further divided into a number of subcategories by the author.

[79] Ibid., p. 783.

[80] Ibid., pp. 784–789. See also Andresen, S., 2014, p. 120 and p. 125. It is argued here that scientific experts play an important role to connect the international regime with the local and national levels by spreading knowledge among the public about the environmental issues addressed.

their attention to the environmental issues at hand, in contrast to States, which have a much wider variety of interests to take into account. Thus NGOs are important actors in pushing such issues. Furthermore, in international negotiations, NGOs' influence as collaborators is generally strongest in issue framing and agenda setting. Agenda setting is also a negotiating phase where scientific expertise seems most relevant. When it comes to standard setting, on the other hand, States are more reluctant to give NGOs influence.[81]

As with stakeholder participation in general, a number of reasons can be pointed out to explain why and how NGOs exert influence. One fundamental role of NGOs in this regard is that they can serve as experts on certain issues. They provide information, policy analysis and scientific or technological expertise in many central environmental matters.[82] Another obvious source of influence is connected to the idea of NGOs as representing public interests, because NGOs are not only generally considered to have a narrower agenda than States but are also – if it is an environmental NGO – considered as being an impartial voice for the environment. Some would argue, however, that this role of NGOs is doubtful: NGOs also have their own agenda setting and other interests to take into account – and not least economic interests. Just as other organizations or collaborative institutions, NGOs are a composition of individuals with their own specific incentives to act. Therefore, their actions are not always fully in the interest of the general public. Their participation in itself, however, is often seen as a public interest, or could at least be framed us such from a democratic and accountability perspective.[83] In addition, financial resources are of course important and affect incentives. The budgets also affect the ability of NGOs to engage with their focus issues and, in the long run, their level of influence to some extent. Some NGOs with larger budgets can even lead projects that are valuable for international processes.[84]

7.4.1 *Forms of Participation and Perspectives on the Role of Nonstate Actors*

As noted earlier, nonstate actors (mainly NGOs) participate in different ways and in different parts of the international system – that is, in addition to exerting pressure on States, they are also their own actors in the international

[81] Bodansky, D., 2010, pp. 123–125; Andresen, S., 2014, pp. 114–115 and pp. 124–125.
[82] See e.g. Raustiala, K., 1997a; Raustiala, K., 1997b.
[83] See also Spiro, P. J., 2007, p. 773.
[84] Bodansky, D., 2010, pp. 125–126.

legal system.[85] This categorization of NGO participation in terms of international environmental law is important when it comes to discussing the role and features of NGO participation. It has significance for the ways an NGO contributes or affects international cooperation and in the discussions on accountability, legitimacy and effectiveness. Therefore, it is also important in a comparison of the role of NGOs in international environmental law with stakeholder participation in social-ecological resilience. It is possible, and probably more fruitful, to view the different categories of NGO or stakeholder participation primarily as complementary. NGOs have many different roles and play many parallel parts in the international system. The reason why some would argue against this is that the idea of NGOs as free actors in the international system paints a picture of the traditional notions of international law as a system built only on the State Parties as sovereign States acting in the international community (Section 3.1).[86]

The role and functions played out by NGOs acting mainly through States, or on the permission given by States, are many. One function suggested by research is that their participation enhances the ability of States to regulate through the treaty process, both in technocratic and political terms. NGO participation provides policy advice, helps monitor commitments and delegations, minimizes risks involved with approval of ratification and facilitates effective communication between governments and constituents.[87] It is sometimes implied that NGOs work in opposition to States; it has also been claimed, however, that States actually gain from the involvement of NGOs. The role and the functions played out by NGO participation depend on the nature of the NGO and vary between States, as does the attitude toward NGO participation.[88]

In the positivist and State-centric view, there are claims that NGO participation is a trade-off for inter alia legitimacy and transparency. One could probably argue that additional assets would be those also argued for in resilience research (i.e., democratic legitimacy, accountability and effectiveness), although that is a debated issue. Moreover, it is claimed that NGO participation provides an important contribution to the linkages between global and local needs and actors – a feature that is very important in the context of stakeholders in management for social-ecological resilience. Others also point

85 Spiro, J. P., "Nongovernmental Organizations in International Relations (Theory)," in Dunoff, J. L. and Pollack, M. A. (eds.), *Interdisciplinary Perspectives on International Law and International Relations – The State of the Art*, Cambridge University Press, 2013, pp. 228ff.

86 On this matter, see Spiro, P. J., 2007, pp. 770ff.

87 Raustiala, K., 1997a, p. 720.

88 Raustiala, K., 1997a, pp. 724–725.

to NGOs as so-called agents of social learning and actors in social movement theory, which is also close to the features argued for in resilience research on stakeholders. However, it must be stated that such functions and features are not necessarily less prominent when NGOs act on their own. An important connection to the resilience perspective on stakeholder participation is the explanation that the rise of NGO participation is due to the political implications of biophysical trends. Thus, although it may be a challenge to the traditional State-centric system, participation could be seen as a natural development for the need of institutional fit in a system where the biophysical and institutional frames have changed in pace with the increased complexity of environmental problems.[89]

7.4.2 *Functions and Features Provided by Participation*

Whatever perspective is chosen, there are many direct and apparent ways that NGOs contribute to international systems. Some of the main contributions by NGOs in relation to governments are to provide information and policy options. If there is a multitude of participating NGOs, they will provide both breadth and depth and a variety of information. The evaluations provided are plentiful and provide States with many options or ideas – ideas that probably would not have emerged solely from an ordinary bureaucratic review. This is a feature that parallels the feature of redundancy and diversity in social-ecological resilience (Section 6.5). In addition, it all comes down to much less cost and resources than would otherwise have been necessary. Ideally, of course, this multitude of options and information also provides a good basis for State decisions and negotiations.[90]

Another important function provided by NGOs is monitoring. State sovereignty puts up a rather strict limit for the possibility of State Parties or international organizations to obtain information from another State or to review their implementation of an agreement. Instead, most agreements rely on self-reporting.[91] This means that the States that are Parties to an agreement will report on their own compliance (i.e., the progress in implementing the agreement). This is not the most effective model for reviewing compliance in cases where a State might not be fully compliant. Although it may depend on and vary with the design of the compliance mechanism connected to the agreement in question, the State will have obvious incentives to somehow

89 Raustiala, K., 1997a, p. 725.
90 Raustiala, K., 1997a, pp. 726–728.
91 See e.g. Handl, G., 1997, p. 32. See also Sands, P., et al., 2012, pp. 143f.

delay or report untruthfully in such cases, which also happens repeatedly. The role of NGOs then becomes important as an alternative means for retrieving this information. Many NGOs act transnationally and thus are represented in many different States. They have the expertise to make independent compliance assessments in the States where they are represented, as well as to gather other kinds of data that can be valuable for international cooperation. Generally, NGOs are indeed also willing to make such contributions, seeing it as an important role, and they also spend a significant amount of effort and resources on these tasks. The NGOs in turn report these findings to other States or the relevant international bodies, which can actively review the compliance report made by the State in question. Some international organizations even have a mechanism for reporting or for submissions from NGOs in this regard. Not all States appreciate these new routines, but they are much harder to oppose than a direct interference by another State or international organization. One possible critique of NGOs as agents for reviewing compliance is that they are often less interested in compliance in the strict legal sense and more interested in specific actions that the NGO may oppose, even though these actions are not in violation of the agreement.[92] However, this behavior would support the idea of NGOs working independently of their State influence, and instead according to their own agenda.

This monitoring function presumes nevertheless that NGOs can gain such access to States. This obviously is not always the case in some parts of the world. There are, for example, restrictions on NGO rights in the Russian Federation, which in 2012 adopted a law regulating NGO operations (the NGO Law). This legislation gives the government power inter alia to audit NGOs and mandate reporting from foreign NGOs. Furthermore, NGOs engaged in alleged political activities and receiving foreign funding must register as "foreign agents."[93]

Another function resulting from NGO participation includes monitoring of the actual negotiations and keeping watch both over and on behalf of governments. They can also provide information about what is going on in different parts or groups of a large negotiation process. Through such vigilance, NGOs can push negotiations in different directions, depending on their own interests. The sheer number and variation of NGOs can provide thorough monitoring in many different dimensions. It also means that NGOs push in

92 Raustiala, K., 1997a, pp. 728–729.

93 Sofrononva, E., Holley, C. and Nagarajan, V., "Environmental Non-Governmental Organizations and Russian Environmental Governance: Accountability, Participation and Collaboration," *Transnational Environmental Law*, Vol. 3, No. 2, 2014, pp. 4–5. The author also states that the term "foreign agent" historically has a negative connotation in Russia often associated with a spy (p. 5, note 31).

different directions, and thus their pressure on negotiations does not necessarily mean that they will have a crucial influence on the outcomes. Furthermore, NGOs are seen in the international legal system as important actors in bridging the gap between the international and national spheres of decision-making, which is important in a comparison with resilience theories. NGOs have this bridging role mainly because they often have a strong position both with the public and local industries. Thus NGOs can help States gain acceptance for new legislation and increase the possibilities for positive response to ratification. In many negotiation situations, however, NGOs also use their influence to strengthen weaker, less politically influential States in their positions toward other States. That is, they help States that might lack the resources or technical development necessary to comply with a strict and far-reaching agreement. What the NGOs often do in this case is to influence the negotiations so that weaker Parties' lack of resources and other such circumstances are accounted for. This also signifies another effect of NGO influence from a State-centric perspective. While not all States gain from the participation of NGOs, the overall collective result may be better and more efficient, since no one will gain from the non-compliance due to lack of resources.[94] Another perspective on the impact of NGOs in international environmental law, as mentioned earlier, is their role as free actors or stakeholders in international organizations. Many treaty regimes provide rights to participate at different levels. Such formal pathways for participation are increasingly important, and some argue that they enhance the legitimacy of international environmental institutions.[95] It is also through such direct participation that NGOs can help secretariats and compliance bodies with information on compliance in some regimes, and help overcome deficiencies in implementation that otherwise would have led to non-compliance. At the same time, NGOs can also directly push their own agendas.[96]

7.5 PUBLIC PARTICIPATION AND THE AARHUS CONVENTION

Public participation in its most common form within law implies a pathway for the general public and environmental NGOs to have access to environmental information and the right to take part in decision-making. It is thus a question of formal and direct pathways for participation. In some cases, these rights are also combined with a general right for the same group to make an

94 Raustiala, K., 1997a, pp. 729–732.
95 Spiro, P. J., 2007, p. 782.
96 Ibid., p. 782.

appeal on these decisions. The function typically connected to public participation is to create environmental democracy in all regulatory regimes and at all levels of regulation. Public participation is thus seen as a significant factor for increasing legitimacy and accountability.[97] Pathways for public participation are important in this review, because they are the most common reflection of what is termed to be stakeholder participation within resilience governance. Pathways for public participation are provided for in different ways and through different instruments. Beyond the formal channels that can be provided directly within international agreements or EU legal acts, there are also instruments specifically regulating participation. The purpose of this section is to review these different forms, pathways and delimitations for public participation. One of the most significant instruments for public participation in environmental law is the 1998 Aarhus Convention on Access to Information, Public Participation in Decision-Making and Access to Justice in Environmental Matters[98] (the Aarhus Convention), which will therefore also be presented to the extent that it is relevant for the given context.

As presented previously in this chapter, participation has been an increasingly important issue in environmental law since the 1970s, and this development also includes more specific forms of participation such as public participation.[99] In the EU, focus on participation arose in the 1990s, primarily as an issue of transparency, legitimacy and democracy. Eventually, however, the environmental protection aspects have also gained focus within the EU, which may be seen as a natural development with regard to the development of the EU EAPs and EU environmental law.[100]

Public participation is different from stakeholder participation primarily in terms of whom it includes (Sections 7.1 and 7.3), although the two sometimes overlap. However, the different forms of participation could also be seen as serving somewhat different purposes with regard to the kind of participation involved. Public participation aims to create formal pathways to involve the public in administrative decision-making. The focus is thus more on creating formal and direct participation in the institutional work and decision-making, as opposed to the wider aspects of stakeholder participation that is not necessarily formalized in this way and therefore can take many different forms. The Aarhus Convention took public participation even further; it emphasizes its

97 See e.g. Ebbesson, J., 2007a, n. 330, pp. 686ff.

98 2161 UNTS 447.

99 See e.g. Stone, C. D., "Should Trees Have Legal Standing? – Toward Legal Rights for Natural Objects," *Southern California Law Review*, Vol. 45, 1972, pp. 450–501.

100 See e.g. Langlet, D. and Mahmoudi, S., pp. 27ff.

importance for environmental governance and management. To enable public participation in decision-making, the knowledge and information of environmental status and the like are crucial. Therefore, the right of access to environmental information is also an included right, seen as a prerequisite associated with the right of the public to participate. From a legal perspective, the possibility to have the right to appeal such environmental decisions (i.e., to have access to redress) is also very significant. Thus public participation generally, and especially as in the Aarhus Convention, is seen as one part of a concept relying on three interdependent components: access to information, public participation and access to justice.

7.5.1 *Background, Purpose and Application of the Aarhus Convention*

As its title implies, the Aarhus Convention rests on three so-called pillars and includes a general right of access to or knowledge of environmental information, the right for the public to participate in various environmental decisions and a right of access to legal review; it also includes the right to appeal such matters under certain circumstances. The Aarhus Convention also includes a Protocol on Pollutant Release and Transfer Registers[101] (the PRTRs Protocol); this was adopted in 2003 but did not become binding on its Parties until 2009. Pollutant release and transfer registers are inventories of pollution from industrial sites and other sources.[102] The objective of the PRTRs Protocol is for Parties to establish such registers nationwide, in order to enhance public access to such information on pollutants.[103]

The aim of the Convention is increased openness and democratic legitimacy in policies on environmental protection. It aims to create a system where the public not only has a right, but through this also a direct responsibility to monitor public authorities and decisions through participation and through legal action to protect the environment.[104] In December 2019, the Aarhus Convention had 47 Parties, including the EU. Of these had 36 Parties also ratified the PRTRs Protocol by this point, including the EU. A large and significant number of the convention Parties are former Soviet States in

101 UN Doc No. MP.PP/2003/1.

102 See the 2003 Kiev Protocol on Pollutant Release and Transfer Registers to the UNECE Convention on Access to Information, Public Participation in Decision-Making and Access to Justice in Environmental Matters (Official UN Doc No. Doc. MP.PP/2003/1); further information about the protocol can be found at www.unece.org/env/pp/prtr.html.

103 The 2003 Kiev Protocol on Pollutant Release and Transfer Registers, Article 1.

104 Pallemaerts, M., "Introduction," in Pallemaerts, M. (ed.), *The Aarhus Convention at Ten – Interactions and Tensions between Conventional International Law and EU Environmental Law*, Vol. 9, Avosetta series, Europa Law, 2011a, p. 4.

Central Asia.[105] The Aarhus Convention is the largest and most important environmental convention of its kind, and it has had a great influence on other regulatory instruments and regimes.[106] It has impacted the interpretation and application of both EU law (which is also a consequence of the EU being a Party to the Convention), as well as the 1950 Convention for the Protection of Human Rights and Fundamental Freedoms[107] (the European Convention on Human Rights), where the European Court of Human Rights (the European Court) has referred to the Aarhus Convention in its judgments.

The EU has adopted both a *Decision on the Conclusion of the Aarhus Convention* (Decision 2005/370/EC; the Aarhus Decision)[108] and a number of directives concerning access to environmental information, some aspects of public participation in environmental matters and access to justice.[109] In addition, a Regulation on the Application of the Provisions of the Aarhus Convention on Access to Information, Public Participation in Decision-Making and Access to Justice in Environmental Matters to Community Institutions and Bodies (EC; No. 1367/2006; the Aarhus Regulation)[110] was adopted in 2006. The European Court has referred in a number of cases to Principle 10 of the Rio Declaration and the rights invoked by the Aarhus Convention.[111] The Council of Europe, administrating the European Convention and the European Court, has even adopted a Recommendation (1614 [2003]) on Environment and Human Rights that focuses on how the human rights system can contribute to protection of the environment and includes a paragraph that expressively confirms that the rights established in the Aarhus Convention shall be safeguarded.[112] It refers to inter alia the Aarhus Convention and the role that individual rights of access to justice and legal

105 Information found at the UNECE webpage: www.unece.org/env/pp/ratification.html (Official UN Doc No. Ch_XXVII_13 Environment, United Nations, Treaty Series, Vol. 2161, p. 447).

106 Pallemaerts, M., 2011a, p. 3.

107 213 UNTS 221.

108 OJ L 124, 17.5.2005, p. 1–3.

109 Primarily Directive 2003/4/EC on public access to environmental information and Directive 2003/35/EC providing for public participation in respect of the drawing up of certain plans and programs; in addition, a regulation incorporating the PRTRs Protocol has also been adopted: Regulation no (EC) 166/2006 establishing the European Pollutant Release and Transfer Register (E-PRTR).

110 OJ L 264, 25.9.2006, p. 13–19.

111 See e.g. *Okyay and others* v. *Turkey* (Application no. 36220/97), Judgment of 12 July 2005; *Taşkın and Others* v. *Turkey* (Application no. 46117/99) [2004] ECHR 621, Judgment of 10 November 2004; *Tatar* v. *Romania* (Application no. 67021/01), Judgment of 27 January 2009.

112 Council of Europe Recommendation 1614 (2003) on Environment and Human Rights, paragraphs 3, 6 and 9. The relevant part of this recommendation states:

"9. The Assembly recommends that the Governments of member States:

...

review procedures play for environmental protection.[113] The council also recommends ministers to draw up an additional protocol to the European Convention regarding individual procedural rights to enhance environmental protection, as set out in the Aarhus Convention.[114]

The Aarhus Convention has also been influential in the case-law of the European Court. In the case of *Okyay and Others against Turkey*,[115] for example, it is stated that the right to a healthy environment and the right to defend it, as it was formulated under domestic law, constituted a civil right. As a consequence, even though the claimants did not argue that they were personally injured by the pollution of the local environment, the rejection by the local courts of the applicants' request to halt the operation constituted a dispute.[116] The applicants in the case lived within the radius where the polluting gases would end up, and the European Court did not answer the question of whether it would have made the same ruling if they had not lived in that area. The European Court does refer, however, to the Recommendation on Environment and Human Rights and the Aarhus Convention, as well as to the Rio Declaration Principle 10 as relevant law, which may mean that this would be the case.[117] Indeed, because the Aarhus Convention is now ratified by a majority of the European States together with the EU, which promotes this development, this also creates a basis on which the European Court can found its judgments – as one of the official methods of assessing relevant laws used by the European Court is the evolutionary method. This method suggests that the general conception or minimum levels of rights in all European Convention Member States should be considered as the norm in that field of law. The court is thus to focus on the significance of the Convention articles in the society of today rather than at the time of adoption. In practice, this means that the judges will consider whether there is a new general view in the Member States as well as whether there may be significant laws or international agreements to be taken into consideration.[118]

In addition to these influences on other regimes, the Parties of the Aarhus Convention adopted the Almaty Guidelines in 2005. The Almaty Guidelines

iii. safeguard the individual procedural rights to access to information, public participation in decision making and access to justice in environmental matters set out in the Aarhus Convention."

113 Ibid., paragraph 6.

114 Ibid., paragraph 10i.

115 *Okyay and Others* v. *Turkey* (Application no. 36220/97), Judgment of 12 July 2005.

116 *Okyay and Others* v. *Turkey*, paragraphs 61–68.

117 *Okyay and Others* v. *Turkey*, paragraphs 51–52 and 72–75.

118 Palm, E., "Rättspraxis och tolkningsmetoder i Europadomstolen för de mänskliga rättigheterna," Juridisk Tidskrift, No. 4, 2003, pp. 742–743.

seek to promote public participation in international forums. The purpose of the guidelines is to provide general guidance to the Parties on how to promote and apply the principles of the Aarhus Convention in international forums in matters relating to the environment.[119] This is connected to Article 3(7), which also states that each Party shall promote the principles of the Aarhus Convention in international decision-making and international organizations. The Almaty Guidelines furthermore state that they may serve as a source of inspiration for the same purpose, for other interested States, international environmental agreements and other international forums, nongovernmental organizations or other members of the public.[120] The intention is thus to further the ideas of the Aarhus Convention to other international organizations.

7.5.2 *The Aarhus Convention Provisions*

The objective of the Aarhus Conventions is as follows:

> In order to contribute to the protection of the right of every person of present and future generations to live in an environment adequate to his or her health and well-being, each Party shall guarantee the rights of access to information, public participation in decision-making, and access to justice in environmental matters in accordance with the provisions of this Convention.[121]

How the Parties are to guarantee these rights is developed in more detail throughout the Convention. While most international environmental agreements concern obligations between States, the Aarhus Convention concerns obligations that the State Parties have toward the public (i.e., civil society), within their respective national territory. The States are obliged to ensure that the public or civil society has participatory and procedural rights, also including access to the information that makes this possible. The Convention therefore can be said to deal with issues that are usually considered to belong to the States' internal affairs. This is also one of the reasons why the Aarhus Convention is considered to be closely related to human rights. It provides means for participation by the public in decision-making in the Member States, hence adding a democratic dimension to such procedures.[122] A significant feature of the

119 UNECE 2005 Aarhus Convention, Report of the second meeting of the Parties, DECISION II/4, Promoting the Application of the Principles of the Aarhus Convention in International Forum, ECE/MP.PP/2005/2/Add.5, Annex, p. 4, Article 1.

120 UNECE 2005 Aarhus Convention, Annex, p. 4, Article 3.

121 The Aarhus Convention, Article 1.

122 Ebbesson, J., "The Notion of Public Participation in International Environmental Law," in Brunnée, J. and Hey, E. (eds.), *Yearbook of International Environmental Law*, Vol. 8, 1997, generally, for a detailed introduction to the Aarhus Convention.

Aarhus Convention is the idea that environmental NGOs can act on behalf of public environmental interests.[123] However, the issue is contested by others, who say that it means that NGOs do not necessarily act or contribute to public interests, at least not solely and exclusively or as a single purpose.[124]

The public, according to the Convention, is defined as "one or more natural or legal persons, and, in accordance with national legislation or practice, their associations, organizations or groups."[125] The Aarhus Convention can be seen as aiming to formalize or regulate different forms of public participation, including public access to justice. The Convention has taken a middle way, however, between private and public interests. First of all, the Convention sets some limits as to who belongs to the public. It furthermore limits the group of the public in some aspects and situations, to provide rights only for *the public concerned*, which means that in some situations the rights of this group extend further. The public concerned, then, is described as "the public affected or likely to be affected by, or having an interest in, the environmental decision-making; for the purposes of this definition, non-governmental organizations promoting environmental protection and meeting any requirements under national law shall be deemed to have an interest."[126]

In some situations, then, the rights of the public concerned extend further than those of the general public. This regards inter alia the right to be notified, retrieve information and review an environmental decision. This must be seen as opposed to providing for general standing for anyone through what is usually called actio popularis. This can also be regarded as another step of narrowing the concept in comparison to the concept of stakeholder participation.

The Convention establishes only minimum standards, and any Party is free to take further measures.[127] As a contrast to the limitations set out which allow only certain rights to the public concerned, the Aarhus Convention also sets out a nondiscrimination principle.[128] This principle means that as long as the other criteria for access and participation are fulfilled, there are no other requirements or limitations set out with regard to citizenship, nationality or other domicile, and the like. Therefore, if someone is concerned about, for example, a certain environmental matter or practice going on in a neighboring

[123] Ebbesson, J., 1997, p. 53.
[124] See for example argumentation by Bodansky, D., 2010, pp. 125–126; Spiro, P. J., 2007, p. 775. See also Raustiala, K., 1997, pp. 724ff.
[125] The Aarhus Convention, Article 2(4).
[126] The Aarhus Convention, Article 2(5).
[127] The Aarhus Convention, Article 3(5).
[128] The Aarhus Convention, Article 3(9).

State in which they do not have citizenship (and the neighboring State is also a Party to the Aarhus Convention), then this person could claim their right to participation and, if belonging to the public concerned, claim access to judicial review of the matter in that State.[129]

This nondiscrimination principle entails interesting possibilities for the public in one Party to then interfere in the environmental practices of another. Of course, this is applicable only within the limits of the environmental laws in that State – that is, the Aarhus Convention is applicable only in relation to the current internal environmental laws of a State. It cannot as such perform a review or make demands for stricter environmental legislation, beyond the implementation of the Convention itself. However, if a State is reviewed under the Aarhus Convention, that can still be a sign of potentially poor environmental protection. This in turn can set other mechanisms in action, perhaps in relation to other conventions with more substantial obligations on environmental protection or by pressures from NGOs.

The PRTRs Protocol requires that the Parties establish and maintain a publicly accessible national pollutant release and transfer register, and it includes a number of quite specific requirements to make these clear and accessible.[130] In practice, this is to be done by the operators of certain activities in the jurisdiction.[131] The purpose of these registers is inter alia to provide an important mechanism to increase corporate accountability, reduce pollution and promote sustainable development through increased transparency on the risk of pollution – and better management – as results of better environmental information systems.[132] The requirements on these registers include many kinds of pollution, and concern both point sources and diffuse pollution.[133] The definitions of the protocol clarify that *releasing pollution* means any introduction of pollutants into the environment as a result of any human activity. Furthermore, this applies regardless of whether the release is deliberate or accidental.[134] It also includes pollution that moves beyond the boundaries of the facility.[135] The PRTR is a kind of register that could be a good tool to show the origins of potential inefficiencies in pollution prevention, as in line with the purpose of the protocol. The register may also increase incentives for operators themselves to ensure better management and preventive action.

129 See also Ebbesson, J., 1997, p. 66.
130 The Aarhus Protocol on Pollutant Release and Transfer Registers, Article 4.
131 The Aarhus Protocol on Pollutant Release and Transfer Registers, Article 7.
132 See the Aarhus Protocol on Pollutant Release and Transfer Registers, Preamble.
133 The Aarhus Protocol on Pollutant Release and Transfer Registers, Article 6.
134 The Aarhus Protocol on Pollutant Release and Transfer Registers, Article 2(7).
135 The Aarhus Protocol on Pollutant Release and Transfer Registers, Article 2(8).

The primary focus of the Aarhus Convention, then, is mechanisms for public participation and access to justice available on a domestic level. The Convention also sets an example by providing for public participation at its meetings (although with some limitations) and not least by including an international mechanism for access to justice in the Convention regime. As a tool for effective implementation of the Aarhus Convention, the Meeting of the Parties of the Convention has established a mechanism for compliance review, the Aarhus Convention Compliance Committee (the ACCC). The ACCC reviews cases of alleged noncompliance submitted to the Aarhus Convention Secretariat and decides on findings and in some cases recommendations to the Parties (i.e., the Member States concerned).[136] The ACCC has even reviewed the EU implementation of the Aarhus Convention.[137] This kind of mechanism for communication and compliance review, which compensates for the gap between levels by being open to the public, is a very good example of how to communicate and connect a pluralistic and multiregulatory regime. It also reflects some important purposes of stakeholder participation in multilevel governance.

7.5.3 *EU Implementation of the Aarhus Convention*

The EU became Party to the Aarhus Convention in 2005.[138] Directives on the first and second parts of the Convention (i.e., access to information and public participation in decision-making) were adopted already in 2003.[139] Both

[136] See UNECE 2002, Meeting of the Parties to the Convention on Access to Information, Public Participation in Decision-Making and Access to Justice in Environmental Matters (the Aarhus Convention), "Report of the First Meeting of the Parties," Decision I/7 on *Review of Compliance*, adopted at the first meeting of the Parties held in Lucca, Italy, October 2002, ECE/MP.PP/2/Add.8.

[137] See e.g. ACCC/C/2005/17, submitted by the nongovernmental organization Association Kazokiskes Community (Lithuania), alleging noncompliance by the European Community with its obligations under article 6, paragraphs 2 and 4, and article 9, paragraph 2, ECE/MP.PP/2008/5/Add.10, and ACCC/C/2010/54, communication alleging a failure by the European Union (EU) to comply with its obligations under articles 5 and 7 of the of the Convention, in relation to Ireland's renewable, especially wind, energy policy, ECE/MP.PP/2014/2/Add.1, Decision V/9g. See also Ebbesson, J., Briefing to European Parliament, "The EU and the Aarhus Convention: Access to Information, Public Participation in Decision-Making and Access to Justice in Environmental Matters," Policy Department C: Citizens' Rights and Constitutional Affairs, European Parliament, PE 571.357, 2016.

[138] Council Decision of 17 February 2005 on the conclusion, on behalf of the European Community, of the Convention on access to information, public participation in decision-making and access to justice in environmental matters, 2005/370/EC (OJ L 124, 17.5.2005, p. 1).

[139] Directive 2003/4/EC and Directive 2003/35/EC.

directives also include some provision on access to justice, but only with regard to the rights they establish. These, just like all directives, are to be implemented as national law in the EU Member States, so that those States which are not Parties to the Aarhus Convention will still integrate some of its provisions. In addition, the EU also adopted a regulation to implement the PRTRs Protocol.[140]

The Directive 2003/4/EC on Public Access to Environmental Information (the Directive on Environmental Information)[141] replaced the Directive 90/313/EEC on the Freedom of Access to Information on the Environment, which had revealed certain shortcomings.[142] The definition of environmental information in the directive is the same as the definition in the Aarhus Convention. Correct classification is important, because it aims to provide broader access than that available to general administrative information. Other significant aspects are inter alia that the information shall be received upon request in a timely manner and that certain practical and structural issues thus be met.[143] Because the Directive on Environmental Information was drafted at the time that the EU was also preparing to become a Party to the Aarhus Convention, it was formulated in line with the Convention.[144] The Directive was to be transposed into the national legislation of the Member States by February 2005, but many of the States were delayed in their internal process of this task. This delay initiated infringement procedures by the Commission and subsequent proceedings in the EU Court. However, most of the States that were brought before the court for infringement did implement the directive in the interim, and thus the cases were closed. Nevertheless, Austria and Ireland were judged by the EU Court as not fulfilling their obligations in accordance with the directive.[145] This is interesting with regard to the direct implementation of the Aarhus Convention itself. Ireland did not ratify the Convention until 2012 and thus was not obliged by the Aarhus Convention at the time. Austria, however, did ratify the Aarhus Convention in 2005 and must have had the intention to comply with all of the

140 EU Regulation ((EC) No. 166/2006) establishing the European Pollutant Release and Transfer Register (E-PRTR), and amending Council Directives 91/689/EEC and 96/61/EC, OJ L 033, 4.2.2006, p. 1.

141 OJ L 41, 14.2.2003, p. 26–32.

142 EU COM Report (2012a), Report from the Commission to the Council and the European Parliament, "On the Experience Gained in the Application of the Directive 2003/4/EC on Public Access to Environmental Information," Brussels, 17.12.2012, COM(2012) 774 final, pp. 2–3.

143 Ibid., pp. 5–7.

144 Ibid., p. 3.

145 Ibid., p. 4.

Aarhus Convention provisions – not only those covered by the EU directive on public access to information. Over time, however, all Member States did eventually comply, and the EU Commission asserts that the directive has clearly improved access to environmental information in the EU Member States.[146]

The Directive 2003/35/EC Providing for Public Participation in Respect of the Drawing Up of Certain Plans and Programmes Relating to the Environment and Amending with Regard to Public Participation and Access to Justice Council Directives 85/337/EEC and 96/61/EC (the Public Participation Directive)[147] focuses primarily on public participation and notification of the public with regard to certain environmental matters. Just like the Directive on Environmental Information, the Public Participation Directive also refers directly to the Aarhus Convention and uses largely the same concepts and definitions. The definition of the public is thus the same as the one found in the Aarhus Convention.[148] The application, however, is much narrower, since the possibilities for the public to participate in the preparation and modification or review of the plans or programs are limited to specific activities listed in Annex I of the directive.[149] The list includes specific provisions from six different directives.

In addition to the directives on access to environmental information and public participation, the EU Commission proposed a directive on access to justice.[150] The proposed directive was planned as a part of a package of legislation intended to fully implement the Aarhus Convention. The proposal also had the objective to eliminate well-known shortcomings in the general enforcement of environmental law in the EU. Even before the signing of the Aarhus Convention, the importance of public participation in enforcing environmental law had been stressed at the EU level on several occasions.[151] The Commission argued that better access to justice in environmental matters for representative groups advocating environmental protection would have numerous positive effects, and that the most significant effect would be the improvement of the practical application of environmental law. The Commission also stated that since environmental law will

146 Ibid., pp. 4 and 12.

147 OJ L 156, 25.6.2003, p. 17–25.

148 The Public Participation Directive, Article 2(1).

149 The Public Participation Directive, Article 2(2).

150 EU COM (2003), Commission Proposal for a Directive of the European Parliament and of the Council on Access to Justice in Environmental Matters (presented by the Commission), Brussels, 24.10.2003, COM(2003) 624 final, 2003/0246 (COD), C5-0513-03.

151 Ibid., p. 2.

only have its desired effects if its enforcement is guaranteed throughout the whole EU, it is crucial to ensure that environmental law can be reviewed in court.[152] The proposed directive was never approved, and in the end, it was withdrawn by the Commission.[153] Hence, the extent to which the Member States have an obligation of offering access to justice in environmental matters in accordance with EU law is limited to the provisions found in the Directive on Environmental Information and the Public Participation Directive. Although the Member States are also directly bound by the Aarhus Convention since the EU has ratified it, the Commission could still force a Member State to comply with its provisions nevertheless.[154] It is also stated in the EUT that the Member States shall provide remedies sufficient to ensure effective legal protection in the fields covered by Union law.[155] The general impression still is that the EU implementation of the Aarhus Convention has been less than satisfactory.

The Commission, however, also proposed to formally apply the provisions of the Aarhus Convention to EU institutions and bodies.[156] This proposal was adopted in September 2006 through the Aarhus Regulation, whose objective is to contribute to the implementation of the Aarhus Convention obligations in the EU institutions and bodies.[157] This is also in accordance with the provisions of the Aarhus Convention that states in its definitions that a *public authority* means inter alia the institutions of any regional economic integration organization that is a Party to the Convention (i.e., the institutions of the EU). It is important to note, however, that the definition excludes bodies of judicial or legislative capacity.[158] The Aarhus Regulation also makes this distinction, stating that institution or body in accordance with the regulation means any public institution, body, office or agency established by or founded on the basis of the EC Treaty, except when the institution is acting in a judicial

152 Ibid., p. 4.

153 2003/0246/COD, Withdrawal of Obsolete Commission Proposals (2014/C 153/03), OJ C 153, 21.5.2014, p. 3–7.

154 The Commission can do this based on Article 258 TFEU. See also Brakeland, J-F., "Access to Justice in Environmental Matters – Developments at the EU Level," published in the *Gyeseiho-Kenkyu*, 2014, No. 5, p. 2.

155 Article 19(1), EUT.

156 EU COM (2003a), Commission Proposal for a Regulation of the European Parliament and of the Council on the Application of the Provisions of the Aarhus Convention on Access to Information, Public Participation in Decision-Making and Access to Justice in Environmental Matters to EC Institutions and Bodies (presented by the Commission), Brussels, 24.10.2003, COM(2003) 622 final, 2003/0242 (COD).

157 The Aarhus Regulation, Article 1(1).

158 Aarhus Convention, Article 2(d).

or legislative capacity. There are, however, some exceptions to this rule with regard to the access to environmental information.[159]

Most of the definitions and concepts included in the Aarhus Regulation are similar to or the same as those in the Aarhus Convention.[160] Where there are divergences, these seem to be due to the structures and specific conditions that accompany EU law and the EU Treaties. It is interesting to note that according to the Aarhus Regulation, the definition of environmental law is legislation that, regardless of the legal basis, contributes to the pursuit of the environmental objectives found in the EU Treaties.[161]

The Aarhus Regulation is divided into five different sections or titles. The first describes the general obligations with objective and definitions, while the middle three sections represent the three pillars of the Aarhus Convention. The second section thus includes rules on access to environmental information. The first article in this section refers to Regulation (EC) No 1049/2001 Regarding Public Access to European Parliament, Council and Commission Documents (the Regulation on Public Access),[162] which was adopted with the purpose to facilitate better access to documents of EU institutions.[163] The Aarhus Regulation thus states that the Regulation on Public Access shall also apply to any request for access to environmental information held by Community institutions and bodies.[164] Moreover, this section includes a number of rules on inter alia the collection of data, organization of environmental information, the quality of such information and how to make it available.[165]

The third section of the Aarhus Regulation concerns public participation concerning plans and programs relating to the environment – those which are subject to preparation and adoption by one such institution or body. It must also be required under legislative, regulatory or administrative provisions and contribute in some way to the environmental policy of the EU and the sixth EAPs. In addition, general environmental action programs are also applicable.[166] The most significant provisions in this section state that institutions and bodies shall provide early and effective opportunities for the public

159 The Aarhus Regulation, Article 2(1)(c).

160 The Aarhus Regulation, Article 2.

161 The Aarhus Regulation, Article 2(1)(f). In addition, there are a number of proceedings and bodies that in their pursuit of such proceedings are excepted from review of the acts and omission they might do in this capacity. See The Aarhus Regulation, Article 2(2)

162 OJ L 145, 31.5.2001, p. 43–48.

163 The Regulation on Public Access, Article 1.

164 The Aarhus Regulation, Article 3.

165 The Aarhus Regulation, Articles 4–5.

166 The Aarhus Regulation, Article 2(1)e.

to participate during the preparation, modification or review of plans or programs relating to the environment, and that the public shall have this possibility while all options are still open.[167] Furthermore, the public likely to be affected is to be informed in appropriate and timely ways of such plans and programs, draft proposals, relevant environmental information and how to participate, and so forth.[168]

In the fourth section on internal review and access to justice, it is stated that an NGO has the right to request an internal review of an EU institution or body that has adopted an administrative act under environmental law or, in case of an alleged administrative omission, should have adopted such an act.[169] To exercise this right, however, the NGO has to be an independent, nonprofit legal person, have the objective of protecting the environment, and demonstrate that this objective is in line with the subject matter to be reviewed. In addition, the NGO has to have existed for more than two years.[170] When these requirements on an NGO are met, however, the NGO making such a request for internal review may initiate proceedings before the EU Court in accordance with the relevant provisions of the EU Treaties.[171]

7.6 PUBLIC PARTICIPATION IN A GLOBAL PERSPECTIVE

The Aarhus Convention is a convention under the United Nations Economic Commission for Europe (UNECE), which is a regional commission with the main aim to promote pan-European economic integration. This means that it is primarily open for European States that are members of the UNECE.[172] However, it is also open for any United Nations member State to accede the Convention.[173] Still, as was clear from the previously provided review of the Aarhus Convention, most Parties are European, with the addition of a number of former Soviet States in Central Asia. The Convention has had an important impact in these countries, including the EU. However, similar instruments can also be found in other parts of the world.

As a start the UN Environmental Programme (UNEP) adopted nonbinding guidelines in 2010; the 2010 UNEP Guidelines for the Development of National Legislation on Access to Information, Public Participation and

167 The Aarhus Regulation, Article 9(1).
168 The Aarhus Regulation, Article 9(2)–(5).
169 The Aarhus Regulation, Article 10.
170 The Aarhus Regulation, Article 11(1) a–d.
171 The Aarhus Regulation, Article 12(1).
172 The Aarhus Convention, Article 17.
173 The Aarhus Convention, Article 19(3).

Access to Justice in Environmental Matters (the Bali Guidelines). The Guidelines are ambitious, and they aim to implement the Rio Declaration, Principle 10, as mentioned previously. Although they are not binding, they are universal since they are adopted by UNEP and such guidelines can inspire and help develop more binding requirements as part of formal instruments. The implementation guide to the Bali Guidelines states that the purpose of the guidelines is to assist countries in their pursuit of adopting broad access to inter alia participation.[174]

The African Union has adopted an agreement, the Revised African Convention on the Conservation of Nature and Natural Resources[175] (the African Convention on the Conservation of Nature) that includes some rather strong rules on participation and access to justice. Under the "Procedural Rights," the Convention states the following:

> 1. The Parties shall adopt legislative and regulatory measures necessary to ensure timely and appropriate
>   a) dissemination of environmental information;
>   b) access of the public to environmental information;
>   c) participation of the public in decision-making with a potentially significant environmental impact; and
>   d) access to justice in matters related to protection of environment and natural resources.[176]

The article furthermore establishes rights in relation to transboundary harm, in a similar way to the Aarhus Convention. However, the provisions are far more general and open than the Aarhus Convention in defining these obligations. In this situation, though, the Bali Guidelines could provide guidance on developing the implementation.[177]

Another agreement that is an important example of similar regional instruments promoting participation is the 2018 Regional Agreement on Access to Information, Public Participation and Justice in Environmental Matters in Latin America and the Caribbean (the Escazú Agreement). This agreement was adopted under the sister organization to the UNECE; the Economic

174 UNEP, "Putting Rio Principle 10 into Action: An Implementation Guide," published by the United Nations Environment Programme (UNEP), October 2015.

175 This can be found at https://au.int/en/treaties/african-convention-conservation-nature-and-natural-resources-revised-version.

176 The African Convention on the Conservation of Nature, Article 16.

177 Ebbesson, J., "Public Participation in Environmental Matters – International Human Rights Developments in Europe and Africa," 2018, Faculty of Law, Stockholm University Research Paper No. 58. Available at https://ssrn.com/abstract=3164785.

Commission for Latin America and the Caribbean (ECLAC). The agreement is not yet in force but it is the result of a long negotiation process, and it has been signed by twenty-two States and is so far ratified by five.[178] It will enter into force after eleven ratifications.[179] It is the second regional agreement beside the Aarhus Convention that is dedicated to the Rio Declaration Principle 10 and to access to information, participation and justice. The objective of the Escazú Agreement is:

> to guarantee the full and effective implementation in Latin America and the Caribbean of the rights of access to environmental information, public participation in the environmental decision-making process and access to justice in environmental matters, and the creation and strengthening of capacities and cooperation, contributing to the protection of the right of every person of present and future generations to live in a healthy environment and to sustainable development.[180]

The following provisions are very similar to the provisions of the Aarhus Convention and are also dedicated to implementing Rio Declaration Principle 10. It even includes provisions to establish a "Committee to Support Implementation and Compliance."[181] It is possible to assume that although the term used is not a compliance committee as in the Aarhus Convention, this committee could have a similar role once the agreements enter into force.

In the end, the effective implementation will be dependent on how the agreement is interpreted once it is adopted. The Committee to Support implementation will of course play an important role here. However, another factor that can affect this is that some of the provisions are less precise than the Aarhus Convention. Another significant difference is one that may also reflect the importance of the resilience features in legal structures. That is the engagement of civil society and NGOs. For an agreement like the Escazú and for the Aarhus Convention, the civil society is key for making them effective. The ECLAC region does not have the same strong network of NGOs as the UNECE or the EU has. Nevertheless, it is not too late for such a network of civil society and NGOs to grow and organize in a way that will exert strong pressure on governments to implement the agreement effectively.[182]

178 This was on December 30, 2019.
179 The Escazú Agreement, Article 22(1).
180 The Escazú Agreement, Article 1.
181 The Escazú Agreement, Article 18.
182 Stec, S. and Jendrośka, J., "The Escazú Agreement and the Regional Approach to Rio Principle 10: Process, Innovation, and Shortcomings," *Journal of Environmental Law*, Vol. 31, 2019, pp. 533–545.

7.7 PARTICIPATION IN EU LAW AND EU INSTITUTIONS

As mentioned in Section 7.3.4, stakeholder involvement and public participation in environmental decision processes are also common features in the EU, although the process of creating structures for participation started later than it did in international law. The background and development of such structures primarily have not been the result of efforts to enforce environmental protection. The main debate and rise of formal stakeholder involvement in decision-making and legislative procedures in the EU started in the 1990s, as a result of increased focus on general legitimacy and the need for better support by citizens of the EU Member States. It can also be assumed that the institutional system in the EU and the Member States was also influenced by the developments in international law. All these events triggered a process toward new governance of the EU (Section 2.4.4).[183]

The result of the new governance approaches has been that many regulatory acts in EU environmental law provide for wide stakeholder participation and especially the inclusion of many corporate actors in regulatory decision-making. This may have a good effect on the effectiveness and enforcement of regulatory acts, but it also entails legitimacy problems.[184] In addition to these new governance measures, the EU implementation of the Aarhus Convention in 2005 opened up for pathways and structures for access to environmental information, participation and judicial review in environmental matters. Hence, this was a road to introducing environmental perspectives on the role of participatory rights. As a result, the importance of participation for environmental protection also received more attention at this time. This was emphasized in the fifth and sixth EAPs, which were developed for the periods of 1992–2000 and 2002–2012, respectively.[185] These developments of the EAPs were also likely a consequence of the international developments in this regard. However, the Commission white paper on new governance also included a number of features, which have shown to be of importance for

183 EU White Paper (2001).

184 See e.g. Abbot, C. and Lee, M., 2015, pp. 1–34.

185 EU 5th EAP, Fifth Environmental Action Programme, "Toward Sustainability – A European Community programme of policy and action in relation to the environment and sustainable development," OJ No C138, 17.5.93; EU 6th EAP, Sixth Environmental Action Programme, Decision No. 1600/2002/EC of the European Parliament and of the Council of July 2002 laying down the Sixth Community Environment Action Programme, OJ L 242, 10.9.2002, p. 1–15. See also EU COM (1999), Communication from the Commission, "Europe's Environment: What directions for the future? – The Global Assessment of the European Community Programme of Policy and Action in relation to the environment and sustainable development, 'Toward Sustainability,'" Brussels, 24.11.1999 COM(1999) 543 final, pp. 2–3.

environmental governance and protection.[186] In addition to the general call for broader participation by stakeholders and the general public, the new governance approaches presented in the white paper included open framework structures in legislation and policy that would make room for further regional, national or local influence.[187]

The EU regime is based on a structure of independent EU institutions and bodies (Section 2.2). Some of the most significant institutions are the Commission, the Council, the European Council, the European Parliament and of course the EU Court. Despite the white paper on new governance and the general attitude toward openness and transparency, the direct pathways for participation in the EU institutional structure are few. Nevertheless, due to its specific supranational structure, the EU regime is ruled by democratic principles to a greater extent than the international community. Although international bodies are also run by the ministers from each State Party, the system built up in the EU offers another structure for decisions and lawmaking. For example, the citizens in each Member State elect the European Parliament. Additionally, the Council as well as the European Council are represented by the European ministers. Therefore, the participatory pathways are also an indirect result of the possibilities for participation at the national level. On the other hand, it can also be argued that the nature of the EU regime – where Member State citizens also have citizenship in the EU – demands an even higher level of democratic rights and pathways for participation or judicial review.

Numerous actors, operators, organizations and so forth are represented in Brussels with the intention of keeping the Commission informed about their respective issues and exerting influence on Commission decision-making.[188] The Commission has an important role in the EU institutional structure. Not only does it have the exclusive role of proposing new legislation; it also supervises and enforces compliance.[189] The Commission thus has the additional and exclusive right to initiate (and determine) infringement procedures (Section 2.2.1 and Section 8.3.4).[190] Still, there are no direct formal pathways for the public to participate or review the Commission's decisions and work. The special role and tasks of the EU Commission and the lack of formal participatory pathways are probably the main reasons for the external

186 EU White Paper (2001).

187 EU White Paper (2001), p. 3.

188 Krämer, L., 2011, pp. 45–46.

189 Article 17(1) and (2), EUT.

190 Article 17(1) EUT, and additionally 258 TFEU about the right to take a member stat to the EU Court.

pressures on Commissioners. To a large extent, this is also how environmental NGOs and other actors work to have compliance reviewed in matters, where they believe that a State is not abiding by EU law.[191]

In general, the channels available for judicial review under EU law are rare. In the context of EU institutions, the issue of access to justice is important since it is connected to the possibility to influence decisions that will have an effect on the supranational level. Access concerns the role of NGOs as actors for both monitoring and reviewing or verifying that relevant knowledge is taken into account when important decisions are adopted. In this way, access also connects to the idea of stakeholder participation in resilience governance. The possibilities to have a case tried directly in the EU court are very limited for *natural or legal persons*, except for the possibilities provided for certain environmental NGOs according to the Aarhus Regulation.[192] Such NGOs are also permitted to have an internal review of certain administrative acts.[193] The only other option for review is if the act is directly addressed to a person or of direct and individual concern.[194] However, decisions addressed directly to a natural or legal person are rare in environmental matters.[195] Hence, it is unlikely that an environmental decision will be reviewed this way.

The Charter of Fundamental Rights of the European Union (2010/C 83/02),[196] originally proclaimed in the year 2000, states: "Any citizen of the Union, and any natural or legal person residing or having its registered office in a Member State, has a right of access to documents of the institutions, bodies, offices and agencies of the Union."[197] Since the entry into force of the Treaty of Lisbon in 2009, these provisions are legally binding. The Lisbon Treaty also enlarge this right of access to justice to some degree, for natural or legal persons to challenge the legality of acts decided by EU institutions before the EU courts. The Lisbon Treaty made a change in what is now Article 263 TFEU, which means that regulatory acts not involving implementing

191 The European Environmental Bureau (the Federation of Environmental Citizens Organizations) states for example on their homepage that "Our policy officers are in almost constant dialogue with the European institutions (Commission, Parliament and Council)"; www.eeb.org/index.cfm/about-eeb/how-the-eeb-works/.

192 The Aarhus Regulation, Article 12(1).

193 The Aarhus Regulation, Article 10(1).

194 Article 263 TFEU.

195 Pallemaerts, M., "Access to Environmental Justice at EU Level. Has the 'Aarhus Regulation' Improved the Situation?," in Pallemaerts, M. (ed.), *The Aarhus Convention at Ten – Interactions and Tensions between Conventional International Law and EU Environmental Law*, Vol. 9 Avosetta Series, Europa Law Publishing, 2011b, p. 294.

196 OJ C 83, 30.3.2010, p. 389–403.

197 Charter of Fundamental Rights of the European Union, Article 42.

measures are open to review by any person to whom they are of direct concern. Previously, the act also had to be of individual concern, a criterion that remains with regard to acts that requires implementation measures if the act is not addressed to the person.[198] For a long time, however, the only rules to be found regarding internal review were the rules of procedure for the Council and the Commission. The EU Court made it its task to formulate precedence in this area, but in 2001 the Commission adopted the Regulation on Public Access – that is, with emphasis on public access to European Parliament, Council and Commission documents.[199] This regulation thus formalizes much of the precedence created by the EU Court, and contains more specific rules on openness and access to documents. The purpose of the Regulation on Public Access is to define the principles, conditions and limits on the grounds of public or private interest governing the right of access to documents in EU institutions.[200] Similar to the Charter of Fundamental Rights of the EU, the Regulation states: "Any citizen of the Union, and any natural or legal person residing or having its registered office in a Member State, has a right of access to documents of the institutions."[201]

The Regulation on Public Access was an important step toward more openness and transparency in the EU institutional structure; it became an important tool to operationalize the general principles stated inter alia in TEU and the EU Charter of Fundamental Rights. It has also been important in realizing the initiatives reflected in the governance white paper. Nevertheless, it also contains a number of exceptions from the general claims of openness, which make it less forceful.[202] Dubious grounds for such exceptions are commercial interests, which will be an exception from the rule as long as there is no overriding public interest in disclosure.[203] Assessing overriding public interest beforehand may be difficult when it comes to environmental information. In addition to transferring the Aarhus Convention into secondary law to be implemented by the EU Member States, the EU Commission also took decisions on implementing it directly in the EU institutions and bodies.[204] This also paved the way for additional openness to the structures set by the Regulation on Public Access, the decisions taken as a result of the

198 Pallemaerts, M., 2011b, note 1067, p. 293.
199 The Regulation (EC) No 1049/2001.
200 The Regulation on Public Access, Article 1.
201 The Regulation on Public Access, Article 2(1).
202 The Regulation on Public Access, Article 4(1)(a) and (b).
203 The Regulation on Public Access, Article 4(2).
204 The Directive 2003/4/EC on public access to environmental information; the Directive 2003/35/EC providing for public participation in respect of the drawing up of certain plans and programmes relating to the environment and amending with regard to public participation

new governance white paper, and the channels for judicial review and communication in matters originally found in the EU legal regime.

The Aarhus Regulation directly refers to the Regulation on Public Access. It states that the provisions of the Regulation on Public Access shall also be applicable with regard to environmental information.[205] It also adds a somewhat wider application by stipulating that the word *institution*, which is the general target for the provisions in the Regulation on Public Access, shall be read as *institution or body*.[206] As described previously, the Aarhus Regulation furthermore states rules for public participation and access for NGOs to judicial review, internal review of administrative acts and review in the EU Court.[207]

The criteria set up for an NGO to be qualified to request this kind of review are found in Article 11(1) of the Aarhus Regulation. First of all, the NGO in question must be an independent, nonprofit legal person. The NGO must be devoted to promoting environmental protection in the context of environmental law, and this must be its primary objective. An additional requirement is that the organization has existed for more than two years and that the subject matter of the request for review is within the scope of the NGO's general objective and activities.[208] Furthermore, according to the Aarhus Regulation definitions, an *administrative act* means any *measure of individual scope* under environmental law.[209] Thus, to be able to have an act reviewed, the act must also concern *measures of individual scope*.[210]

In recent years, there have been a number of cases tried in the EU Court regarding access to justice and the application of the Aarhus Convention. To a large extent, these cases have been raised with regard to implementation in Member States and often involve matters under directives with specific provisions on public participation, such as the EIA Directive and the IPPC/IE Directives. There have also been a number of cases on matters regarding the Aarhus Convention itself. Again, many cases have concerned access to justice and standing in the Member States, and Member States' implementation of

and access to justice Council Directives 85/337/EEC and 96/61/EC; Regulation (EC) No 1367/2006 on the application of the provisions of the Aarhus Convention on Access to Information, Public Participation in Decision-Making and Access to Justice in Environmental Matters to Community institutions and bodies.

205 The Aarhus Regulation, Article 3.

206 The Aarhus Regulation, Article 3, last section.

207 The Aarhus Regulation, Article 12 (1).

208 The Aarhus Regulation, Article 11(1)(a)–(d).

209 The Aarhus Regulation, Article 2(1)(g).

210 The Aarhus Regulation, Article 2(1)(g).

the Aarhus Convention provisions. The EU Court has often found that Member States do not sufficiently provide access to environmental justice.[211] The reason for the large number of cases concerning implementation of these provisions is probably that access to justice in environmental matters for the public, including NGOs, in the Member States is still far from satisfactory, nor is it satisfactory at the level of the EU itself.[212] In an important case from 2011, however, the EU Court stated that the obligations following from the Aarhus Convention and access to justice have indirect effect (but not direct effect, since the Convention is not sufficiently clear in its formulation). The indirect effect meant that the interpretation of national law should still be made in conformity with the objectives of the Convention.[213]

The internal application of access to justice provisions in the EU institutional structure has also been reviewed. In a submission sent to the ACCC on alleged noncompliance under the Aarhus Convention, for example, a number of NGOs claimed that the EU and the EU Court were not applying the Convention provision on access to justice in accordance with the intent of the Convention. The NGOs had a number of concerns; they claimed inter alia that the limitation of the internal review procedure in the EU to appeals against administrative acts of an individual nature was effectively stopping NGOs from access. As an argument, the NGOs referred to a number of cases where NGOs had been denied access to judicial review.[214] In 2011 the ACCC issued findings and recommendations in the matter. The ACCC did not state that the EU was definitely noncompliant. However, its main findings were that if this jurisprudence of the EU Courts were to continue, the EU would fail to comply with Aarhus Convention Article 9(3) and (4) on access to justice, unless this was compensated by adequate

211 See inter alia Case C-427/07 *Commission* v. *Ireland* (ECLI:EU:C:2009:457) and Case C-263/08 Djurgården-Lilla Värtans Miljöskyddsförening (ECLI:EU:C:2009:631). See also Darpö, J., "Article 9(2) of the Aarhus Convention and EU Law – Some Remarks on CJEUs Case-Law on Access to Justice in Environmental Decision-Making," *Journal for European Environmental and Planning Law*, Vol. 11, No. 4, 2014.

212 Pallemaerts, M., 2011a, p. 7.

213 Case C-240-09 *Lesoochranárske zoskupenie VLK* v. *Ministerstvo životného prostredia Slovenskej republiky*, "Slovak Brown Bears Case" (ECLI:EU:C:2011:125).

214 Some of the cases were Case T-91/07 *WWF-UK Ltd* v. *Council of the European Union* (ECLI:EU:T:2008:170); Case C-355/08 P *WWF-UK Ltd* v. *Council of the European Union and the Commission of the European Communities* (ECLI:EU:C:2009:286); Joined Cases T-236/04 and T-241/04 *European Environmental Bureau (EEB) and Stichting Natuur en Milieu* v. *Commission* (ECLI:EU:T:2005:426). See also ACCC/C/2008/32 (Part I), Report of the Compliance Committee: Findings and recommendations with regard to communication concerning compliance by the European Union, adopted on 14 April 2011, ECE/MP.PP/C.1/2011/4/Add.1, paragraph 3, p. 3.

administrative review procedures.[215] The recommendations provided by the ACCC included a call for a new direction of EU Court jurisprudence to be established in order to ensure compliance with the Aarhus Convention.[216] The communication has continued between the Parties in the matter and the ACCC after these findings and recommendations. The EU has successively approved their implementation and compliance in a number of issues where it has received critique from the ACCC. In January 2015, the EU Court handed down a ruling where access to judicial review of EU institutional acts and omissions were limited even further. In a joint case, two environmental NGOs had challenged a decision by the Commission to grant extended exemptions from the Directive 2008/50/EC on ambient air quality and cleaner air for Europe[217] (The Air Quality Directive). The EU Court found that the NGOs, which referred to the provisions of the Aarhus Convention and the Aarhus Regulation, could not be granted access to the court since the challenged acts could not be considered as acts of *individual scope.*[218] Therefore, although the EU Court has gone far in making Member States apply a broad interpretation of the Aarhus Convention provision on access to justice, this is apparently not the approach taken internally when it comes to the EU internal review.[219] However, in another submission addressing noncompliance with the rules on access to justice by the EU the ACCC in its findings from 2017 again concluded that the facts presented were not sufficient amount to non-compliance.[220]

7.8 SUMMARY AND CONCLUSIONS

Stakeholder participation, as presented in theories on resilience in social-ecological systems, represents many features and functions of great importance.

[215] ACCC/C/2008/32 (Part I), Report of the Compliance Committee: Findings and recommendations with regard to communication concerning compliance by the European Union, adopted on 14 April 2011, ECE/MP.PP/C.1/2011/4/Add.1, paragraph 94, p. 22.

[216] ACCC/C/2008/32 (Part I), Report of the Compliance Committee: Findings and recommendations with regard to communication concerning compliance by the European Union, adopted on 14 April 2011, ECE/MP.PP/C.1/2011/4/Add.1, paragraph 97, p. 22.

[217] OJ L 152, p. 1–44.

[218] Joined Cases C-401/12 P to C-403/12 P *Council of the European Union and Others* v. *Vereniging Milieudefensie and Stichting Stop Luchtverontreiniging Utrecht* (ECLI:EU:C:2015:4).

[219] See also Jendroska, J., "Citizen's Rights in European Environmental Law: Stock-Taking of Key Challenges and Current Developments in Relation to Public Access to Information, Participation and Access to Justice," *Journal for European Environmental and Planning Law*, Vol. 9, No. 1, 2012, pp. 71–90.

[220] Findings and recommendations with regard to communication ACCC/C/2014/123 concerning compliance by the European Union in document ECE/MP.PP/C.1/2017/21, p. 19.

In the resilience theories, participation is primarily about assuring that those concerned and closely connected to the environment at different levels are involved in the measures taken. From a legal perspective, participation is similarly meant to involve those concerned in measures and decision-making regarding environmental matters. However, in a legal structure, the concept of participation is often defined in a narrower sense and provided for in more formal pathways. What it means for a party to be concerned in legal terms is a formal requirement defined by certain criteria specifically set out in different regulatory regimes and instruments. Stakeholders contribute to a number of significant and partly interconnected functions in management for social-ecological resilience, in both larger and more local scales. The overview presented in this chapter shows that different forms of participation in law also provide for many of the features and functions presented, in both the management context as well as a strict legal context. Since the 1970s, different forms of participation have increasingly become a natural part of many international law regimes, and since the 1990s most (East) European States, as well as the EU, are also Parties to the Aarhus Convention. This can be regarded as a significant statement regarding States' attitude toward participatory rights and the role of the public – and not least NGOs – in monitoring environmental decision-making.

In addition to involving those concerned in decisions taken, the feature of participation in different levels of the legal system provides for other important functions, such as legitimacy and democracy. As implied in the research on resilience governance, participation also provides mechanisms to bridge institutional gaps and better adjust measures or approaches to specific ecological or environmental prerequisites.

There are many aspects that could be included in a review of participation. This chapter focused on different concepts of participation and how participation is formally defined within law. Furthermore, pathways for participation and how participation is provided for in legal structures at regional, international and, in part, national levels were examined. The chapter also explored the role and functions connected to participation within law, in comparison and in contrast, to the functions of participation in governance for social-ecological resilience, as well as the role and function of participation in law, connected to creating democracy, legitimacy and institutional ecosystem fit or ecosystem approach.

Although the concept of stakeholders varies between different regulatory situations, it can be concluded that to a large extent stakeholder participation is reflected in law and legal institutional structures. Aside from the Aarhus Convention, many international agreements and international organizations provide the opportunity for NGOs to observe and participate in meetings under certain circumstances. It is also obvious that beyond NGOs there are within international and EU law, also much space for the involvement of many different kinds of stakeholders, such as scientists, regional interest groups and possibly business organizations.

In the EU, lobbying organizations are fully engaged in trying to influence the decisions made, primarily by the EU Commission. Additionally, EU environmental laws often have structures that emphasize the need to involve stakeholders in their implementation. Along with the general public and NGOs, corporate economic actors are key in decision-making, in the EU and these instruments. Nevertheless, the review presented here of transparency and the general openness to NGOs in the larger decision-making perspective, and not least in the EU Court, revealed a disappointing result. Despite promoting so-called new governance and emphasizing the role of stakeholders in governance, the EU is not implementing the Aarhus Convention principles properly. The EU Aarhus Regulation does not really reflect the Aarhus Convention, although this is the aim. This excludes many NGOs from reviewing decisions.

Stakeholder participation is found to be a wider concept of participation in a legal context, and one that does not directly limit the actors that may participate. It is this kind of participation that is primarily referred to in the EU legal system and EU legal instruments. Generally, all kinds of participation, whether formalized and more restricted or wider and more participatory, are important as a legal form of adaptive governance. Many participatory pathways are formalized; they cannot be directly compared to the kind of participation that is referred or that emphasizes self-organization. Still wider access to participation may demonstrate such features. All forms of participation can be seen and compared as inter alia pathways for distribution and application of social/local knowledge. All these features are important for achieving an institutional fit and in creating a bridge between local, regional and international levels of organization in multilevel systems such as those of international and EU law.

To a large extent, the legal structures create prerequisites for the implementation of laws that have often been determined on other and generally higher levels than those on which implementation is being enforced. Where participation is enabled, the participatory role will often be to scrutinize such laws, related decisions and the implementation measures. This role is thus comparable not only to bridging functions, but is also important in monitoring and serving as a buffer to legitimize laws. This role of participation in legal structures or legal instruments becomes a legitimizing factor for laws that need to be adjusted to the specific circumstances in which they are implemented. Thus, even if the legal act is established and decided on in the EU, there are still opportunities for important influence by concerned actors on its measures for implementation. These are important features for the legal system, and at the same time, they are also similar to the functions and features presented in resilience research.

The aims of bridging, and of monitoring implementation, benefit from improved access for actors concerned at the top levels of regulatory governance systems. Accomplishing institutional fit is a tricky issue, and there is no guarantee that these kinds of participatory structures will create this fit at the right scales. It also depends on other factors of an administrative nature, such as coordination and coherence. Factors that reflect how biophysical or ecological indicators and other scientific knowledge are obtained and presented among different levels of regulation, without being transformed due to regulatory administrative and structural issues. However, without participation and transfer of knowledge between different levels in these regulatory structures, and the attempt to connect different scales in the regulatory process, institutional fit would be impossible.

Generally, it can be stated that democratic features are also connected to stakeholder participation – as proposed in social-ecological resilience research, and then especially to issues of legitimacy and accountability. Institutions described in resilience research as those bridging different levels of management are held to generate or provide prerequisites for legitimacy, accountability and effectiveness. As stated, in some aspects these institutions also closely resemble those of law and general legal structures. All kinds of structures that promote formalized participation must be regarded as contributing to democratic legitimacy and accountability. Although the concept of legitimacy can be described, defined and interpreted from different perspectives, the legal system and the rule of law can generally be regarded also as relying and depending on such features, and then especially to aspects of democracy. In law, public participation and access to information are important aspects of the democratic system. The legal structures and pathways for participation therefore have a significant impact on issues of democratic legitimacy and could be regarded as increasing accountability and transparency in the system, although questions of legitimacy and accountability in the system of international law go far beyond this. Problems of perspectives on legitimacy and accountability may emerge when discussing the broader kind of stakeholder participation and the involvement of economic actors. Including corporate economic actors in participation runs the risk that democratic features will be weakened, since corporate economic actors represent other interests and the information provided by such actors may lack objectivity; they may not represent public interests, at least to the same extent as

NGOs, for example. This is of course a complex issue represented by a diversity of opinions and views. However, few seem to consider refraining from involving economic actors as a solution. Corporate economic actors also provide important knowledge and insights. As discussed, the involvement of corporate economic actors may still be valuable and important for many regulatory processes. In that case, however, other features promoting legitimacy, accountability and transparency become even more important as a complement. Having more formal pathways for public participation may thus be important in these systems, as a feature designed to strengthen democratic values. In the legal system, the possibility to appeal and review decisions is a crucial safeguard in these cases, and this is difficult to create in an effective way without setting up some limits as to what or who can have such access. One problem in this context is of course the fact that it is difficult for other kinds of actors to validate and review many of the facts and industrial state-of-the-art processes that are central to much of this regulatory decision-making.

The Resilience Feature of Stakeholders and Structures for Participation is a feature that both is an important component in itself but also plays a significant role in the operationalization of other resilience features. The inclusion of different forms of participation is crucial for fully enabling adaptive governance and adaptive legal structures. Stakeholders will be both carriers of knowledge; in addition, they are important actors in the adaptive monitoring cycle. Moreover, stakeholders play an important role in multidimensional legal structures. In such diverse and polycentric structures, stakeholders can be bridges between different institutions and institutional levels. Also, in this case, stakeholders are inter alia important as information carriers. So, here, the design starts to become clear – how the different components are interlinked and will be interdependent and dependent on how the other features are included.

When reviewed also in terms of an independent component in resilience law, it is obvious that creating active pathways for participation is both a significant role of law, just as it is an important part of how law can contribute to resilience governance.

8

Operationalization, Monitoring, Compliance and Trust Building

This chapter aims to evaluate effectiveness and compliance in the legal system. In resilience, the factors to be addressed in this regard are to control and monitor slow ecological variables and feedbacks, and to ensure trust building, including structures for sanctions and institutional fit (Section 4.4). However, translated into what law can accomplish, the focus will be on operationalization, monitoring, compliance and trust building. This also reflects the fact that if the legal structures, as seen in this study, are designed to focus on the ecosystem or have flexible and adaptive features, then it is also important to review mechanisms for compliance and control in relation to such features. In regard to social-ecological resilience, it is also important to review how the legal system is or could be adjusted to assess ecological variables, the demands that this ecosystem focus place on the legal system, and whether this lies within the potential of what law can accomplish. These questions connect the different features previously reviewed in the study. They are all part of a structure where the main intention is to focus on the ecosystem. Central in these kinds of legal structures are adaptive intertwined, flexible features and the ecosystem approach as a basis for regulation. Legal structures will only be fully effective when these features are viewed in relation to each other and operationalized under some form of coordinated control or review mechanism and through relevant enforcement. In short, the effectiveness and problem-solving potential in law will be discussed in terms of compliance, enforcement and monitoring. Different perspectives on compliance, compliance control, implementation, enforcement and regulatory effects will be reflected upon. As part of this discussion, the matter of trust building and organizational connections will also be touched upon.

As can be concluded from the aim described previously, the final category of features to be reviewed in this study consists of a nest of factors that – compared to the other resilience features – are less concrete in their role in governance. These features are less directly instrumental and more accurately represent what is to be achieved by governance and in this context by law. To some extent, it can even be regarded as a collection of features that tie into and connect with the other features reviewed in this study. This category reflects how important it is for resilience governance to control so-called slow ecological variables and thereby their feedbacks (i.e., the environmental consequences). Therefore, in this context, it is also necessary to review whether these results can be achieved with law, and the prerequisites for achieving such results. This effect is partly the aim of all the resilience features reviewed, in combination, and cannot be evaluated only in regard to these features as single components.

The chapter outline is as follows. This first section provides a general introduction, where the concepts and perspectives within resilience governance are presented in the relation to the legal context. After this, different perspectives of legal enforcement, implementation, compliance and effectiveness are discussed from a more general perspective.

8.1 A LEGAL PERSPECTIVE ON SLOW ECOLOGICAL VARIABLES, FEEDBACKS AND TRUST BUILDING

Evaluating effectiveness of the role of law and legal governance for resilience (i.e., the possibility for law to contribute to resilience governance) is not just a question of compliance and control in a traditional sense. Also, the effectiveness of law in this context is connected to the ecological factors – just like the different components of resilience governance are all partly connected to an aim of effectiveness in this regard. The features of resilience governance must be seen and evaluated as components of effectiveness tied to one another.

Adaptive and flexible features in law are important for resilience and the ecosystem approach – that is, for adjusting measures to fit the problem (Chapter 5). However, as concluded in Chapter 5, they demand effective monitoring and review in order to function as intended. Adjusting measures to fit the problem also relates to evaluating whether a multidimensional legal system is appropriate when it comes to operationalizing measures (Chapter 6), and not least to different aspects of integrating pathways for participation. As discussed (Chapter 7), participatory actors are important in both operationalization and adjusting measures at different scales, as well as in monitoring and review structures. Last but not least, the questions of controlling ecological variables are also directly related to the concept of ecosystem approach. Therefore, these features must also be evaluated in the context of operationalization, control and effectiveness.

To better understand complex systems, they can be divided into categories of fast and slow variables.[1] According to resilience theories, slow, controlling variables regulate the fundament of a social-ecological system and thus whether or not a critical threshold is exceeded (which is in turn a factor related to fast variables).[2] In terms of resilience governance and effectiveness, this could be interpreted to mean the extent to which law manages to control slow variables through legislation. Controlling slow variables then means reducing the level of pollution or habitats destruction, for example. This can be evaluated from different perspectives. The effectiveness is connected to some degree to the other governance features reviewed in this study, as discussed previously. It also relates to the effectiveness of the legal system in relation to the ecological or environmental results of regulation.[3] Ultimately, this concerns the effectiveness of the legal instruments and their ability to achieve their goals. The main perspectives on legal effectiveness in controlling, for example, pollution could be regarded either in terms of results or in terms of conduct.[4] In other words, one aspect could be to assess the differences in pollution load that might be the result of legislation; another more strictly legal view could be to evaluate legal compliance without a direct connection to the environmental result. Taken even further, results of legislation could also be assessed by behavioral change (i.e., the actions taken by the States in their efforts of implementation and enforcement). These different perspectives and their applicability will be discussed and evaluated throughout the chapter.

The basis for this reasoning on slow variables is that social-ecological systems are affected by a multitude of variables that change and interact on a range of timescales. The system as a whole is changed by changes made to the steering of slow variables, and thus different forms of feedback are created. These changes or the steering of slow variables can be reinforcing a changing trend, or they can dampen such change.[5] An example of how slow variables can be controlled is through sanctions in levied due to misbehavior by an

[1] See e.g. Chapin, F. S., Folke, C. and Kofinas, G. P., 2009, pp. 12ff.; Walker, B. H., et al., "Drivers, 'Slow' Variables, 'Fast' Variables, Shocks, and Resilience," *Ecology and Society*, Vol. 17, No. 3, 2012, p. 30.

[2] Biggs, R., et al., 2015, p. 109; Walker, B. H., et al., 2012.

[3] See e.g. Mitchell, R. B., "International Environmental Agreements: A Survey of Their Features, Formation, and Effects," *Annual Review of Environment and Resources*, Vol. 28, 2003, pp. 444ff. See also Young, O. R. and Levy, M. A., "The Effectiveness of International Environmental Regimes," in Young, O. R. (ed.), *The Effectiveness Of International Environmental Regimes: Causal Connections and Behavioral Mechanisms*, MIT Press, 1999, pp. 1–7.

[4] See e.g. Bodansky, D., 2010, p. 253.

[5] Biggs, R., et al., 2015, pp. 109–120 and 127ff.

actor, which is seen as a measure having a dampening effect on the feedback. Sanctions as a way of steering variables and feedbacks also put these issues in a perspective that is interesting from a legal point of view. It is stated within resilience research that effective punishment of offenders acts as a dampening feedback by discouraging further misbehavior by the individual as well as discouraging others from repeating the undesirable behavior.[6] Although the example stated refers to local-scale informal or formal social sanctioning, the effects and purposes of sanctions or other forms of control mechanisms are much the same in the legal system.

The resilience theories furthermore state that reinforcing slow variables at a local scale is connected to trust building and knowledge generation, which are additional factors that prepare the system for more abrupt and rapid changes.[7] Although rarely discussed in the same terms, trust and leadership are also central components in the system of international law. Trust could be regarded as a cornerstone for making international or transboundary cooperation work and one main reason to enter into an agreement in the first place.[8] States usually enter into agreements because they have common interests, or common resources, and success depends on the active participation of all States concerned. However, for States to take, sometimes costly, measures and comply with an agreement, they must be able to rely on the other Parties to do the same. This perspective is connected to rational choice and an opposite would be the problem of free-riders and the prisoner's dilemma. From a legal perspective, trust and compliance are closely tied concepts. Parties' compliance with an international agreement creates trust in the agreement and between the Parties, but in many respects, trust is also a prerequisite for compliance. If Parties to an agreement trust that the others will comply, the incentives for complying becomes much stronger than if Parties suspect a large degree of so-called free-riding.[9]

In resilience thinking, trust building is seen as an important factor for institutional stability and continuity in management actions, and between actors as well as institutions. These facts are also an argument for a monitoring and sanctioning system, since such mechanisms are intended to guarantee compliance by all. Leadership is then often represented either by active States

6 Biggs, R., et al., 2015, pp. 109–110. See also Ostrom, E., 1990, pp. 36–55.

7 See e.g. Hahn, T., et al., 2006; Folke, C., et al., 2005, pp. 448ff.

8 Mitchell, R. B., 2007, p. 906.

9 See e.g. Matz, N., "Financial and Other Incentives for Complying with MEA Obligations," in Beyerlin, U., Stoll, P-T. and Wolfrum, R. (eds.), *Ensuring Compliance with Multilateral Environmental Agreements – A Dialouge between Practitioners and Academia*, Martinus Nijhoff Publishers, 2006, pp. 305–306. See also Guzman, A. T., 2008, pp. 63–68.

or the governing body. However, it is also frequently argued that legitimacy, as an expression of trust, is the basis for compliance.[10] Continuity and trust building can then be governed by the supervisory body and active involvement of different kinds of stakeholders.[11] Thus, in governance systems formed by a legal system, it is important to sustain trust, leadership and continuity. The same mechanisms or capacities are important in forming a bridging organization. Bridging organizations, or bridging structures, are especially important with regard to multilevel systems with diverse actors. Although the purpose of a bridging organization may never be entirely the same as a legal system structure, it is still possible to identify similar characteristics in the two. To a large extent, the legal system of international or transboundary law also aims to coordinate and bridge different levels and forms of measures, action and participation (Section 7.2). Creating trust between actors and institutions involved in governance and management permeates most of the other prerequisites for resilience governance. It is needed between the actors on the same levels and between the different vertical and horizontal levels. At a local scale, trust building is dependent to a large extent on participatory actors and NGOs. They contribute to transparency and monitoring, and create a basis for legitimacy – features which also provided for on the international scale. In addition, the regulatory approaches at the international scale depend on monitoring and participation at all levels, down to the very local scale. These factors could thus be part of creating structures for bridging organizations.[12]

As stated, this chapter aims to evaluate effectiveness and compliance in the legal system in relation to the ecological variables. This includes issues of compliance, enforcement and monitoring. More specifically, the chapter focuses on perspectives and theories about what constitutes compliance, and how it is achieved. Enforcement is also discussed, including aspects on arbitration, supervisory bodies and other control mechanisms, as are dispute settlement procedures, effectiveness in terms of goal achievement, and legal measures that can be related to environmental results and ecological factors.

10 See e.g. Franck, T. M., 1988, generally.

11 See e.g. Brunnée, J., "Enforcement Mechanisms in International Law and International Environmental Law," in Beyerlin, U., Stoll, P-T. and Wolfrum, R. (eds.), *Ensuring Compliance with Multilateral Environmental Agreements – A Dialogue between Practitioners and Academia*, Martinus Nijhoff Publishers, 2006, pp. 7–12. See Jacobson, H. K. and Brown Weiss, E., "Compliance with International Environmental Accords," in Rolén, M., Sjöberg, H. and Svedin, U. (eds.), *International Governance on Environmental Issues*, Environment and Policy, Volume 9, Springer Science+Business Media, 1997, p. 107f., regarding improving compliance and the role of leader countries.

12 Brunnée, J., 2006, pp. 12–22.

8.2 COMPLIANCE

Both the form and substance of international agreements vary considerably. They can vary in terms of level and clarity of obligations, as well as in the structures for monitoring and compliance review and so forth. These differences or varieties in combinations in different instruments are also important for the effectiveness of the agreement in question. If the depth of the substance of an agreement is measured in terms of the extent to which it demands major changes to national law and policy. However, as stated, the combination of form and substance creates the agreement. This means that if requirements are vague, they may need to be compensated by other features of the agreement for it to be effective.[13] This idea of complementary features and effectiveness is also important in the capabilities of an agreement to achieve true transformability – meaning that for law to be a substantial driver for change in the social-ecological system, features other than substantial requirements are also important.

Compliance is an important indicator for the possibility to achieve the goals of an agreement on abating environmental problems, although there is not necessarily a direct connection or causality between the two. Put simply, a high-level compliance can also just be a consequence of a low level of requirements. At the same time, there is no guarantee at all that behavioral change or compliance with any legal measures will bring about ecosystem change and that environmental problems will be effectively reduced. Still, this is the most direct contribution that a legal system can accomplish in this regard. Compliance with international environmental agreements is an important factor in controlling so-called slow variables and establishing social-ecological resilience. Indeed, the point of environmental agreements would be lost completely if no attention was given to compliance and implementation. Still, this assumption is valid only when compliance is equal to effective implementation and behavioral change by the central actors in environmental management. However, there are many ways to analyze and discuss compliance and what compliance actually is or entails, just as there are many definitions of effectiveness in this regard.[14]

In the following, different perspectives of compliance, enforcement and effectiveness are reviewed and discussed. The aim is to evaluate what

[13] Raustiala, K., 2005, pp. 584–586.

[14] See e.g. Bodansky, D., 2010, pp. 205–251; Victor, D. G., Raustiala, K. and Skolnikoff, E. B., "Introduction and Overview," in Victor, D. G., Raustiala, K. and Skolnikoff, E. B. (eds.), *The Implementation and Effectiveness of International Environmental Commitments: Theory and Practice*, MIT Press, 1998, pp. 6–15. See also Chambers, W. B., 2004, which provides an overview of different perspectives on effectiveness in international environmental law.

international and EU regulatory structures entail in terms of compliance and implementation, and the potential for achieving the goals of regulations and thus potentially affect the slow variables of an ecosystem.

8.2.1 *Assessing Compliance*

The most common way for lawyers and legal scholars to assess the effectiveness of an agreement has been primarily to pay attention to the extent to which States comply with their commitments.[15] To assess the extent of compliance with commitments, it must first be clarified in the agreement what the commitments are. As discussed previously in this study, however, States often have a rather large margin of discretion to interpret and implement an international agreement and thus in how to interpret and transpose commitments (Section 5.2). Therefore, in some cases, it may be difficult to precisely define the implications of an agreed-upon commitment for a State. What is agreed upon usually lies in what can be considered a reasonable frame seen in relation to general legal principles, but this does not mean that States will understand an agreement equally. Furthermore, uncertainty is added by the fact that to a large extent, and due to the difficult and political negotiation process leading to a binding document, international agreements form vague requirements.

In addition, many international environmental treaty regimes contain both hard law and what could be regarded as soft law. These agreements are considered quite flexible and even less precise in terms of what the States are obligated to do. They are even more flexible if they are action- or goal-oriented, as is often the case with framework legislation and new adaptive law approaches. Environmental complexity often blurs the situation even more with regard to both assessments of what to do and what to accomplish. This may be more complicated if the law in question relies on EQS. Aside from the fact that all this complicates the determination of whether a State is in compliance, compliance is also dependent on States' possibilities to assess and understand which actions are appropriate.[16] Compliance is not a sharp line; together with follow-up and review by convention bodies, it is possible to define a somewhat common

[15] See e.g. Mitchell, R. B., 2007, p. 894. Cf. Martin, L. L., "Against Compliance," in Dunoff, J. L. and Pollack, M. A. (eds.), *Interdisciplinary Perspectives on International Law and International Relations – The State of the Art*, Cambridge University Press, 2012, pp. 591ff. generally, and pp. 605–607. The author argues that compliance is a legal concept ill-suited to identify or measure casual effects of behavior.

[16] See also Kirk, E. A., "Noncompliance and the Development of Regimes Addressing Marine Pollution from Land-Based Activities," *Ocean Development and International law*, Vol. 39, No. 3, 2008, pp. 235–236.

picture or frame of what is expected of the States as Parties. Thus compliance is considered to be conduct that lies in this frame. Nevertheless, many factors affect State behavior, and can either further compliance or present obstacles. Such factors include resources, national strategies for implementation, local incentives and not least sanctions or other forms of enforcement control.

Another perspective on the question of whether international law creates change is that international law is effective if it influences State behavior.[17] International relations scholars are concerned with any behavioral or environmental changes that can be attributed to an agreement, regardless of whether the changes involve compliance. Their focus is instead on the reasons why States would change their behavior and the aspects of an agreement that could explain those changes.[18] Compliance is then viewed as an indicator of the influence that international law has on the States. Compliance with international rules implies that these States have assumed a certain behavior.[19] From this perspective, the effectiveness of environmental agreements is determined in relation to the level of compliance by the Parties. It is also important, however, to assess what effectiveness means in relation to the environment (i.e., if compliance also implies goal achievement). An even wider approach to compliance could also be taken, considering that a number of factors influence compliance – from the negotiating stages to the specific characteristics of the agreement as well as of the Parties. Seen from this perspective, an international agreement is defined as effective if it successfully achieves its overall policy goals.[20]

8.2.2 *Implementation, Effectiveness, Behavioral and Problem-Solving Compliance*

Generally, and in somewhat simple terms, the effectiveness of an agreement is judged in relation to whether it achieves compliance. It is ineffective if States

17 Mitchell, R. B., 2007, p. 894; Martin, L. L., 2012, p. 602; Schiele, S., *Evolution of International Environmental Regimes – The Case of Climate Change*, Cambridge University Press, 2014. See also Downs, G. W., Rocke, D. M. and Barsoom, P. N., "Is the Good News about Compliance Good News about Cooperation?," *International Organization*, Vol. 50, No. 3, 1996, generally.

18 Mitchell, R. B., 2007, pp. 894–895 and 901ff. See also Raustiala, K. and Slaugther, A-M., "International Law, International Relations and Compliance," in Carlsnaes, W., Risse, T. and Simmons, B. A. (eds.), *Handbook of international Relations*, SAGE Publications, 2002 p. 539.

19 Mitchell, R. B., 2007, pp. 896ff.; Schiele, S., 2014, p. 92.

20 Victor, D. G., Raustiala K. and Skolnikoff, E. B., 1998, pp. 7–14; Chambers, W. B., 2004, p. 531; Jacobson, H. K. and Brown Weiss, E., "A Framework for Analysis," in Brown Weiss, E. and Jacobson, H. K. (eds.), *Engaging Countries – Strengthening Compliance with International Environmental Accords*, MIT Press, 1998a, pp. 4–6. This broader concept of compliance is included in the question of "whether countries in fact adhere to the provisions of the accord and to the implementing measures that they have instituted," as well as "the spirit of the treaty."

fail to meet their obligations. Compliance is thus seen as a function of two factors: (1) the obligation established by a rule, and (2) the actual conduct of or results created by those subject to the obligation. However, this view of effectiveness is based on that what a rule imposes is clear and that the goal of the rule must be measurable. When reviewing complex environmental problems, new governance approaches and the ecosystem approach, however, one can conclude that this is not always the case. If the obligations are unclear, it will be difficult to identify the required (or prohibited) conduct. If measures taken in regard to the given obligations do not immediately show a result because of time-lags, complexity or other natural factors, then as a consequence it will be impossible to categorize the behavior of the States concerned in terms of compliance or noncompliance.[21]

Another issue that needs to be taken into account when discussing compliance is the nature of obligations or measures stated by the agreement. Depending on the design and the obligations established by the agreement, compliance alone can be a poor indicator of a treaty's value. The agreement as such may be either unnecessary or insufficient for dealing with the problems encountered. It might not demand any significant changes to be made by the Parties. When this is the case, it is more interesting to evaluate the effectiveness of the obligations or the measures that are agreed upon.[22] This makes it interesting to compare the effectiveness of legal rules with the degree to which international environmental agreements lead to changes in behavior that in turn contribute to solving environmental problems. This perspective is considered relevant to investigate law in the context of slow variables and feedbacks, since it is connected to the ability of law to affect those environmental variables that control the foundations of a social-ecological system.

Implementation is naturally directly related to the assessment of compliance and can be seen as the first step in a process through which the intent of an agreement is translated into action. Some even argue that it is not legislation alone but also the implementation process that determines whether a commitment has any practical influence.[23] Implementation is not the only factor that affects behavior, but it is one of the most important. Although international environmental agreements primarily obligate State governments, they also constrain a wide range of actors, whose behavior does not change automatically because governments adopt international commitments. Thus, in order to operationalize such an agreement, a complex process

21 Bodansky, D., 2010, p. 254.
22 Downs, G. W., Rocke, D. M. and Barsoom, P. N., 1996, p. 380.
23 Jacobson, H. K. and Brown Weiss, E., 1998a, pp. 4–5.

begins in order to shape and adjust domestic policy to conform to international standards. This process is combined with the added complexity of coordinating activities among many governments implementing different policies in parallel. This is why the implementation process is so central. The targets of implementation are all those actors who affect the environmental problem in focus. It is ultimately their behavior that must change. Still, international agreement implementation usually goes through several stages or levels before it influences these groups of actors. The concept or process of implementation includes not only the many acts of governments, such as adopting regulations and new laws, but also the activities of non-State actors, such as firms, scientists, consumer and environmental pressure groups, and trade associations. In addition to this, implementation is also assisted by the actions of international institutions – such as monitoring and assistance provided to national governments to realize international requirements and put commitments into practice.[24]

It is important to realize, however, that there are other limitations to behavioral effectiveness beyond the complexity of implementation and compliance. Behavioral change as a result of compliance does not automatically imply that the agreement is effective with regard to environmental change, or in reducing or eliminating the environmental threat. Although the pollution load may decrease as a result of implementation, the problems still might not be automatically abated.[25] One example is the agreements to limit pollution that causes acid precipitation in Europe. These agreements influenced the behavior of polluters, and as a consequence, emissions of some pollutants became lower than they would be without the accords. Nonetheless, the accumulation of acid in European ecosystems continued and environmental impacts are still compounded, although at a slower pace than without the accords.[26]

It is also important to be aware of other factors that influence behavior and the effectiveness of agreements. If the factors causing change are not carefully assessed, it could lead to invalid conclusions about ways to improve the implementation and effectiveness of international agreements. Law plays a central role in regulating social behavior, but even in domestic settings,

[24] Victor, D. G., Raustiala K. and Skolnikoff, E. B., 1998, pp. 1–2 and pp. 16ff. See also Jacobson, H. K. and Brown Weiss, E., "Assessing the Record and Designing Strategies to Engage Countries," in Brown Weiss, E. and Jacobson, H. K. (eds.), *Engaging Countries – Strengthening Compliance with International Environmental Accords*, MIT Press, 1998b, pp. 535–542.

[25] See e.g. Mitchell, R. B., 2003, pp. 444ff.

[26] Victor, D. G., Raustiala K. and Skolnikoff, E. B., 1998, p. 6.

where legal institutions are well established and enforcement powers are readily available, the definition of what leads to effective laws is debated. It could even be said that international law never acts without external pressures and influences, and thus it is never the only factor affecting change. In addition, the nature of the problem will have significant effects on implementation, compliance and effectiveness of an agreement.[27]

In light of complex environmental problems and adaptive legal approaches, behavioral effectiveness is more difficult to measure than legal effectiveness. Environmental problems are easier to address when strong scientific consensus exists, when the costs of addressing the problems are low and when relatively few countries are involved.[28] If an adaptive agreement imposes integration of a number of governance measures and structures, with the aim to create operational space for self-organization in a pluralistic, multilevel scaled system – like the structures set up in the framework of a goal-based instrument, for example – it is difficult to define how effectiveness can be measured.

Legal effectiveness demands only a comparison of what is required with what actually takes place. In contrast, behavioral effectiveness requires a comparison of what takes place with what would have occurred in the absence of the agreement. This entails completely different kinds of assessments. The concept of problem-solving effectiveness, however, requires even more. It requires a focus on and assessment of the causal chain. It is not enough to establish that an international agreement affects behavior; whether the behavioral change affects the environmental outcomes must also be evaluated.[29] This is a challenging task with regard to complex, transboundary environmental problems and adaptive approaches to governance. Therefore, such environmental structures need to be evaluated in a way so that measures taken can be weighed against something other than direct environmental effects. Another challenge in the light of new governance approaches that makes effectiveness and compliance a problematic issue is that such governance approaches are predicated on distribution and fragmentation of authority. However, the new approaches may also be structured to better handle and solve such problems. In new governance, adaptive and flexible rules are designed to be able to meet new challenges and resolve unexpected problems. In relation to this, while a traditional conception of law may be regarded as being founded upon existing knowledge, new governance places emphasis

[27] Bodansky, D., 2010, p. 266; Victor, D. G., Raustiala K. and Skolnikoff, E. B., 1998, pp. 8–9.
[28] Bodansky, D., 2010, pp. 262–265.
[29] Ibid., pp. 255–256.

upon the need to facilitate the continuous generation of new knowledge.[30] Thus, if new legal approaches function as intended (i.e., by adapting and giving rise to new measures and requirements), then this could be a regulatory structure with more potential to actually affect the environmental problems in focus.

Regarding compliance and effectiveness, some studies even suggest that there may be an inverse relationship between the effectiveness of and compliance with some types of standards. All else being equal, more compliance is preferable to less compliance. But this inverse relationship suggests that full and perfect compliance may mean that the requirements in an agreement are set at a very low level. Therefore, less strict compliance may be preferable if it is related to the ambitious aims and obligations of the agreement. Viewed from this perspective, the effectiveness of an agreement with a low compliance standard may be better than one with perfect compliance. Although attention to compliance is important, it must be understood and evaluated in context. In addition, a low level of compliance may be of importance for the implementation process and can thus contribute inversely to higher environmental effectiveness. Noncompliance and the procedures initiated to address the problems thus becomes a vehicle for enhancing effectiveness. In this regard – and this may be important to emphasize – compliance is not an end but a means to achieve effectiveness.[31]

8.2.2.1 Rational Choice Perspectives

So-called rational choice theories establish a somewhat challenging view on compliance. This theoretical perspective, connected to economic theories and inter alia game theory, argues that a State that is Party to an agreement only complies with the obligations of the agreement when it is in the State's interest to do so. This, according to these theories, means that States are always calculating and deliberating – even after having entered into an agreement – whether it is worthwhile from a cost-benefit perspective to comply.[32]

In relation to compliance with international law, this theoretical perspective means that in order to make States comply, an international agreement has to be combined with strict compliance review and a possibility to sanction

[30] Scott, J. and Trubek, D. M., 2002, p 8.

[31] Victor, D. G., Raustiala K. and Skolnikoff, E. B., 1998, p. 7.

[32] Mitchell, R. B., 2007, pp. 901–902; Barrett, S., 2003, generally. See also Snidal, D., "Rational Choice and International Relations," in Simmons, B. A., Risse-Kappen, T. and Carlsnaes, W. (eds.), *Handbook of International Relations*, SAGE Publications, 2013; and Guzman, A. T., 2008, pp. 25–70 and generally.

unwanted behavior. However, an opposite perspective is that when States agree to form and adopt an agreement in a specific issue area, it is a sign that States have made the assessment that they will benefit from cooperation on the issue in question. Still, rationalists argue that if not all Parties to an agreement comply and some instead act as free-riders, then the remaining Parties will lose rather than benefit from such cooperation. These kinds of scenarios are typically described as the "prisoner's dilemma."[33] In studies of domestic law, however, it is established that individuals obey because they view rules as legitimate, not because they fear punishment. In this view of law, violations are deterred more by informal social mechanisms than by top-down imposed sanctions.[34]

Within the logic of the perspective of rational choice theory, State actors behave as they do owing to explicit and instrumental calculations. The consequences of their actions and the alternatives available will thus influence their interests and choices. Typically, they will base their chosen behavior and actions only on what they deem to be best for them. They will therefore be strongly invested in determining the actions that are in their interests, gathering information and calculating the relative costs and benefits.[35] According to these ideas, then, an environmental treaty regime could influence this process of decision-making by affecting the consequences of engaging in certain desired actions or behaviors. Factors that could affect such decision-making are inter alia the State's position in the world relative to other States; material, economic, political and social resources; and the preferences and dispositions of its citizens.[36]

Another approach that is increasingly common among lawyers is the theoretical views on international relations stating that State behavior is more a response to the interplay of norms and identity. According to these theories, States will calculate their assessments of available choices and behavior based on how their choice would harm or help their interests. They will base these assessments on their apprehension of right and wrong, in relation to their position and the given situation. In such situations, international environmental agreements can also affect the choices and assessments made by States by codifying requirements to signal right or wrong and what is thereby

33 Barrett, S., 2003, pp. 3–4 and 53–61. See also Brunnée, J., 2006, pp. 7–10; Mitchell R. B., 2007, pp. 901–902.

34 Thompson, A., "Coercive Enforcement of International Law," in Dunoff, J. L. and Pollack, M. A. (eds.), *Interdisciplinary Perspectives on International Law and International Relations – The State of the Art*, Cambridge University Press, 2013, p. 507.

35 See e.g. Barrett, S., 2003, pp. 1–18.

36 Mitchell, R. B., 2007, pp. 901–902.

appropriate or inappropriate in different situations. This results in an understanding of compliance and noncompliance based on these factors and the States' desire to have a reputation of being appropriate. Thus, even if the environmental agreement as such does not establish any direct consequences for compliance or violation of the agreement, the placement of different behaviors into categories of right or wrong can have a significant influence on most actors.[37]

The negotiating process is in focus for this promotion of values, because States often negotiate agreements not only to regulate a common problem but also to promote their national interests. To the extent that States negotiate because they see that reaching an agreement on some issue is in their interests, it is likely that they will also adjust to it. The subsequent conforming behavior should thus be interpreted as a probable reflection of those interests, rather than as the influence of international law that codified those interests. This is also related to the inverse relationship of compliance and effectiveness. When agreements require little or no change in behavior or require behavioral changes the Parties planned to make anyway, we should expect high compliance – but we should not interpret this compliance as evidence of agreement influence. Agreements often reflect the lowest common denominator negotiations, so most States and companies will find themselves already in compliance.[38] Seen in the light of this reasoning, it would not mean much, since according to these theories, States adopt only laws with which they are already complying in some way.

8.2.2.2 Managerial Compliance

An opposite perspective to the rational approach is the compliance theories called the managerial approach.[39] One fundamental stepping-stone in this model is that it disregards rational choice theories and rather assumes that States have a propensity to comply. It is stated that even the most dedicated among rational choice theorists are beginning to acknowledge that they have set themselves an impossible task. The basic problem is that, on the assumption of

37 Mitchell, R. B., 2007, p. 902. See also March, J. G. and Olsen, J. P., "The Institutional Dynamics of International Political Orders," *International Organization*, Vol. 52, No. 4, 1998, pp. 948–954.

38 Mitchell, R. B., 2007, p. 904. See also Henkin, L., *How Nations Behave: Law and Foreign Policy*, Columbia University Press, 1979, p. 47, with the famous statement that "almost all nations observe almost all principles of international law and almost all of their obligations almost all of the time."

39 Chayes, A. and Handler Chayes, A., 1995, p. 3.

rational choice theory, most of the interesting situations generate not one determinate solution but a number of possible equilibriums. The theory cannot predict within its own terms which of these possible equilibriums will be chosen. Thus, as described previously, the choice finally made is not a product of simple, self-regarding value maximization, but of decisions made in a social and institutional context.[40] The opposite perspective of rational choice is the assumption that States are generally inclined to comply with international obligations. It seems logical to assume that this is the case in most situations, since States invest an enormous amount of time and effort in inter alia preparing, drafting and negotiating agreements. They then devote a lot of effort to monitoring, reporting and so forth. It seems unlikely that a State would put itself through such a huge process and debate provisions of the agreement if it did not take the view when signing the agreement that it would also be bound by such provisions, and thus, be limited in its actions. This combination of factors is not claimed to always lead automatically to compliance but supports the assumption of a general propensity among States to comply. These factors could thus also lead to better understanding and conclusion about what the real problems behind noncompliance involve.[41]

Even though there are occasions where States obviously have been deliberately and calculatedly noncompliant, the most common reasons for noncompliance are often more causal, such as ambiguity and indeterminate nature of treaty language, limitation on the capacity of Parties to carry out their undertakings, and the temporal dimension of the social, economic, and political changes contemplated by regulatory treaties.[42] As opposed to the idea of strict control, sanctioning, and the fear of punishment, these factors behind noncompliance explain and provide valid reasons that could excuse why a State's noncompliance. They may even justify a State behavior that is not at all compatible with compliance. It could even be compared with a plea, which, if successful, implies that the conduct is not a violation of agreement after all. It also puts a different light on what is necessary to help States with implementation and achieving compliance.[43] The managerial approach means that the

40 Ibid., 1995, p. 115.

41 Chayes, A. and Handler Chayes, A., 1995, pp. 3–4. See also e.g. Raustiala, K. and Slaugther, A-M., 2002, pp. 546ff; Downs, G. W., Rocke, D. M. and Barsoom, P. N., 1996, pp. 379–406.

42 See also Koskenniemi, M., "Environmental Cooperation in the Baltic Region," *Tulane Journal of International and Comparative Law*, Vol. 1, 1993, at p. 106, which argues that open-ended treaties such as the Helsinki Convention also creates increased probability for noncompliance, even making it difficult to assess what the obligations are.

43 Chayes, A. and Handler Chayes, A., 1995, pp. 10–11. See also Kirk, E. A., 2008, p. 236, where the author argues that treaties that meet noncompliance are embraced as part of an iterative process of developing understanding and the like are stronger.

best way of dealing with noncompliance in this regard is to help States overcome the deficits that obstruct compliance. This can be done through capacity-building, negotiating interpretations and providing other necessary resources and so forth.

With regard to implementation, interpretation and compliance, the managerial approach also suggests that if there is a degree of trust in those who are to apply the rules, a broader standard may be more effective than a series of detailed regulations, when it comes to realizing the general policy behind the law. If an agreement is too detailed, other kinds of problems could appear. A more precise rule may, for example, exclude a range of alternative scenarios, although these scenarios may be within the frame of regulatory application. Moreover, the more complex a problem is, the more extensive the regulatory structures will be. Having more inclusive regulatory formulations is also a way to avoid excessively complex rule systems and too much political friction. On the other hand, such indeterminate treaty language can also be exploited by States to justify their preferred course of action. However, if compliance is reviewed in some way and issues of interpretation arise and are handled with authority, a general debate often emerges that can further application of the laws, instead of the matter being assessed only in a two-party dispute. When such debate arises in the absence of intentional bad faith, a well-founded structure with expertise can be a good path or mechanism for clarifying the meaning of the rules.[44]

As discussed previously, the production of legal rules is linked to the apparatus of government, and compliance often involves public coercive action. One common attribute of almost all legislation is that it carries an obligation of obedience. Still, the appreciation of that obedience is felt at different intensities and differently depending on the object concerned.[45] In theory, the sovereign State is entitled to pursue its choices without regard to the reactions of others – at least as long as there is no comprehensive dispute settlement. However, this is no longer how the international community works in practice. Instead, the international community includes wide ranges of audiences – foreign and domestic – too many relationships, and too many linkages to other issues, and in practice a State cannot ignore them. Therefore, if a State is challenged as to implementation or conduct with regard to a legal regulation, the State must respond, almost by necessity. The State must then

44 Chayes, A. and Handler Chayes, A., 1995, pp. 11–12. See also Thompson, A., 2013, pp. 506–513, on similar theories on why States comply and the potential obstacles as well as incentives for effective enforcement.

45 Chayes, A. and Handler Chayes, A., 1995, p. 116; Raustiala, K. and Slaugther, A-M., 2002, pp. 544–545.

demonstrate that it has undertaken proper interpretation of the applicable rules and regulations.[46]

Efficiency in this regard is connected to the same ideas that are brought as arguments against rational choice theories on compliance. Since governmental resources for policy analysis and decision-making are costly and also often in short supply, a standard economic analysis tells us that States are unlikely to pursue continuous recalculations of costs and benefits of convention obligations, if circumstances have not changed significantly since the time of signing. The alternative – to follow a treaty rule – seems more likely, since it reduces costs and is more in line with traditional, routine-based bureaucratic State behavior. This in turn relates to the assumption that the State's interests were met in the treaty, since such an instrument does not have any power if it is not signed. States generally spend considerable effort and resources on defining and preparing State positions in international treaty negotiations. Hence, it could be assumed that State Parties would generally not enter into an agreement if that agreement went against its interests. Still, this position may be in relation to a vague notion that States also explore and learn more about the issue in question and discover what their interests are.[47] This process and the results are of course made more transparent due to the significant involvement of participants and their role in the negotiating process (Section 7.3). As a contrast, however, the international treaty-making process leaves a good deal of room for accommodating divergent interests. The treaty is in some measure a compromise. Still, problems of endemic noncompliance are likely to be more a result of the fact that the negotiating process did not succeed in incorporating a sufficiently broad range of the Parties' interests and less a result of willful disobedience.[48] Understanding this aspect is very important when evaluating and assessing compliance, enforcement and effectiveness of treaties.

8.3 ENFORCEMENT AND COMPLIANCE CONTROL IN INTERNATIONAL LAW AND THE EU

Together with the different aspects of compliance and perhaps with a parallel to the rational choice perspective, a common question of debate is whether international law matters at all if it is not enforceable.[49] International law and

46 Chayes, A. and Handler Chayes, A., 1995, p. 119.

47 Ibid., pp. 4–5, and ff.

48 Ibid., 1995, p. 7.

49 Mitchell, R. B., 2007, p. 894; D'Amato, A., "Is International Law Really 'Law'?," *Northwestern University Law Review*, Vol. 79, 1984–1985,p. 1293. Martin, L. L., 2012, p. 602.

international legal agreements are often compared to national legal systems, and thus, when it comes to compliance, the immediate thought is that a binding agreement needs to be accompanied by a mechanism for strict compliance control and sanctions.[50] This is rarely the case, however, when it comes to international agreements. It is furthermore a general principle in accordance with Article 33 of the UN Charter that disputes must be settled peacefully, although how that settlement will be carried out is to be decided by the Parties.

The EU legal regime is fundamentally different when it comes to enforcement: it is a supranational system and has its own court system. The EU Member States cannot choose to not be scrutinized by the EU Commission and the EU Court, since they have provided this competence and thus have given up some of their sovereignty in this regard (Section 2.2). In the system of international law, on the other hand, States themselves decide in relation to each other, and to each separate treaty, as to whether there should be a sanctioning or dispute settlement mechanism, including a referral of potential conflicts to an international court or tribunal.[51] This is rarely seen, however, mainly because States are generally unwilling to involve third Parties and put themselves at risk of being taken to trial. In addition, such actions are generally seen as an inefficient way to resolve conflicts arising from noncompliance, especially noncompliance in relation to environmental governance. Hence, it is viewed as particularly ineffective with regard to multilateral environmental agreements.[52]

According to theories of managerial compliance, as discussed previously, it is most often a lack of resources that makes States noncompliant, rather than intentional misinterpretation of the treaty or intentional desire to not comply.[53] It is also often difficult to claim or identify any specific State as directly responsible for noncompliance with environmental treaties in comparison to the case of trade, military or economic treaties, for example. In such treaties, the effects of noncompliance often create a more direct harm to other States, in comparison to noncompliance with protecting the environment. Despite this, a few environmental law cases have been brought to the International Court of Justice (ICJ).[54] However, the ICJ has been reluctant

[50] See, for example, the discussion in D'Amato, A., 1984–1985, pp. 1293–1301; Chayes, A. and Handler Chayes, A., 1995, pp. 1–4.

[51] Sands, P., et al., 2012, p. 159.

[52] Birnie, P., Boyle, A. and Redgwell, C., 2009, pp. 211–213 and pp. 237–239; Fitzmaurice, M. A. and Redgwell, C., "Environmental Non-compliance Procedures and International Law," *Netherlands Yearbook of International Law*, Vol. 31, 2000, pp. 36–38.

[53] Mitchell, R. B., 2007, pp. 908–910.

[54] For example, Argentina versus Uruguay in a case regarding Pulp Mills on the River Uruguay, *Pulp Mills on the River Uruguay (Argentina* v. *Uruguay)*, Judgment, ICJ Reports 2010, p. 14;

to apply and interpret international environmental law.[55] One reason is that legal proceedings are very costly, and it is claimed that the political and ad hoc nature of such sanctioning systems would also be insufficient from a legitimacy perspective.[56]

Dispute settlement through arbitration is primarily suited for scenarios where an apparent object is injured, or one specific State suffers the injuries and thus has its rights violated. Such scenarios are often difficult to identify in environmental law cases. The obstacles are often so grave that States have preferred to avoid the law of State responsibility and have instead tried their cases by other methods of establishing liability, using national law. For example, no modern pollution disaster has resulted in the adjudication of an international claim against the State concerned.[57] Dispute settlements through court procedures are not a very common or particularly effective way to solve such conflicts in practice. However, it is still important to discuss the potential as well as the limitations of this form of enforcement. An understanding of what it can and cannot offer could be essential in explaining other developments in the international legal system – not least the understanding related to the increase in focus and presence of other forms of compliance control in international environmental regimes.[58]

An environmental treaty must be able to ensure compliance with obligations – for example, of pollution control, cooperation and assessing transboundary risks. The difference between enforcement by arbitration or international court compared to more elaborated and nuanced nonconfrontational mechanisms, is significant in dealing with these facts. If an agreement provides a procedural right for a Party only when it is being injured in an event of breach or pollution damage, this agreement must be seen as inappropriate in relation to actions for controlling pollution. In this context with polycentric and diverse governance structures, with the large range of actors that are involved by such governance, such enforcement mechanisms would not contribute much to reducing pollution. The multiplicity of complex interrelated features and problems must be handled in a better way with regard to

Hungary versus Slovakia, regarding the Gabčíkovo–Nagymaros Dam Project, *Gabcikovo-Nagymaros Project (Hungary* v. *Slovakia)*, Judgement, ICJ Reports 1997, p. 7; and *Whaling in the Antarctic (Australia* v. *Japan: New Zealand intervening)*, Judgment, ICJ. Reports 2014, p. 226.

55 Zengerling, C., *Greening International Jurisprudence: Environmental NGOs before International Courts, Tribunals, and Compliance Committees*, Martinus Nijhoff Publishers, 2013, p. 191.

56 Chayes, A. and Handler Chayes, A., 1995, pp. 2–3.

57 Birnie, P., Boyle, A. and Redgwell, C., 2009, pp. 211–212; Thompson, A., 2013, pp. 510–513.

58 See, for example, the reasoning in: Fitzmaurice, M. A. and Redgwell, C., 2000, pp. 35–65.

complexity, if the protection of common interests – such as common resources or future generations – are to be guaranteed. Many environmental problems involve harm, which is subtle, cumulative, and manifested only after a long period of time. In these circumstances, a court procedure is not truly equipped to initiate the change or negotiations needed to create change. Instead, a mechanism, which is in a more constant dialogue with the States concerned, must be more appropriate.

Because of aspects like these, the development of international environmental law has moved toward a situation where States increasingly rely on intergovernmental commissions and meetings of treaty Parties as means of coordinating policy, developing the law, supervising its implementation, putting community pressure on individual States and resolving conflicts of interest. Such bodies also have greater flexibility and may be better at securing compliance than traditional forms of dispute settlement.[59] In short, this treaty mechanism is much better suited to large-scale, complex environmental cooperation than international court proceedings.

Liability for loss or damage is an elementary feature of a legal system. In international law, liability for transboundary damage is, in a similar way, also one of the oldest concepts in interstate disputes. Ever since the Trail Smelter case in 1941,[60] the no-harm principle has also been seen as a general principle of international environmental law. This principle implies that States are not allowed to cause environmental harm to other territories. As a fundamental feature of any kind of dispute settlement or compliance control mechanism in international legal systems, modern monitoring and sampling techniques have made it possible to track and calculate, with reasonable accuracy the amounts of transboundary pollution. Generally, structures for compliance review comprise rules and procedures, by which the Parties to international agreements exchange data, share information on implementation, monitor activities, assess the adequacy of existing commitments and handle problems of poor implementation.[61] This must therefore be seen as a highly important basis or platform for any environmental treaty.

59 Birnie, P., Boyle, A. and Redgwell, C., 2009, pp. 212–213. See also Brunnée, J., 2002, pp. 8–10.

60 *The Trail Smelter Arbitration Case* (*United States* v. *Canada*) 1941: The Trail Smelter case was a dispute regarding transboundary air-pollution involving Canada and the United States. It was one of the first international cases on environmental law and became the first step toward establishing the No-Harm Principle. See also Birnie, P., Boyle, A. and Redgwell, C., 2009, pp. 216–219.

61 Victor, D. G., Raustiala, K. and Skolnikoff, E. B., 1998, p. 16; Sands, P., et al., 2012, pp. 143–144 and pp. 161–167.

8.3.1 *Monitoring and Supervision*

From both the precautionary principle and the no-harm principle, it follows that States must have an overview of any actions, causes and potential effects from their activities that may harm the environment, both nationally and internationally. Environmental agreements generally incorporate some kind of obligation to track results or measures, and not least to report on the progress of implementation and its effects. Therefore, most States monitor their pollution and biodiversity in different ways, and through such monitoring, it is also possible to track breaches of agreements or environmental harm in other aspects due to inter alia pollution.[62]

Pollution can be defined as "the introduction by man of substances or energy, whether directly or indirectly, into the environment."[63] It is the relationship between these substances and their effects that combine to constitute pollution. This implies inter alia that overuse of resources or the impact of urban development on ecosystems – however harmful it may be – is not to be regarded as pollution according to the definition reflected here. In practice, however, what is considered as pollution is mostly limited to the substances of discharge that States have specifically agreed to control. Threats to the evironment from other activities are often monitored in other ways though. Not least the biodiversity conventions and directives require monitoring certain species, for example. The agreements and their annexes with details about the substances that should be controlled are often crucial in identifying the thresholds for pollution, before reaching harmful levels (i.e., threshold and limits for controlling slow variables, as discussed in the introduction).[64]

The key tasks that treaty supervisory bodies perform are those of information and data collection, receiving and reviewing reports on implementation by States, overseeing independent monitoring and inspection, and facilitating compliance with agreed standards of conduct. These obligations or standards will usually have a treaty basis, but the technique is also capable of applying rules of customary law or soft law.[65] Activities required by treaties and their programs for monitoring of different substances or activities are often crucial components in identifying and addressing international environmental problems. Treaty programs to monitor and model environmental processes may, for example, improve the quality of data on emissions and implementation and make it easier to set regulatory priorities.[66] In all treaty supervisory bodies, special attention is paid to how data is gathered

62 Birnie, P., Boyle, A. and Redgwell, C., 2009, p. 189.
63 Ibid., p. 189.
64 Ibid., p. 189.
65 See e.g. Sands, P., et al., 2012, pp. 624–636; Birnie, P., Boyle, A. and Redgwell, C., 2009, p. 240.
66 Victor, D. G., Raustiala, K. and Skolnikoff, E. B., 1998, p. 8.

and assessed. Many environmental agreements suffer from poor data collection, but data is also the main basis for treaty supervision bodies and functional compliance control. Although data collection may be lacking, requirements to report and compare data on a regular basis can still lead to improvements of the quality and quantity of the data reported.[67]

8.3.2 *Adjudication and Court Proceedings in International Environmental Law*

One obvious form of judicial review in international law that must also be considered when discussing enforcement and compliance procedures is settlement through court proceedings. As stated previously, one of the probably most famous examples of legal dispute settlement in international environmental law is the arbitration of the Trail Smelter case from 1941. This case concerned transboundary air pollution and involved only two States: the United States and Canada. Thus it was a less complex situation than most environmental harm cases that occur today. Although State responsibility for environmental harm is still tried in court or settled in arbitration, there are many reasons (Section 8.2) why this way of enforcing environmental law is not the most suitable and effective, especially if it is compulsory in nature.[68]

The inclusion of rules for a compulsory, binding, third-party dispute settlement in multilateral treaty regimes is often intended to provide an authoritative mechanism for resolving matters relating to compliance and implementation. It thus provides answers regarding interpretation or application of agreements, because defining the interpretation and application is a crucial step in deciding whether a State is in breach of the agreement obligations. The dispute settlement can involve the application of other rules of international law if the agreement so provides, or interpretation and application where other rules are taken into account. In accordance with general principles on treaty interpretation and the Vienna Convention, an element of evolutionary interpretation may thus be possible.[69] One of the disadvantages of this approach to enforcement is the adverse effect it has on

67 Ibid., pp. 18–19. See also Greene, O., "Implementation Review and the Baltic Sea Regime," in in Victor, D. G., Raustiala, K. and Skolnikoff, E. B. (eds.), *The Implementation and Effectiveness of International Environmental Commitments: Theory and Practice*, MIT Press, 1998, pp. 182ff.

68 Birnie, P., Boyle, A. and Redgwell, C., 2009, p. 211; Koskenniemi, M., "Peaceful Settlement of Environmental Disputes," *Nordic Journal of International Law*, Vol. 60, No. 1, 1991, pp. 74–80.

69 Birnie, P., Boyle, A. and Redgwell, C., 2009, p. 257, referring primarily to the Vienna Convention, Article 31(3). See also Linderfalk, U., 2007, pp. 161–195.

relations between States concerned; States are generally reluctant to provoke other States, even if a treaty violation has been established. Moreover, the complexity, length and expense of international litigation make bringing action a less attractive alternative – just like the technical character of environmental problems and the difficulties of proof that legal proceedings may entail also contribute to making bringing action less attractive. Yet another complicating factor is that many international agreements are vague and of an unsettled character, which makes it difficult to conclude when a breach has actually taken place.[70] One of the main concerns with court proceedings, however, may be a focus on granting of reparation as a response to violations of international law, rather than preventing environmental harm before it happens – especially considering that noncompliance often is related to a lack of resources or similar problematic reasons that are not mended by a court judgment.[71]

Despite having a status as the principal judicial organ of the UN, the ICJ enjoys no priority as a forum for dispute settlement. Instead, the jurisdiction of the ICJ – with regard to all international judicial and arbitral tribunals – is based on the consent of the State Parties to each dispute. Thus, there is no obligation to take any disputes to the ICJ. The ICJ is not the preferred forum under agreements that provide for compulsory binding settlement.[72] The LOSC, for example, has extensive provisions for compulsory settlement of disputes. LOSC allows the Parties to choose from various forums, including conciliation, several forms of arbitration, the ICJ and a specialized court called the International Tribunal for the Law of the Sea (ITLOS; Section 6.2).[73] While most scholars see this possibility to choose different forums as unproblematic, this part of international law causes concern for those who argue that international law is becoming increasingly fragmented and thus

[70] Birnie, P., Boyle, A. and Redgwell, C., 2009, p. 211; Jacobson, H. K. and Brown Weiss, E., 1998a, pp. 4–5. Cf. also the contrasting view in: Brunnée, J., 2002, pp. 37 ff., where a more dynamic system for development of environmental agreements is emphasized. See also Bodansky, D., 1999, pp. 606–611, on the need for nonconsensus decision-making.

[71] Handl, G., "Compliance Control Mechanisms and International Environmental Obligations," *Tulane Journal of International and Comparative Law*, Vol. 5, 1997, pp. 34–35. See also Chayes, A. and Handler Chayes, A., 1995, pp. 9–17.

[72] Sands, P., et al., 2012, pp. 169–172.

[73] LOSC, Part XV, includes different provisions on settlement of disputes. LOSC Article 287, provides for choice of procedures. According to this Article, a State party shall choose one or more means listed in the article for the settlement of disputes concerning the interpretation or application of the Convention. See also Birnie, P., Boyle, A. and Redgwell, C., 2009, pp. 250–251. See also Boyle, A. E., "Dispute Settlement and the Law of the Sea Convention: Problems of Fragmentation and Jurisdiction," *International and Comparative Law Quarterly*, Vol. 46, No. 1, 1997, pp. 37–54.

means that there is a risk to the basic foundation of law as a coherent system with coherent judgments and proceedings. Some also argue that free choice of forum diminishes the authority of the ICJ.[74]

Though the LOSC is an umbrella convention and refers most of the more specific regulation in marine regions to implementation of regional agreements, there are still some provisions regarding the environment that are directly applicable.[75] One example of application and assessment of these provisions by judicial process is the MOX Plant case, as discussed in Section 6.2.1.[76] As a provisional measure, ITLOS ordered that the UK and Ireland should cooperate and thus exchange information, monitor risks and effects and devise measures to prevent pollution generated by the operation of the plant.[77] In 2007 Ireland withdraw its claim and the case was thus terminated in 2008.[78]

As mentioned previously, however, a few environmental law cases have been brought before the ICJ. Most of the environmental law cases brought before this court have also involved procedural issues, such as issues related to the interpretation of the agreement or the obligation to notify States concerned and provide an Environmental Impact Assessment (EIA), rather than actual, identified environmental harm – although, of course, these are related issues. An EIA is an important tool to establish whether the rights of other States have been violated through breach of the no-harm principle, and for that reason, it is important in any environmental case.[79] Nevertheless, the ICJ has been reluctant to apply and interpret international environmental law.[80] Legal proceedings through courts have also had a limited role in developing international environmental law. In addition to the reluctance by the States to

74 See e.g. UN ILC Report 2006; Hafner, G., 2000; Koskenniemi, M. and Leino, P., 2002; Hafner, G., 2004; Dupuy, P-M., 2007.

75 LOSC, Article 197.

76 *Dispute Concerning Access to Information Under Article 9 of the OSPAR Convention, Final Award (Ireland* v. *the United Kingdom)* (2 July 2003) Permanent Court of Arbitration, ILM Vol. 42 (2003) p. 1118.

77 *The MOX Plant Case, Ireland* v. *United Kingdom*, Order No 3, Suspension of Proceedings on Jurisdiction and Merits, and Request for Further Provisional Measures, June 24, 2003.

78 Ireland formally notified the Arbitral Tribunal of the withdrawal of its claim against the United Kingdom on February 15, 2007. On June 6, 2008, the Tribunal issued Order No. 6, terminating proceedings. *The MOX Plant Case, Ireland* v. *United Kingdom*, Order No. 6, Termination of Proceedings, June 6, 2008.

79 For example, the case of *Gabcikovo-Nagymaros Project (Hungary* v. *Slovakia)*, Judgement, ICJ Reports 1997, p 7; *Pulp Mills on the River Uruguay (Argentina* v. *Uruguay)*, Judgment, ICJ Reports 2010, p. 14. See also more on the ICJ environmental case law in Zengerling, C., 2013, pp. 179–188.

80 Zengerling, C., 2013, pp. 191–194.

include such forms of dispute settlement into environmental agreements, arbitration or any other kind of judicial dispute settlements are also unfit to provide real solutions to environmental problems. An important decision of the ICJ, the Advisory Opinion Concerning the Threat or Use of Nuclear Weapons,[81] provides a good example. The decision concerned control of environmental risk and shows that it is possible to accommodate issues that are of public interest and which concern multilateral interests. The ICJ did stress the no-harm principle but did not in any other way take this opportunity to use environmental law principles and the position of the ICJ so as to bring about further progress on nuclear disarmament.[82]

For all the reasons mentioned above, enforcement through court procedure is generally seen as unfit for environmental law. The low number of cases brought before the court might also be due to uncertainty about the proper forum or the applicable law if the dispute straddles several treaties or the jurisdiction of the forum is limited. These uncertainties make the legal process difficult and hard to predict. This can result in precedents with unwelcome implications. Moreover, judicial proceedings and arbitration are generally less well adapted to the multidimensional character of many environmental problems and governance structures. More informal supervision through Meetings of the Parties to treaty regimes, including noncompliance procedures, are often more in line with the problems and causes of legal breach and are thus increasingly preferred – meaning that negotiated solutions are often preferred. In addition, the negotiated, nonconfrontational mechanisms often provide more dynamic forms of participation and standing. In arbitration, it is rare to find any provision for third-Party intervention. Before the ICJ and the ITLOS, third Parties may intervene only when the interpretation or application of a treaty to which they are Party is called into question.[83]

8.3.3 *Alternative Forms for Dispute Settlement and Compliance Control*

Court procedures, as stated, are rather ineffective and not particularly well adjusted to noncompliance with multilateral environmental agreements. Several additional reasons explain why this dispute settlement mechanism is rarely used by State Parties. There are several other mechanisms or noncompliance procedures that are more commonly applied. Their proceedings and

81 *Legality of the Threat or Use of Nuclear Weapons*, Advisory Opinion, ICJ Reports 1996, p. 226.
82 Birnie, P., Boyle, A. and Redgwell, C., 2009, pp. 212–213. See also Zengerling, C., 2013, p. 191.
83 See also Birnie, P., Boyle, A. and Redgwell, C., 2009, pp. 252–253.

decisions are often less strict and considered as nonconfrontational in comparison with a court procedure and ruling, which actually represents an exclusive competence given to a court. A number of environmental treaties have introduced formal noncompliance procedures in this other less confrontational form.[84] The most developed environmental agreements all include regular reporting by the Parties, reviews of these reports, and often on-site inspections. Many agreements also include procedures that allow for some enforcement of international commitments. Still, there is no single pattern by which such review structures develop.[85]

In contrast to bilateral arbitration and court procedures, alternative forms of treaty supervisory bodies perform a kind of supervision of compliance that could be seen as collective. The collective approach enables individual States to be held accountable for noncompliance in relation to all the other treaty Parties, and the review process may also involve NGOs as observers. The purpose of these treaty bodies is to move away from strict and authoritative interpretation of compliance with an agreement, toward a nonconfrontational mechanism that provides for more negotiation and mutual assistance.[86] Some of the features that are specific for such nonconfrontational compliance mechanisms are, for example, that the supervisory body does not need the consent of the respondent State before a process can be initiated.

Furthermore, standing – in the traditional, formal sense of a person being directly concerned – is not required to make a complaint. In most cases, any Party to the agreement or the secretariat of such instrument has the right to complain, and in some cases, NGOs and members of the public may also complain or provide information to the secretariats.[87] Pressures and scrutiny of other States in such intergovernmental forums may be effective, given that these

84 Sands, P., et al., 2012, pp. 163–167; Klabbers, J., "Compliance Procedures," in Bodansky, D., Brunnée, J. and Hey, E. (eds.), *The Oxford Handbook of International Environmental Law*, Oxford University Press, 2007, pp. 995–1003; Fitzmaurice, M. A. and Redgwell, C., 2000, pp. 35–65; Chambers, W. B., 2004, pp. 501–532.

85 Victor, D. G., Raustiala K. and Skolnikoff, E. B., 1998, p. 17.

86 Koskenniemi, M., 1991, pp. 81–86; Fitzmaurice, M. A. and Redgwell, C., 2000, pp. 39–43; Handl, G., 1997, pp. 32–37; Chayes, A. and Handler Chayes, A., 1995, pp. 17–28 and pp. 135–153. See also Kirk, E. A., 2008, on embracing noncompliance as a tool for developing environmental regimes and controlling marine pollution.

87 Birnie, P., Boyle, A. and Redgwell, C., 2009, p. 246; Handl, G., 1997, pp. 32–37; Zengerling, C., 2013, pp. 82–89. See also Chayes, A. and Handler Chayes, A., 1995, pp. 259–270; Epiney, A., "The Role of NGOs in the Process of Ensuring Compliance with MEAs," in Beyerlin, U., Stoll, P-T. and Wolfrum, R. (eds.), *Ensuring Compliance with Multilateral Environmental Agreements – A Dialouge between Practitioners and Academia*, Martinus Nijhoff Publishers, 2006, pp. 324–334; and, Ebbesson, J., 1997, pp. 57–61.

relations with other States are important to sustain.[88] A nonconfrontational compliance procedure could be seen as a way to avoid dispute or as alternative dispute resolution in the sense that a binding third-party court procedure is avoided. Thus, a strict binding decision is also avoided. It is easier to form a noncompliance review in these alternative compliance mechanisms, because more formal and strict dispute settlement is something that most States are very reluctant to accept – for several reasons. These procedures are based to a large extent on the managerial approach to compliance and the assumption that States normally intend to comply once they have ratified a treaty. The treaty Parties will usually seek consensus on the issue in dispute, and the process is a way to reinforce the stability, transparency, and legitimacy of the regime as a whole.[89]

Noncompliance procedures could be regarded as a logical extension of information gathering, monitoring and supervision by the MOP. In these procedures, there is an important difference: there is no formally independent third party involved in facilitating the agreement. The outcome of a negotiating noncompliance procedure can be focused on assistance or other inducements to encourage future compliance, but if necessary, more compelling responses are also possible.[90] In addition, compliance reviews in these nonconfrontational procedures are performed by a wide array of institutions, even if only some of them are formally dedicated to such tasks. Viewing functions of implementation and review, also as a system wider than just the specific task of a supervisory body, is crucial to performing an accurate assessment of how such functions contribute to the implementation and effectiveness of an international agreement. Studies suggest that decentralized systems work well because they distribute tasks according to capacity.[91]

One of the more famous nonconfrontational compliance procedures in this fashion is the noncompliance procedure adopted by the Parties to the Montreal Protocol on reducing the ozone-depleting substances – the first of

88 Birnie, P., Boyle, A. and Redgwell, C., 2009, p. 240.

89 Klabbers, J., 2007, pp. 1000–1005; Birnie, P., Boyle, A. and Redgwell, C., 2009, pp. 245ff.; Handl, G., 1997, pp. 34–37; Fitzmaurice, M. A. and Redgwell, C., 2000; Chayes, A. and Handler Chayes, A., 1995, generally. See also Franck, T. M., *Fairness in International Law and Institutions*, Clarendon Press, 1995, pp. 7–8 and pp. 380–412, where it is argued that legitimacy contributes to compliance. The elements of legitimacy described are equal fairness among States, which managerial noncompliance mechanisms and stakeholder participation contribute to.

90 Handl, G., 1997, pp. 30–45; Sands, P., et al., 2012, pp. 143–144 and pp. 161–167; Koskenniemi, M., 1991, pp. 81–86.

91 Victor, D. G., Raustiala K. and Skolnikoff, E. B., 1998, p. 17.

its kind when established in 1990.[92] The LRTAP against air pollution has a similar procedure.[93] The compliance procedure of the Montreal Protocol, based on the Implementation Committee, has been established on a permanent basis. The Committee is composed of ten Parties elected by the Meeting of the Parties, for two years, on the basis of equitable geographical distribution.[94] The compliance procedure can be invoked by any Party to the protocol or by the secretariat, which can submit information if there are alleged problems with compliance. The Implementation Committee receives the complaint and seeks further information. It is also the main task of the Committee to consider submissions, information and observations made to it and then seek an appropriate solution on the basis of respect for the provision of the Protocol. However, the final decision in such matters is taken by the Meeting of the Parties, to which a report on the Committee's recommendations is sent. The Meeting of the Parties will thus decide formally on steps to take to bring about full compliance. These can include the provision of appropriate financial, technical, or training assistance to help the Party comply.[95] The Climate Change Convention also provides this kind of compliance review, but this is a softer multilateral consultative process to resolve questions regarding implementation. Conducted by a panel of experts, rather than by other Member States, it remains nonjudicial, nonconfrontational and advisory rather than supervisory. No sanctions of any kind can be imposed, not even suspension of rights and privileges; there is power only to recommend measures to facilitate cooperation and implementation, and to clarify issues and promote understanding of the Convention.[96]

Another kind of compliance review process, and one that is even more innovative, is the Compliance Committee for the 1998 Aarhus Convention. The Aarhus Convention Compliance Committee (ACCC) has also

92 Bodansky, D., 2010, p. 248. The Implementation Committee was established in accordance with Article 8 of the Montreal Protocol and with decision II/5 of the Second Meeting of the Parties to the Montreal Protocol.

93 See e.g. Kuokkanen, T., "Practice of the Implementation Committee under the Convention on Long-Range Transboundary Air Pollution," in Beyerlin, U., Stoll, P-T. and Wolfrum, R. (eds.), *Ensuring Compliance with Multilateral Environmental Agreements – A Dialouge between Practitioners and Academia*, Martinus Nijhoff Publishers, 2006, pp. 39–51.

94 Decision IV/5 of the Fourth Meeting of the Parties to the Montreal Protocol.

95 See the Montreal Protocol Secretariat at http://ozone.unep.org/en/institutions. See also e.g. Sarma, K. M., "Compliance with the Multilateral Environmental Agreement to Protect the Ozone Layer," in Beyerlin, U., Stoll, P-T. and Wolfrum, R. (eds.), *Ensuring Compliance with Multilateral Environmental Agreements – A Dialouge between Practitioners and Academia*, Martinus Nijhoff Publishers, 2006, pp. 28–38.

96 Birnie, P., Boyle, A. and Redgwell, C., 2009, pp. 246–247.

established a non-confrontational, non-judicial, and consultative procedure.[97] This compliance procedure is also open for members of the public and NGOs to bring complaints before the Committee. The Compliance Committee produces recommendations to the Parties with suggestions for the development of the implementation of the Aarhus Convention, or inter alia capacity building. The rulings by the ACCC also interpret and clarify the provisions of the convention, and a body that could be regarded as case law is emerging (Section 7.5.2). Generally, the ACCC is an independent committee with an aim of transparency and NGO involvement compliance procedures. In all of these respects, the Aarhus procedure is significantly stronger than any other currently in operation.[98]

As in the case of climate change or ozone depletion, as well as ocean pollution, noncompliance affects all Parties to the treaty. Therefore, a mechanism for securing compliance that is multilateral in character and allows all Parties, as well as NGOs, to participate is a great merit. Although it is possible to accommodate a multiplicity of participants in judicial proceedings, as has been shown by the ICJ, it is not easy to do so.[99] Instead, nonconfrontational settlements typically facilitate more readily than judicial processes the necessary input of scientific and technical expertise required to deal with issues of compliance under agreements of this kind, while also guiding Parties to better performance in accordance with the treaty.[100]

8.3.4 *Enforcement and Compliance Control in the EU*

As stated previously (Chapter 3 and 7), the EU regime is different from the control systems connected to international law and international treaties. As noted, the EU structure is based on the competence of conferred powers by the Member States. This means that in some issue areas, the Member States have transferred parts of their own sovereign rights (i.e., the rights of lawmaking and decision-making) to the EU.[101] In comparison to international law that must first be accepted and ratified by the State before it becomes binding, the

97 In accordance with the Aarhus Convention, Article 15.

98 Kravchenko, S., "The Aarhus Convention and Innovations in Compliance with Multilateral Environmental Agreements," *Colorado Journal of International Environmental Law and Policy*, Vol. 18, No. 1, 2007, pp. 1–50.

99 As in the case of the *Legality of the Threat or Use of Nuclear Weapons*, Advisory Opinion, ICJ Reports 1996, p. 226.

100 Birnie, P., Boyle, A. and Redgwell, C., 2009, pp. 247–248; Handl, G., 1997.

101 In accordance with Article 5(1) and (2), as well as 4(1) TEU.

EU legal order entails that the laws adopted become binding on the Member States without individual State approval or ratification. The new law is already indirectly accepted with the transfer of competence. In this way, individual Member States have abandoned the ability to block legislation adopted by the EU. However, it is only legislation that is supported by a qualified majority of Member States representing a qualified majority of the EU citizens that can be adopted.[102]

The European Commission has an important role in the EU institutional structure, especially in regard to compliance – since it has the responsibility to supervise and enforce compliance.[103] It is the task of the Commission to ensure that all EU primary and secondary environmental law is applied.[104] Moreover, the Commission has the exclusive right to initiate (and bring) a case before the EU Court.[105] Still, as discussed in Chapter 7 (Sections 7.3.4 and 7.5.3), and in comparison to most compliance review mechanisms in international environmental law, there are no direct, formal pathways for the public to participate in or review Commission decisions and work. The monitoring is ensured by the general Commission administration.[106] Administrative units do not make active reviews of the implementation; they are heavily dependent on information from the public through so-called citizen complaints. There are no formal requirements on how such a complaint should be formulated, since the Commission has broad competence to act and start an inquiry even if there is no express suspicion or evidence according to Article 17 TFEU. The Commission also has no obligation to take such complaints into consideration. Environmental NGOs and other actors put significant external pressure on Commissioners through such complaints in order to have compliance reviewed in matters where they believe that a State is not abiding by EU law.[107]

Since it is primarily the EU Commission that is responsible for controlling compliance and enforcement, most breaches of EU legislation are also primarily handled by the EU Commission. The Commission publishes inter alia annual reports on monitoring and application of EU law, including

[102] Article 289 TFEU. See more in Langlet, D. and Mahmoudi, S., 2016, pp. 22–23.

[103] Article 17(1) and (2) EUT.

[104] Krämer, L., 2011, p. 400.

[105] Article 17(1) EUT, and additionally Article 258 TFEU about the right to take a member stat to the EU Court.

[106] Krämer, L., 2011, p. 400.

[107] Ibid., pp. 402–405. For example, the European Environmental Bureau (the Federation of Environmental Citizens Organizations) states on their home page, "Our policy officers are in almost constant dialogue with the European institutions (Commission, Parliament and Council)," at www.eeb.org/index.cfm/about-eeb/how-the-eeb-works/.

environmental regulation, but these reports do not provide complete transparency or coherent, reliable data. Nor do any other EU institutions contribute to any extent to the monitoring.[108] If the Commission suspects that a Member State is noncompliant with a legal act adopted by the EU, the Commission shall first approach the State concerned and initiate communication in the matter. The State is given an opportunity to explain their intentions through such communication with the EU Commission, and the commission will respond, providing statements on the EU position regarding proper interpretation and implementation. During such communication, the EU Commission can also provide suggestions on how the State in question could change their application of the law in order to comply. Communications between the EU Commission and a Member State can proceed for a long time. As a last resort, the Commission can refer such matters to the EU Court for a more authoritative interpretation of the law (as stated previously). The Court will deliver a judgement and may also decide on remedies in the form of a penalty payment (Section 2.2.1).[109]

The court proceedings in the EU are important in the sense that the Court actively contributes to the development and interpretation of EU law. Just like international treaties, the law adopted in the EU is often vague as a result of compromise during the negotiations. Thus further interpretation by the Court defines the law in important ways, although this should be done in light of the original treaty; it may still be controversial because it could strike out the agreements made in negotiations. Taken further, with regard to the EU legislation resulting from the international treaties to which the EU is a Party, the EU Court will also indirectly interpret these treaties.[110]

8.4 SUMMARY AND CONCLUSIONS

As stated in the introduction to this chapter, an important issue for resilience governance is to control slow ecological variables and thereby their resulting feedbacks. This must also be the aim of law for resilience. Ultimately, this concerns the effectiveness of and compliance with the legal instruments, and their potential goal achievement. Just as stated regarding stakeholder compliance, the Resilience Feature of Operationalization, Monitoring, Compliance

108 Krämer, L., 2011, pp. 400–401.

109 This is according Article 258 TFEU. See also Krämer, L., 2011, pp. 406–408.

110 Article 216 TFEU. To some extent, this depends on the given circumstances of the treaty; see Langlet, D. and Mahmoudi, S., 2016, pp. 128–129.

and Trust Building, is also connected and dependent on the other components of the legal design for resilience. The first component addressed and analyzed in this study are reflecting functions that aim to create institutional structures that are compatible with the ecosystem, thus being able to create an ecosystem fit in measures applied. This involves structures that are dynamic and not necessarily stable – as opposed to how law traditionally is created. Moreover, the role of stakeholders and pathways for participation are both to be part of these dynamic structures, as well as participating in monitoring. Thus, pathways for participation may be a bridge between the first two components and the last.

It has also been stated in this chapter that compliance and effectiveness are important and related issues when reviewing environmental law approaches in regulatory instruments. They are also important concepts to discuss in regard to environmental complexity. Generally, the effectiveness of a treaty is assessed in relation to the extent that compliance is achieved; it is ineffective if States fail to meet their obligations. Effectiveness can also be assessed in relation to whether States change behavior, or more specifically, it can be assessed in relation to the environmental effects that can be identified as a result of measures taken. However, the latter kind of effectiveness is particularly difficult to assess in relation to new adaptive legal approaches, framework legislation and measures taken with the ecosystem approach.

Compliance in its most direct form is seen as a function of two factors: the obligation established by a rule and the actual conduct or results of those subject to an obligation. However, as stated, this view is based on two conditions. The first condition is that it must be clear what a rule imposes and the second is that the goal of the rule is measurable. However, when reviewing complex environmental problems, new governance approaches and the ecosystem approach – as in resilience law – these conditions cannot always be met. As described previously, there are a number of factors that complicate such evaluations of compliance. If the obligations established are unclear, it will be difficult to identify the required (or prohibited) conduct, or if measures taken within the given obligations do not immediately show a result because of time lags or other natural factors, then as a consequence, it will be impossible to categorize the behavior conducted by the States concerned in terms of compliance or noncompliance. For this reason, different forms of monitoring and reporting have been developed. In addition to a number of ways to assess compliance and effectiveness, it has also been made clear that there are different definitions of what signifies compliance and how laws are best enforced.

There is an important divide in perspectives on compliance, where the first perspective reflects the theory that strong enforcement mechanisms are needed to ensure implementation and compliance. This perspective, however, includes a somewhat controversial presumption that States will generally be intentionally noncompliant.[111] The opposing theory is that States have a predisposition for compliance, and therefore noncompliance should be met with a softer managerial approach.[112] Very bluntly, these perspectives can be seen as representing either a legal system with competence to impose sanctions and take States to some kind of tribunal for dispute settlement or a legal structure that promotes a system of supervision and negotiation-based, nonconfrontational compliance mechanisms. The latter is built on the assumption that noncompliance is generally due to factors other than intent – for example, political changes, a lack of resources or even a misinterpretation of the agreement.

The more negotiation-based managerial approach to compliance is increasingly common, with different forms of nonconfrontational compliance mechanisms in international environmental treaties. Still, even if they are not that common, the more traditional kind of compliance control tribunals still dominates the view on compliance review. However, even where they exist, tribunal mechanisms are rarely applied to enforce compliance. The reasons for this are many. States are generally very reluctant to engage in a court procedure where they risk a loss of sovereignty and authority. Most of these dispute settlement procedures therefore build on the prior acceptance by States and cannot be triggered spontaneously without consent, and this makes them difficult to initiate. Another reason is that a bilateral procedure is usually not quite sufficient to solve problems occurring with regard to a multilateral treaty and with regard to complex problems in common areas. However, another form of more comprehensive court procedure is established in the EU – which always follows a process of EU Commission mediation and communication with Parties on their implementation. The environmental laws of the EU are enforced differently than international environmental treaties. The EU legal regime has a stricter compliance structure with the potential to put significant pressure on the Member States to comply, thereby adding another layer of complexity to the issues of compliance in international settings. The EU legal regime is often perceived as more effective in achieving a higher level of compliance. The review of compliance with EU law is not

111 See e.g. Mitchell, R. B., 2007.

112 The most famous and widely applicable example of this approach is presented in Chayes, A. and Chayes, A. H., 1995.

comprehensive in its evidence that the enforcement is more effective, although it does show that States have respect for the EU court procedure.

It is important to emphasize in this context that there is no guarantee that compliance also leads to effectiveness and changes in relation to the problem (i.e., that it truly affects the slow variables). The obligations or measures stated by the treaty must be taken into account when discussing compliance. Depending on the treaty design and the obligations established by the treaty, compliance alone could be a poor indication of a treaty's value. The treaty itself might be either unnecessary or insufficient for the problems being addressed, or perhaps it does not demand any significant changes to be made by the Parties. When this is the case, it is more interesting to evaluate the effectiveness of the obligations or measures agreed upon.[113] When it comes to ensuring compliance in terms of behavioral change, or any such assessment of the implementation of legal regulatory measures, this validation does not automatically entail ecosystem change or that environmental problems are also effectively abated. Nevertheless, it is a fact that implementation and compliance are the most direct contributions that the legal system can achieve in this regard.

As stated previously, studies suggest that sometimes there may even be an inverse relationship between effectiveness and compliance with some types of standards (i.e., that full and perfect compliance might mean that the requirements in a treaty are set at a very low level). Therefore, less strict compliance may be preferable if it is related to high aims and obligations of the treaty. Seen in this perspective, the effectiveness of a treaty with a low compliance standard may be better than one with perfect compliance. While attention to compliance is important, it must be understood and evaluated in context.

Since international legal instruments generally are quite vague and flexible, it is difficult to assess not only when States are in compliance but also what is actually required by the States and, in the end, the results of any measures taken. Effectiveness of legal regulations, assessed as to the degree to which they actually lead to changes in behavior, may thus be the most appropriate means for solving environmental problems.

So, in short, the Resilience Feature of Operationalization, Monitoring, Compliance and Trust Building, is not only the last component in a legal design for social-ecological resilience; it is also the one that ties al other features together. If compliance is ineffective, all other efforts are in vain. After all, the main contribution of law to resilience governance overall must be

[113] Bodansky, D., 2010, p. 254.

the fact that law is the only instrument we have that can force States and other actors into action. So, if the operationalization, compliance and trust building is weak, it will affect the whole legal structure. However, at the same time, the mechanisms for Operationalization, Monitoring, Compliance and Trust Building, and how they should be designed, depends on the other components for social-ecological resilience.

9

Conclusions – Effective Legal Design for Resilience Governance

This study has reviewed the compatibility of some of the main features of social-ecological resilience governance with international and EU law. The purpose of this review was to identify legal and extra-legal approaches, mechanisms and other legal components that may create the basis for a legal design that contributes to social-ecological resilience. This is in line with the overall purpose of the book, namely to explore new theories and concepts with a focus on how international and EU environmental law can become more adjusted and effective in relation to the Anthropocene, with increasingly complex threats to the earth system. This purpose included a threefold aim: (1) to explore the possibilities at hand within the scope of already existing legal regimes, (2) to propose a tool for assessing the potential effectiveness or vulnerability of environmental laws and legal systems, and (3) to reveal the necessary components for designing environmental laws or legal regimes equipped for an increasingly unpredictable earth system. The baseline for the study has been the assumption that laws that are compatible with and can contribute to social-ecological resilience governance are more effective and fit for the era of the Anthropocene. Hence, it is an important task is to find out how and by which measures and mechanisms law contributes to effective governance in this regard – a legal design for social-ecological resilience.

Research on governance for social-ecological resilience takes the perspective of the environment as a complex, dynamic, continuously changing and integrated social-ecological system where human actors and institutions are seen as nested and intertwined with the ecological systems. This theoretical perspective also emphasizes that social-ecological systems may change, flip, enter alternative states and cross irreversible thresholds as a result of pressures such as pollution, unless the system is endowed with conditions of strong resilience – or resistance – to such pressures. This perspective entails certain prerequisites for governance approaches. The prerequisites for resilience governance could also be a good basis for answering how law can approach the regulation of complex nonlinear environmental problems. Theories of social-ecological resilience also provide guidance for integrating and operationalizing the ecosystem approach.

In order to make the concept of social-ecological resilience and resilience governance comprehensible in a legal context, the study first established some general governance features that represent the core of resilience governance. these features are adaptivity, flexibility and transformation; multidimensional and polycentric structures; stakeholders and structures for participation; and operationalization, monitoring, compliance and trust building. These features or components of resilience governance can be seen as the core of what a legal design for social-ecological resilience should also reflect in order to be effective. However, to be effective law and legal design must also safeguard some of the legal principles and legal characteristics that form the core of the law and its role as a stable institutional base with binding requirements and the ability to force actors into a certain behavior. Based on these prerequisites, the resilience features were then reviewed from the point of view of international and EU law. Analyzing each feature separately has provided a picture of both obstacles and compatibility with law in each separate part, and as well finding out what kinds of legal measures, approaches and mechanisms that respond to each feature. This was also important in order to find out in more detail how law can also be assessed in relation to each feature. Although, in the end, the legal system as well as the governance system for social-ecological resilience must reflect all features to some extent.

The study reviewed both possible matches and potential obstacles where law may not sufficiently reflect the features of resilience governance. However, it also unveiled legal mechanisms that contribute in other ways than expected. All in all, a general conclusion is that law has many important features that match resilience governance and thus have the potential to form an important basis for resilience governance in many different settings. Of course, law also has limitations, in comparison to the aim of the resilience features. This is often connected to both the overarching roles of law and the purpose of the rule of law; law cannot be unconditionally flexible or adaptive and must guard the prerequisites of a functioning legal system.

There is also a difference between international and EU law. To some extent, these different legal systems also complement each other. Both EU and international law provide for basic adaptivity and flexibility; together with national law, they create both polycentric and multidimensional systems and provide different forms of pathways for participation. An important difference between EU and international law is also the compliance control and enforcement mechanisms. Another significant difference is that EU law has to a much wider extent established adaptive, open and goal-based laws that are often also reviewed in an adaptive cycle. This is not often seen in international law. However, the layer of international laws is often complementary to EU law and can be more strictly implemented through EU law, since incentives for States to implement certain substantive rules are stronger if they are obligated by both international and EU laws; this creates a form of redundancy. The implementation is of course even stronger when the EU is a Party to an international agreement. An important part of coordinating these different levels or systems of legislation is played by stakeholders. Although the strictly legal definition of stakeholders or those formally participating in a legal structure is more limited than if seen from a general governance perspective, the roles of these actors in the institutional structure are equally important.

The legal systems are built according to traditional structures set out both on how laws relate to one another but also by jurisdiction at different levels. Sometimes these limits set out by and for the law also creates limits for governance – not least in a transboundary or international scene. However, it is important to keep in mind that these features of law and legal systems are also what gives law its other unique characteristics. The fact that law is the only tool that can also force actors into certain actions or behaviors. This aspect of law and legal systems is also an important aspect of why law is a necessary part of governance, in addition to the more general steering mechanism of governance systems. It is moreover important to realize that the legal components cannot only be reviewed separately. The legal design that these different components create together is dependent on how the different components are composed and how they affect each other. Hence, the legal design and the role of law for social-ecological resilience also depends on this interplay.

9.1 ADAPTIVITY, FLEXIBILITY AND TRANSFORMATION

The chapter on adaptive and flexible legal mechanisms reviewed adaptability, flexibility and transformability within law. International law can provide for adaptivity and flexibility in many different ways, both directly and indirectly. How this takes shape in a legal instrument is related to issues of institutional design and how the provisions and general obligations are formulated. The development of environmental law, with environmental law principles, new approaches (not least the ecosystem approach), new structures and different kinds of legal mechanisms, has promoted flexible and adaptive features in law. Environmental law has been designed to reflect or integrate both flexibility and adaptability, with the aim of responding to environmental variations and the need for continuous review. Thus legal regulations can also represent the functions of adaptive governance in this regard. In EU environmental law, some directives are designed specifically to be adaptive and flexible in their approach to the regulation of environmental problems. While these directives, just like international law, also include principles or concepts with specific adaptive or flexible features, they primarily integrate flexibility and adaptability through their overall design and their way of imposing requirements. International law can be regarded as flexible and adaptive in its core structure too, but flexibility is then often a result of a wide margin of discretion for the States in implementing the agreement and the fact that the requirements in an international agreement are often vague. Such features are thus not an intentional design but instead often due to the complicated process of agreeing on a treaty text. However, most international agreements do include mechanisms for amending or complementing the provisions, as well as providing other elaborations of the main provisions. This is done in response to environmental change or change in the knowledge about the problem and its solutions – typically an adaptive feature. Regardless of whether these mechanisms were deliberately added to these instruments, the features that follow add important functions to the regulatory system, seen in the light of governance for social-ecological resilience. However, any flexible legal mechanisms must also be seen in relation to the overall structure of the legal regime. Flexibility and a wide margin of discretion could also create leeway for States in their implementation. Thus, the case of wide flexibility – whether intentional or unintentional – should be combined with other complementary features, especially a mechanism for compliance review.

Compliance review is connected to the issue of transformability. International law and international agreements are built on a structure of both form and substance. To accomplish transformability in legal governance (i.e., for law to be a substantial driver for change in a social-ecological system), a combination of form and substance is of importance. The interplay or relation between these different sides to the agreement is significant for its effectiveness. If the requirements are not very clear, as in the case of vague substance, more weight is given to a thorough system for monitoring and enforcement. Otherwise, a high level of flexibility in a legal instrument could contradict the possibility for law to control State behavior.

For a long period of time, the EU has focused on developing open structures and new governance. This has been less acknowledged in international law. However, the role of international governing organizations has changed rapidly in recent decades. This has significant consequences for adaptability and flexibility in international institutional structures. The environmental laws of the EU have developed adaptive features both by creating framework legislation and by opening up for more direct cooperation with stakeholders. Additionally, both international law and the EU legal regime apply environmental law principles, which are definitely an important tool for creating flexible regulatory instruments. They are also important in directing focus to the environment and ecosystem in regulation. Implementation of the ecosystem approach has also brought flexible and open structures into the regulatory instruments.

9.2 MULTIDIMENSIONAL AND POLYCENTRIC STRUCTURES

The next chapter, which is part of the examination of the overarching question of effective measures and mechanisms, explored multidimensional, dynamic legal structures and overlapping regulation and reviewed the resilience features of cross-scale interaction, multilevel structures, diversity and redundancy. A first conclusion is that the combination of multiple applicable legal regimes and instruments expresses a polycentric structure and diversity of measures similar to the structures emphasized in resilience governance. It is also clear that, to some extent, such structures create significant change and diversity in approaches and measures in the legal regimes. These features and questions are directly related to the interplay of international and EU law.

Other related issues are diversity of measures and redundancy, allocation of authority, coordination and ecosystem match. One of the more difficult questions to answer is what a multitude of overlapping regulatory instruments and requirements entail for the States that are to implement these. It is not evident that the implementation is characterized by diversity, although the multiple incentives to take measures accompanying overlapping regulations still resemble a form of redundancy. Due to the flexibility in the system and the nested regulatory structures, coordination is necessary to create incentives for ambitious and more cost-effective implementation. Rational choice theories hold that multiple environmental regimes could trigger a race to the bottom if an issue is not strictly regulated. Furthermore, actors have increasingly emphasized that the sheer proliferation of institutions, issues and agreements places serious stress on the legal system. This, it is suggested, creates a number of obstacles for an effective legal system. However, in practice, nothing seems to verify this position, although different forms of coordination – not least through different forms of participation – is important to counteract the drawbacks of polycentric systems.

One of the reasons from a resilience perspective for having polycentric or multilevel structures is to create ecosystem match. Polycentric and multidimensional legal structures do not in themselves create ecosystem match, as aimed for in resilience theories. While they provide the potential for a more dynamic regulatory approach, they are focused on the environmental or ecological perspective. Thus, the adoption of the ecosystem approach becomes important as a legal mechanism for adjusting measures to the appropriate ecological scale and implementing ecosystem-based measures. The ecosystem approach and goal-centered regulatory instruments also coordinate the polycentric regulatory structures, since they link both the environmental goal and other requirements to very specific ecological targets and indicators. Even if the goal is not achieved according to the timetable set out, it plays a significant role in coordinating polycentric structures. However, in order to create such an ecological match through this coordination, it is of crucial importance that the goals and indicators are relevant and accurately assessed with respect to the problem. Such process also creates a managerial platform for discussion of measures which nevertheless provide incentives and initiatives for new measures and further developments of the plans for measures.

9.3 STAKEHOLDERS AND STRUCTURES FOR PARTICIPATION

In the chapter on participation, the resilience feature of stakeholder participation was reviewed and evaluated. In social-ecological resilience theories, stakeholder participation represents a wide spectrum of features and functions but is primarily about assuring that those concerned and connected to an environmental problem are involved in planning for measures and the like. Similar features and functions are also reflected in international and EU environmental law. From a legal perspective, participation is also meant to involve those concerned in measures and decision-making regarding environmental matters, but the concept of participation is generally framed differently. Stakeholder participation is also a prominent feature in international environmental law, although the term *stakeholder* is less applicable in a legal context. The essence of this term is that someone has an interest in the issues at stake. Sometimes such stakeholders are instead presented as actors, NGOs, the public or those with similar intents but more limited application. Participation or actor involvement takes place in many different ways in legal structures as well, through both formal and informal pathways.

Democratic elements are connected to stakeholder participation, both in law and how participation is proposed in social-ecological resilience research, and especially so in terms of issues of legitimacy and accountability. Where participation is provided for, the participatory role will often be to scrutinize laws, related decisions and the implementation measures, as well as for monitoring and control. Although the concept of legitimacy can be described, defined and interpreted from different perspectives, the legal system and the rule of law generally rely on structures that promote formalized participation. In law, public participation and information are important aspects of the democratic system. Therefore, the legal structures and pathways for participation have a significant impact on issues of democratic legitimacy and could increase accountability and transparency in the system, although questions on legitimacy and accountability in the system of international law go far beyond this. In legal structures, pathways to participation also create an important basis for adaptive measures.

NGOs are often included and provided with legal rights; thus they can represent both the environment itself and broader stakeholder groups. While open channels for participation lead the way for adaptive mechanisms, monitoring and information transfer, the roles of participation and the pathways for such participation in the legal system are different from the concept and form for participation in governance in general. Still, to some extent, all three forms of participation serve similar purposes and are comparable to the features and functions presented with regard to stakeholder participation in resilience theories. The possibility to take local knowledge into account in local management is one such purpose. This is also a way to create an ecosystem match. Actors involved are often referred to as local actors in resilience management. However, since the actors concerned in the legal context are defined by legal criteria, this may sometimes be interpreted differently in law.

Another purpose is to build bridges to actors between different institutional levels. While the similarity may be apparent at first, other forms of similarities are related to the fact that actors concerned still have the possibility to affect at least forms and details in the implementation and often provide significant input. They will thus most likely not experience that laws and management decisions are something imposed only from above, at least to the same extent as otherwise. This is of great importance for the issue of legitimacy (and democracy).

To some degree, there is more direct access to justice on the State level and in the EU institutions, much thanks to the Aarhus Convention. However, judging from ECJ case law, the EU Aarhus Regulation contains limitations in its application. This is problematic in relation to far-reaching mechanisms for decision-making and setting regulatory indicators that are not direct requirements within the directive as such, as found within the EU framework directives, for example. It is crucial for such regulatory structures to rely on broad access to justice if they are to have a chance to review such decisions. The lack of access to justice with regard to the ECJ creates an obstacle, as it largely excludes NGOs from having EU decisions reviewed in practice.

9.4 MONITORING, COMPLIANCE AND TRUST BUILDING

The last question that the study has aimed to answer relates to compliance and the possibilities for ensuring monitoring, enforcement and control in complex environmental governance. As stated previously, most of the resilience features are interdependent and connected. While they have been assessed and reviewed as separate categories or themes, the answer to whether they are effective depends much on how they interact, as well as on how they are operationalized and enforced.

However, the different features also contribute to and affect the possibilities to assess compliance, enforce measures and perform some form of compliance review. Increased flexibility and adaptivity might make it more difficult to assess and enforce compliance. On the other hand, with reasonably clear compliance review, this flexibility will also be an important feature in providing for effectiveness. Flexibility offers the possibility to deal with complexity. The adaptive features serve this purpose; they have also introduced a new system for monitoring.

Generally, assessing compliance comes down to a few crucial issues – that is, whether the State Parties are performing their obligations, whether they are changing behavior as a result of regulation and whether the aims of the regulation are being achieved. In flexible legal structures with a large margin of discretion and without specific requirements on State conduct, it is difficult to assess compliance because it is not fully clear what the States are actually required to do. Further problems may also occur in relation to complex environmental problems where the measures taken are difficult to assess. Besides the fact there is very little on which to base any assessments of effectiveness, it also means that mutual trust in the region will be weaker. The will to take action and implement forceful measures will be less in States if there is a large margin for free-riding and, in addition, if the Parties cannot be sure that there is equity in the measures taken. However, with a shift toward more adaptive cyclic reviews and coordination of different indicators and actors, managerial compliance and nonconfrontational compliance mechanisms may be a new tool to create increased compliance in the future.

9.5 FINAL REMARKS AND REFLECTIONS

The study has sought answers regarding what kind of legal approaches, measures or mechanisms are potentially effective for addressing environmental complexity, based on the theories on social-ecological resilience and resilience governance. The basis for finding such answers has been the resilience features that provide important guidance as to the measures, mechanisms and approaches that are effective. The resilience features reflect structures and functions that governance systems should aim to integrate to bridge the kind of complexity that is inherent in nonlinear and unpredictable social-ecological systems, and the increasing complexity that is entailed to the era of the Anthropocene. Legal governance should then integrate these structures, functions and mechanisms as part of a larger governance framework. However, law and legal structures have other core functions than just providing for effective environmental governance. Law is based on a number of general principles connected to the rule of law and the function of law as a foundation for stability in society and in human interactions. These principles are of fundamental value and the primary aim of any legal system. They could be characterized as features for social resilience in a context where social resilience is seen as a state where social systems are democratic, providing important services or means for its citizens' well-being, economic stability and general development.

The answers found have been based on the resilience features chosen for this study and presented herein. Some of these features are more difficult than others to integrate with general legal principles. The core in most of the legal principles comprises stability and foreseeability, and it can be argued that this creates obstacles to more flexible and adaptive law. This is also true in the international community. The overall issue that is the focus in this study – the increasing complex, nonlinear transboundary environmental problems with unpredictable responses – is thus an area often seen to be in conflict with general regulatory approaches. Still, this is how environmental problems evolve now, and thus matching legal approaches or legal designs must be identified.

Adaptability and flexibility are the features that most directly strike one as being incompatible with legal foundations. Moreover, some of the features are more difficult to translate into a legal context, while others – such as participation – are well-known concepts in law. Still, the function and aim of participation in the general sense differ between law and resilience governance. The overall result of integrating and comparing these features with legal mechanisms has shown that much of what is emphasized within resilience theories is, or could be, reflected by more or less established legal structures and approaches. It also shows that, to a large extent, new legal features and designs manage to balance flexible features with the rule of law. This is also a prominent role of law in relation to social-ecological resilience research, where such issues with important impact for the social system are given little attention. One legal concept that integrates many aspects of the resilience features is the concept of ecosystem approach. It is also clear from the study, however, that the effect and ecosystem match of the legal application of resilience features are very dependent on the way they are pursued, both formally and in regard to operationalization, monitoring and control measures.

References

Abbot, C., and Lee, M., "Economic Actors in EU Environmental Law," *Yearbook of European Law*, Vol. 34, No. 1, 2015.

Adger, W. N., "Social and Ecological Resilience: Are They Related?," *Progress in Human Geography*, Vol. 24, No. 3, 2000, pp. 347–364.

Agné, H., Dellmuth, L. M., and Tallberg, J., "Does Stakeholder Involvement Foster Democratic Legitimacy in International Organizations? An Empirical Assessment of a Normative Theory," *The Review of International Organizations*, Vol. 10, No. 4, 2015.

Ambrus, M., Arts, K., Hey, E., and Raulus, H., "The Role of Experts in International and European Decision-Making Processes: Setting the Scene," in Ambrus, M., Arts, K., Hey, E., and Raulus, H. (eds.), *The Role of "Experts" in International and European Decision-Making Processes: Advisors, Decision Makers or Irrelevant Actors?*, Cambridge University Press, Cambridge, 2014.

Andresen, S., "The Role of Scientific Expertise in Multilateral Environmental Agreements: Influence and Effectiveness," in Ambrus, M., Arts, K., Hey, E., and Raulus, H. (eds.), *The Role of "Experts" in International and European Decision-Making Processes: Advisors, Decision Makers or Irrelevant Actors?*, Cambridge University Press, Cambridge, 2014.

Angelo, M. J., "Harnessing the Power of Science in Environmental Law: Why We Should, Why We Don't, and How We Can," *Texas Law Review*, Vol. 86, 2007–2008.

Armitage, D., "Governance and the Commons in a Multi-level World," *International Journal of the Commons*, Vol. 2, No. 1, 2008.

Arnold, C. A., and Gunderson, L. H., "Adaptive Law and Resilience," originally printed in *Environmental Law Reporter*, Vol. 43, No. 10427, 5–2013; reprinted with copyright to Environmental Law Institute, Washington, DC, 2013, University of Louisville, Legal Studies Research Paper Series, Paper No. 2104–04.

Bäckstrand, K., "Multi-Stakeholder Partnerships for Sustainable Development: Rethinking Legitimacy, Accountability and Effectiveness," *European Environment*, Vol. 16, 2006.

Barrett, S., *Environment and Statecraft: Strategy for Environmental Treaty Making*, Oxford University Press, New York, 2003.

Barstow Magraw, D., and Hawke, L. D., "Sustainable Development," in Bodansky, D., Brunnée, J., and Hey, E. (eds.), *The Oxford Handbook of International Environmental Law*, Oxford University Press, New York, 2007.

Benson, M. H., and Craig, K. R., *The End of Sustainability: Resilience and the Future of Environmental Governance in the Anthropocene*, University Press of Kansas, 2017.

Berkes, F., Colding, J., and Folke, C. (eds.), *Navigating Social-Ecological Systems: Building Resilience for Complexity and Change*, Cambridge University Press, Cambridge, 2003.

Bernstein, S., "Legitimacy in Global Environmental Governance," *Journal of International Law and International Relations*, Vol. 1, No. 1–2, 2005.

Beyerlin, U., "Different Types of Norms in International Environmental Law: Policies, Principles and Rules," in Bodansky, D., Brunnée, J., and Hey, E. (eds.), *The Oxford Handbook of International Environmental Law*, Oxford University Press, New York, 2007.

Biermann, F., et al., "The Fragmentation of Global Governance Architectures: A Framework for Analysis," *Global Environmental Politics*, Vol. 9, No. 4, 2009.

Biermann, F., et al., "Navigating the Anthropocene: Improving Earth System Governance," *Policy Forum, Science*, Vol. 335, No. 6074, 2012.

Biggs, R., et al., "Principle 3 – Manage Slow Variables and Feedbacks," in Biggs R., Schlüter M., and Schoon M. L. (eds.), *Principles for Building Resilience: Sustaining Ecosystem Services in Social-Ecological Systems*, Cambridge University Press, Cambridge, 2015.

Biggs R., Schlüter M., and Schoon M. L., "An Introduction to the Resilience Approach and Principles to Sustain Ecosystem Services in Social-Ecological Systems," in Biggs R., Schlüter M., and Schoon M. L. (eds.), *Principles for Building Resilience – Sustaining Ecosystem Services in Social-Ecological Systems*, Cambridge University Press, Cambridge, 2015a.

Biggs R., Schlüter M., and Schoon M. L. (eds.), *Principles for Building Resilience: Sustaining Ecosystem Services in Social-Ecological Systems*, Cambridge University Press, Cambridge, 2015b.

Birnie, P., Boyle, A., and Redgwell, C., *International Law and the Environment*, 3rd ed., Oxford University Press, New York, 2009.

Bodansky, D., "The Legitimacy of International Governance: A Coming Challenge for International Environmental Law?," *The American Journal of International Law*, Vol. 93, No. 3, 1999.

Bodansky, D., "Legitimacy," in Bodansky, D., Brunnée, J., and Hey, E. (eds.), *The Oxford Handbook of International Environmental Law*, Oxford University Press, New York, 2007.

Bodansky, D., *The Art and Craft of International Environmental Law*, Harvard University Press, Cambridge, 2010.

Bodansky, D., "Legitimacy in International Law and International Relations," in Dunoff, J. L., and Pollack, M. A. (eds.), *Interdisciplinary Perspectives on International Law and International Relations – The State of the Art*, Cambridge University Press, New York, 2012.

Bodansky, D., Brunnée, J., and Hey, E., "International Environmental Law – Mapping the Field," in Bodansky, D., Brunnée, J., and Hey, E. (eds.), *The Oxford Handbook of International Environmental Law*, Oxford University Press, New York, 2007a.

Bodansky, D., Brunnée, J., and Hey, E. (eds.), *The Oxford Handbook of International Environmental Law*, Oxford University Press, New York, 2007b.

Bohman, B., "The Ecosystem Approach as a Basis for Managerial Compliance: An Example from the Regulatory Development in the Baltic Sea Region," in Langlet, D., and Rayfuse, R., (eds.), *The Ecosystem Approach in Ocean Planning and Governance – Perspectives from Europe and Beyond*, Brill/Nijhoff, Leiden, 2018, pp. 80–116.

Bohman, B., "Lessons from the Regulatory Approaches to Combat Eutrophication in the Baltic Sea," *Marine Policy*, Vol. 98, 2018a.

Bohman, B., "Regulating Eutrophication: Flexible Legal Approaches and Environmental Governance in the Baltic Sea Area," in Ringbom, H. (ed.), *Regulatory Gaps in Baltic Sea Governance – Selected Issues*, MARE Publications Series, Springer Cham, 2018b.

Bohman, B., and Langlet, D., "Float or Sinker for Europe's Seas? The Role of Law in Marine Governance," in Gilek, M., and Kern, K. (eds.), *Governing Europe's Marine Environment: Europeanization of Regional Seas or Regionalization of EU Policies?*, Ashgate, Farnham, Surrey, 2015.

Bosselmann, K., *The Principle of Sustainability: Transforming Law and Governance.* Abingdon, Oxon, Ashgate, 2008.

Bosselmann, K., Engel, R., and Taylor, P., *Governance for Sustainability: Issues, Challenges, Successes*, UCN Environmental Policy and Law Paper No. 70, IUCN, Gland, Switzerland, 2008.

Boyle, A. E., "Dispute Settlement and the Law of the Sea Convention: Problems of Fragmentation and Jurisdiction," *International and Comparative Law Quarterly*, Vol. 46, No. 1, 1997.

Boyle, A., "Some Reflections on the Relationship of Treaties and Soft Law," in Gowlland-Debbas, V. (ed.), *Multilateral Treaty-Making – The Current Status of Challenges to and Reforms Needed in the International Legislative Process* (Part of the series Nijhoff Law Specials, Vol. 47), Kluwer Law International, 2000.

Boyle, M., Kay, J., and Pond, B., "Monitoring in Support of Policy: An Adaptive Ecosystem Approach," in Munn, T., *Encyclopedia of Global Environmental Change*, Vol. 4, Wiley, New York, 2001.

Brakeland, J.-F., "Access to Justice in Environmental Matters – Developments at EU Level," published in the *Gyeseiho-Kenkyu*, 2014, No. 5.

Brunnée, J., "Enforcement Mechanisms in International Law and International Environmental Law," in Beyerlin, U., Stoll, P-T., and Wolfrum, R. (eds.), *Ensuring Compliance with Multilateral Environmental Agreements – A Dialogue between Practitioners and Academia*, Martinus Nijhoff Publishers, Leiden/Boston, 2006.

Brunnée, J., "Common Areas, Common Heritage, and Common Concern," in Bodansky, D., Brunnée, J., and Hey, E. (eds.), *The Oxford Handbook of International Environmental Law*, Oxford University Press, New York, 2007.

Carpenter, S., et al., "From Metaphor to Measurement: Resilience of What to What?," *Ecosystems*, Vol. 4, 2001.

Carvalho, W. D., et al., "Deforestation Control in the Brazilian Amazon: A Conservation Struggle Being Lost as Agreements and Regulations Are Subverted and Bypassed," *Perspectives in Ecology and Conservation*, Vol. 17, No. 3, 2019, pp. 122–130.

CBD (1995), CBD II/8, The Second Meeting of the Conference of the Parties (COP) of the Convention on Biological Diversity, held in Jakarta, Indonesia (CBD COP 2) Decision 8, UNEP/CBD/COP/2/19.

CBD, "Ecosystem Approach, Description of the Ecosystem Approach," COP Convention on Biological Diversity, May 2000, in Nairobi, Kenya (CBD, COP 5), Decision V/6, para. 4–5, part A, p. 1. (2000c).

CBD, "The Ecosystem Approach – Operational and Implementation Guidelines," Seventh Ordinary Meeting of the Conference of the Parties to the Convention on Biological Diversity, February 2004 in Kuala Lumpur, Malaysia (CBD COP 7), Decision VII/11, UNEP/CBD/COP/DEC/VII/11.

CBD, "The Malawi Principles," COP Convention on Biological Diversity, May 2000, in Nairobi, Kenya (CBD, COP 5), Decision V/6, para. 4–5, part B. (2000a),

CBD SBSTTA (2000), Subsidiary Body on Scientific, Technical and Technological Advice (SBSTTA), fifth meeting, Montreal, January 2000, Item 4.2.1 of the provisional agenda; *Ecosystem Approach: Further Conceptual Elaboration*, Document: UNEP/CBD/SBSTTA/5/11, October 23, 1999.

Chaffin, B. C., et al., "Transformative Environmental Governance," *Annual Review of Environment and Resources*, Vol. 41:1, 2016, pp. 399–423.

Chaffin, B. C., Gosnell, H., and Cosens, B. A., "A Decade of Adaptive Governance Scholarship: Synthesis and Future Directions," *Ecology and Society*, Vol. 19(3), 2014, p. 56.

Chaffin, B., Gunderson, L., and Cosens, B. C. (eds.), "Practicing Panarchy: Assessing Legal Flexibility, Ecological Resilience, and Adaptive Governance in U.S. Regional Water Systems Experiencing Climate Change," *Ecology and Society*, Vol. 23(1), 2018.

Chambers, W. B., "Towards an Improved Understanding of Legal Effectiveness of International Environmental Treaties," *Georgetown International Environmental Law Review*, Vol. 16, 2004.

Chapin, F. S., et al., "Resilience-Based Stewardship: Strategies for Navigating Sustainable Pathways in a Changing World," in Chapin, F. S., Kofinas, G. P., and Folke, C. (eds.), *Principles of Ecosystem Stewardship – Resilience-Based Natural Resource Management in a Changing World*, Springer, New York, 2009a.

Chapin, F. S., Folke, C., and Kofinas, G. P., "A Framework for Understanding Change," in Chapin, F. S., Kofinas, G. P., and Folke, C. (eds.), *Principles of Ecosystem Stewardship – Resilience-Based Natural Resource Management in a Changing World*, Springer, New York, 2009a.

Chapin, F. S., Kofinas, G. P., and Folke, C. (eds.), *Principles of Ecosystem Stewardship – Resilience-Based Natural Resource Management in a Changing World*, Springer, New York, 2009.

Charney, J. I., "The Impact on the International Legal System of the Growth of International Courts and Tribunals," *NYU Journal of International Law and Politics*, Vol. 31, 1999.

Charnovitz, S., "Two Centuries of Participation: NGOs and International Governance," *Michigan Journal of International Law*, Vol. 18, No. 183, 1996–1997.

Chayes, A., and Chayes, A. H., "On Compliance," *International Organization*, Vol. 47, No. 2, 1993.

Chayes, A., and Chayes, A. H, *The New Sovereignty: Compliance with International Regulatory Agreements*, Harvard University Press, Cambridge, 1995.

Churchill, R., and Ulfstein, G., "Autonomous Institutional Arrangements in Multilateral Environmental Agreements: A Little-Noticed Phenomenon in International Law," *The American Journal of International Law*, Vol. 94, No. 4, 2000.

Coleman, W. T., "Legal Barriers to the Restoration of Aquatic Systems," *Vermont Law Review*, Vol. 23, 1998.

Commission on Global Governance, *Our Global Neighbourhood – The Report of the Commission on Global Governance*, Oxford University Press, Oxford, 1995.

Cosens, B. A., "Transboundary River Governance in the Face of Uncertainty: Resilience Theory and the Columbia River Treaty," *University of Utah Journal of Land Resources, and Environmental Law*, Vol. 30, No. 2, 2011, pp. 229ff.

Cosens, B. A., "Legitimacy, Adaptation, and Resilience in Ecosystem Management," *in Ecology and Society*, Vol. 18, No. 1, 2013.

Cosens, B. A., et al., "The Role of Law in Adaptive Governance," *Ecology and Society*, Vol. 22(1):30, 2017.

Cosens, B., and Gunderson, L. H., "Adaptive Water Governance: Summary and Synthesis," in Cosens, B., and Gunderson, L. H. (eds.), *Practical Panarchy for Adaptive Water Governance*, Springer International Publishing AG, Cham, 2018a.

Cosens, B., and Gunderson, L. H., "An Introduction to Practical Panarchy: Linking Law, Resilience, and Adaptive Water Governance of Regional Scale Social-Ecological Systems," in Cosens, B., and Gunderson, L. H. (eds.), *Practical Panarchy for Adaptive Water Governance – Linking Law to Social-Ecological Resilience*, Springer International Publishing AG, Cham, 2018b.

Cosens, B., and Gunderson, L. H. (eds.), *Practical Panarchy for Adaptive Water Governance – Linking Law to Social-Ecological Resilience*, Springer International Publishing AG, Cham, 2018c.

Craig, P., and De Búrca, G., *EU Law – Text, Cases, and Materials* (5th ed.), Oxford University Press, New York, 2011.

Craig, R. K., et al., "Balancing Stability and Flexibility in Adaptive Governance: An Analysis of Tools Available in U.S. Environmental Law," *Ecology and Society*, Vol. 22, No. 2, 2017, p. 3.

Craig, R. K., et al., "Stability and Flexibility in the Emergence of Adaptive Water Governance," in Cosens, B., and Gunderson, L. H. (eds.), *Practical Panarchy for Adaptive Water Governance*, Springer International Publishing AG, Cham, 2018.

Crutzen, P. J., "Geology of Mankind," *Nature*, Vol. 415, No. 6867, 2002, p.23.

D'Amato, A., "Is International Law Really 'Law'?," *Northwestern University Law Review*, Vol. 79, 1984–1985, pp. 1293ff.

Darpö, J., "Article 9 (2)of the Aarhus Convention and EU Law – Some Remarks on CJEUs Case-Law on Access to Justice in Environmental Decision-Making," *Journal for European Environmental and Planning Law*, Vol. 11, No. 4, 2014.

De Búrca, G., Keohane, R., and Sabel, C., "New Modes of Pluralist Global Governance," *New York University Journal of International Law & Politics*, Vol. 45, No. 3, 2013, pp. 723–786.

De Lucia, V., "Competing Narratives and Complex Genealogies: The Ecosystem Approach in International Environmental Law," *Journal of Environmental Law*, Vol. 27, 2015, pp. 91–117.

Dearing, J. A., et al., "Safe and Just Operating Spaces for Regional Social-Ecological Systems," *Global Environmental Change*, Vol. 28, 2014, pp. 227–238.

Delmas, M. A., and Young, O. R., "Introduction: New Perspectives on Governance for Sustainable Development," in Delmas, M. A., and Young, O. R. (eds.), *Governance for the Environment – New Perspectives*, Cambridge University Press, Cambridge, 2009.

Downs, G. W., Rocke, D. M., and Barsoom, P. N., "Is the Good News about Compliance Good News about Cooperation?," *International Organization*, Vol. 50, No. 3, 1996, pp. 379–406.

Duit, A., and Galaz, V., "Governance and Complexity – Emerging Issues for Governance Theory," *Governance: An International Journal of Policy, Administration and Institutions*, Vol. 21, No. 3, 2008, pp. 311–335.

Duit, A., et al., "Governance, Complexity and Resilience," *Global Environmental Change*, Vol. 20, No. 3, 2010.

Dunoff, J. L., "Levels of Environmental Governance," in Bodansky, D., Brunnée, J., and Hey, E. (eds.), *The Oxford Handbook of International Environmental Law*, Oxford University Press, New York, 2007.

Dupuy, P.-M., "A Doctrinal Debate in the Globalisation Era: On the Fragmentation of International Law," *European Journal of Legal Studies*, Vol. 1, No. 1, 2007.

Ebbesson, J., *Compatibility of International and National Environmental Law*, Iustus Förlag AB, Uppsala, 1996.

Ebbesson, J., "The Notion of Public Participation in International Environmental Law," in Brunnée, J., and Hey, E. (eds.), *Yearbook of International Environmental Law*, Vol. 8, Oxford University Press, New York, 1997.

Ebbesson, J., "Public Participation," in Bodansky, D., Brunnée, J., and Hey, E. (eds.), *The Oxford Handbook of International Environmental Law*, Oxford University Press, New York, 2007a.

Ebbesson, J., "Implementing and Enforcing the Baltic Sea Convention through European Community Law," in Führ, M., Wahl, R., and von Wilmowsky, P. (eds.), *Umweltrecht und Umweltwissenschaft – Festschrift für Eckhard Rehbinder*, Erich Schmidt Verlag, Berlin, 2007b.

Ebbesson, J., "The Rule of Law in Governance of Complex Socio-Ecological Changes," *Global Environmental Change*, Vol. 20(3), 2010, pp. 414–422.

Ebbesson, J., Briefing to European Parliament, "The EU and the Aarhus Convention: Access to Information, Public Participation in Decision-Making and Access to Justice in Environmental Matters, Policy Department C: Citizens' Rights and Constitutional Affairs," European Parliament, PE 571.357, 2016.

Ebbesson, J., "Public Participation in Environmental Matters – International Human Rights Developments in Europe and Africa," 2018, Faculty of Law, Stockholm University Research Paper No. 58. Available at https://ssrn.com/abstract=3164785.

Ebbesson, J., and Folke, C., "Matching Scales of Law with Social-Ecological Contexts to Promote Resilience," in Garmestani, A. S., and Allen, C. R. (eds.), *Social-Ecological Resilience and Law*, Columbia University Press, New York, 2014.

Ebbesson, J., and Hey, E. (eds.), "Special Feature on Law and Social-Ecological Resilience, Part II: Contributions from Law for Social-Ecological Resilience Symposium, Stockholm, Sweden, 2010," *Ecology and Society*, Vol. 18(3) 2013.

Ebbesson, J., and Hey, E., "Introduction: Where in Law Is Social-Ecological Resilience?," *Ecology and Society*, Vol. 18(3):25, 2013.

Epiney, A., "The Role of NGOs in the Process of Ensuring Compliance with MEAs," in Beyerlin, U., Stoll, P-T., and Wolfrum, R. (eds.), *Ensuring Compliance with*

Multilateral Environmental Agreements – A Dialogue between Practitioners and Academia, Martinus Nijhoff Publishers, Leiden/Boston, 2006.

EU 5th EAP, Fifth Environmental Action Programme, "Towards Sustainability – A European Community Programme of Policy and Action in Relation to the Environment and Sustainable Development," OJ No C138, 17. 5.93;EU 6th EAP, Sixth Environmental Action Programme, Decision No. 1600/2002/EC of the European Parliament and of the Council of July 2002 laying down the Sixth Community Environment Action Programme, OJ L 242, 10.9.2002.

EU COM (1999), Communication from the Commission, "Europe's Environment: What Directions for the Future? – The Global Assessment of the European Community Programme of Policy and Action in Relation to the Environment and Sustainable Development, 'Towards Sustainability,'" Brussels, 24.11.1999, COM (1999) 543 final, pp. 2–3.

EU COM (2003), *Commission Proposal for a Directive of the European Parliament and of the Council on Access to Justice in Environmental Matters* (presented by the Commission), Brussels, 24. 10.2003, COM(2003) 624 final, 2003/0246 (COD), C5-0513–03.

EU COM (2003a), *Commission Proposal for a Regulation of the European Parliament and of the Council on the Application of the Provisions of the Aarhus Convention on Access to Information, Public Participation in Decision-Making and Access to Justice in Environmental Matters to EC Institutions and Bodies* (presented by the Commission), Brussels, 24.10.2003, COM(2003) 622 final, 2003/0242 (COD).

EU COM Report (2012a), Report from the Commission to the Council and the European Parliament, "On the Experience Gained in the Application of the Directive 2003/4/EC on Public Access to Environmental Information," Brussels, 17.12.2012, COM(2012) 774 final.

EU COM Report (2014), Report from the Commission to the Council and the European Parliament, "The First Phase of Implementation of the Marine Strategy Framework Directive (2008/56/EC) – The European Commission's Assessment and Guidance [SWD(2014) 49 final]," Brussels, 20.2.2014COM(2014) 97 final.

EU Treaties Office Database of the European External Action Service, http://ec.europa.eu/world/agreements/default.home.do.

EU WFD CIS, Common Implementation Strategy for the Water Framework Directive (2000/60/EC), "Carrying Forward the Common Implementation Strategy for the Water Framework Directive: Progress and Work Programme for 2003 and 2004," as agreed by the Water Directors 17 June 2003.

EU White Paper (2001), Communication from the EU Commission, "European Governance – A White Paper," Brussels, 25. 7.2001, EU COM(2001) 428 final, OJ Document: 2001/C 287/01.

Farber, D. A., "Politics and Procedure in Environmental Law," *Journal of Law, Economics and Organization*, Vol. 8, 1992.

Fitzmaurice, M. A., and Redgwell, C., "Environmental Non-compliance Procedures and International Law," *Netherlands Yearbook of International Law*, Vol. 31, 2000.

Folke, C., "Resilience: The Emergence of a Perspective for Social-Ecological Systems Analysis," *Global Environmental Change*, Vol. 16, No. 3, 2006, pp. 253–267.

Folke, C., Carpenter, S., Elmqvist, T., et al., "Resilience and Sustainable Development: Building Adaptive Capacity in a World of Transformations," *Scientific Background Paper on Resilience for the Process of the World Summit on Sustainable Development on Behalf of the Environmental Advisory Council to the Swedish Government*, Edita Norstedts Tryckeri AB, Stockholm, 2002a.

Folke, C., Chapin, F. S., and Olsson, P., "Transformations in Ecosystem Stewardship," in Chapin, F. S., Kofinas, G. P., and Folke, C. (eds.), *Principles of Ecosystem Stewardship – Resilience-Based Natural Resource Management in a Changing World*, Springer, New York, 2009.

Folke, C., Colding, J., and Berkes, F., "Synthesis: Building Resilience and Adaptive Capacity in Social-Ecological Systems," in Berkes, F., Colding, J., and Folke, C. (eds.), *Navigating Social-Ecological Systems: Building Resilience for Complexity and Change*, Cambridge University Press, Cambridge, 2003.

Folke, C., Jansson, Å., Rockström, J., et al., "Reconnecting to the Biosphere," *Ambio*, Vol. 40:719, 2011.

Folke, C., et al., "Resilience and Sustainable Development: Building Adaptive Capacity in a World of Transformations," *Ambio*, Vol. 31, No. 5, 2002, pp. 437–440.

Folke, C., et al., "Adaptive Governance of Social-Ecological Systems," *Annual Review of Environmental Recourses*, Vol. 30, 2005, pp. 441–473.

Folke, C., et al., "Resilience Thinking: Integrating Resilience, Adaptability and Transformability," *Ecology and Society*, Vol. 15, No. 4, 2010, pp. 20–28.

Folke, C., et al., "Transnational Corporations and the Challenge of Biosphere Stewardship," *Nature Ecology & Evolution*, Vol. 3, 2019, pp. 1396–1403.

Franck, T. M., *Fairness in International Law and Institutions*, Clarendon Press, Oxford, 1995.

Franck, T. M., "Legitimacy in the International System," *American Journal of International Law*, Vol. 82, No. 4, 1988.

Galaz, V., et al., "Analytical Themes: The Problem of Fit among Biophysical Systems, Environmental and Resource Regimes, and Broader Governance Systems: Insights and Emerging Challenges," in Young, O.R., King, L. K., and Schröder, H. (eds.), *Institutions and Environmental Change – Principal Findings, Applications, and Research Frontiers*, MIT Press, Cambridge, 2008, pp. 147–182.

Garmestani, A. S., Allen, C. R., and Benson, M.H. (eds.), "Special Feature on Law and Social-Ecological Resilience, Part I: Contributions from Resilience 2011," *Ecology and Society*, Vol. 18(2), 2013.

Garmestani, A. S., Allen, C. R., and Benson, M. H., "Can Law Foster Social-Ecological Resilience?" *Ecology and Society*, 18 (2):37, 2013.

Garmestani, A. S., Allen, C. R., and Cabezas, H., "Panarchy, Adaptive Management and Governance: Policy Options for Building Resilience," *Nebraska Law Review*, Vol. 87, 2008, pp. 1036ff.

Garmestani, A. S., and Benson, M. H., "A Framework for Resilience-Based Governance of Social- Ecological Systems," *Ecology and Society*, Vol. 18(1): 9, 2013.

Garmestani, A. S., and Allen, C. R. (eds.), *Social-Ecological Resilience and Law*, Columbia University Press, New York, 2014a.

Garmestani, A. S., et al., "Introduction – Social-Ecological Resilience and Law," in Garmestani, A. S., and Allen, C. R. (eds.), *Social-Ecological Resilience and Law*, Columbia University Press, New York, 2014b.

Gehring, T., "Treaty-Making and Treaty Evolution," in Bodansky, D., Brunnée, J., and Hey, E. (eds.), *The Oxford Handbook of International Environmental Law*, Oxford University Press, New York, 2007.

Gonzales, C. G., "Global Justice in the Anthropocene," in Kotzé, L. J. (ed.), *Environmental Law and Governance for the Anthropocene*, Bloomsbury Publishing, Oxford, 2017.

Green, O. O., et al., "EU Water Governance: Striking the Right Balance between Regulatory Flexibility and Enforcement?," *Ecology and Society*, Vol. 18 (2):10, 2013.

Green, O. O., et al., "Barriers and Bridges to the Integration of Social–Ecological Resilience and Law," *Frontiers in Ecology and the Environment*, Vol. 13, 2015a, pp. 332–337.

Green, O. O., et al., "The Role of Bridging Organizations in Enhancing Ecosystem Services and Facilitating Adaptive Management of Social-Ecological Systems," in Allen, C. R., and Garmestani, A. S. (eds.), *Adaptive Management of Social-Ecological Systems*, Springer Science, Dordrecht, 2015b.

Gunningham, N., and Holley, C., "Next-Generation Environmental Regulation: Law, Regulation, and Governance," *Annual Review of Law and Social Science*, Vol. 12:1, 2016, pp. 273–293.

Guzman, A. T., *How International Law Works: A Rational Choice Theory*, Oxford University Press, New York, 2008.

Hafner, G., "Risks Ensuing from Fragmentation of International Law," Volume II (Part 2): Report of the Commission to the General Assembly, Document A/55/10: Report of the International Law Commission on the work of its fifty-second session in UN ILC 2000, *Yearbook of the International Law Commission 2000*.

Hafner, G., "Pros and Cons Ensuing from Fragmentation of International Law," *Michigan Journal of International Law*, Vol. 25, 2004.

Hahn, T., et al., "Trust-Building, Knowledge Generation and Organizational Innovations: The Role of Bridging Organization for Adaptive Comanagment of a Wetland Landscape around Kristianstad, Sweden," *Human Ecology*, Vol. 34, 2006.

Handl, G., "Compliance Control Mechanisms and International Environmental Obligations," *Tulane Journal of International and Comparative Law*, Vol. 5, 1997.

Hardin, G., "The Tragedy of the Commons," *Science*, Vol. 162, No. 3859, 1968, pp. 1243–1248.

Helfner, L. R., "Flexibility in International Agreements," in Dunoff, J., and Pollack, M. A., (eds.), *Interdisciplinary Perspectives on International Law and International Relations – The State of the Art*, Cambridge University Press, Cambridge, 2013.

Henkin, L., *How Nations Behave: Law and Foreign Policy*, Columbia University Press, New York, 1979

Hey, E., "Multi-Dimensional Public Governance Arrangements for the Protection of Transboundary Aquatic Environment in the European Union – The Changing Interplay between European and Public International Law," *International Organizations Law Review*, Vol. 6, 2009.

Holling, C. S., and Meffe, G. K., "Command and Control, and the Pathology of Natural Resource Management," *Conservation Biology*, Vol. 10, No. 2, 1996.

Huitema, D., et al., "Adaptive Water Governance: Assessing the Institutional Prescriptions of Adaptive (Co-)Management from a Governance Perspective and Defining a Research Agenda," *Ecology and Society*, Vol. 14 (1):26, 2009.

Jacobson, H. K., and Brown Weiss, E., "Compliance with International Environmental Accords," in Rolén, M., Sjöberg, H., and Svedin, U. (eds.), *International Governance on Environmental Issues, Environment and Policy*, Vol. 9, Springer Science +Business Media, Dordrecht, 1997.

Jacobson, H. K., and Brown Weiss, E., "A Framework for Analysis," in Brown Weiss, E., and Jacobson, H. K. (eds.), *Engaging Countries – Strengthening Compliance with International Environmental Accords*, MIT Press, Cambridge and London, 1998.

Jacobson, H. K., and Brown Weiss, E., "Assessing the Record and Designing Strategies to Engage Countries," in Brown Weiss, E., and Jacobson, H. K. (eds.), *Engaging Countries – Strengthening Compliance with International Environmental Accords*, MIT Press, Cambridge and London, 1998b.

Jans J.H., et al., "'Gold Plating' of European Environmental Measures?," *Journal for European Environmental and Planning Law*, Vol. 6(4), 2009.

Jans, J. H., and Vedder, H. H. B., *European Environmental Law After Lisbon*, 4th ed., Europa Law Publishing, Groningen, 2012.

Jendroska, J., "Citizen's Rights in European Environmental Law: Stock-Taking of Key Challenges and Current Developments in Relation to Public Access to Information, Participation and Access to Justice," *Journal for European Environmental and Planning Law*, Vol. 9, No. 1, 2012.

Josefsson, H., and Baaner, L., "The Water Framework Directive – A Directive for the Twenty-First Century?," *Journal of Environmental Law*, Vol. 23, No. 3, 2011.

Jänicke, M., and Jörgens, H., "New Approaches to Environmental Governance" in Jänicke, M., and Jacob,K. (eds.), *Environmental Governance in Global Perspective: New Approaches to Ecological Modernisation* (FFU Report 01–2006), Freie Universität, Berlin, 2006. (First published in *Neue Steuerungskonzepte in der Umweltpolitik. Zeitschrift für Umweltpolitik & Umweltrech,*. Jg. 27, H.3, 2004, s. 297–348.)

Jönsson, C., and Tallberg, J., "Transnational Actor Participation in International Institutions: Where, Why, and with What Consequences?," in Jönsson, C., and Tallberg, J. (eds.), *Transnational Actors in Global Governance*, Palgrave Macmillan, New York, 2010.

Juda, L., "Considerations in Developing a Functional Approach to the Governance of Large Marine Ecosystems," *Ocean Development and International Law*, Vol. 30, No. 2, 1999.

Juda, L., "The EU and the Marine Strategy Framework Directive: Continuing the Development of the European Ocean Use Management," *Ocean Development and International Law*, Vol. 41, 2010.

Kim, R. E., "The Emergent Network Structure of the Multilateral Environmental Agreement System," *Global Environmental Change*, Vol. 23, 2013.

Kim, R. E., and Mackey, B., "International Environmental Law as a Complex Adaptive System," *International Environmental Agreements: Politics, Law and Economics*, Vol. 14, No. 1, Springer, 2014, pp. 5–24.

Kirk, E. A., "Noncompliance and the Development of Regimes Addressing Marine Pollution from Land-Based Activities," *Ocean Development and International Law*, Vol. 39, No. 3, 2008, pp. 235–256.

Kiss, A., and Shelton, D., *International Environmental Law*, 2nd ed., Transnational Publishers, Ardsley, New York, 2000.

Klabbers, J., "Compliance Procedures," in Bodansky, D., Brunnée, J., and Hey, E. (eds.), *The Oxford Handbook of International Environmental Law*, Oxford University Press, Oxford, 2007,

Koskenniemi, M., "Peaceful Settlement of Environmental Disputes," *Nordic Journal of International Law*, Vol. 60, No. 1, 1991

Koskenniemi, M., "Environmental Cooperation in the Baltic Region," *Tulane Journal of International and Comparative Law*, Vol. 1, 1993, pp. 81–106.

Koskenniemi, M., and Leino, P., "Fragmentation of International Law? Postmodern Anxieties," *Leiden Journal of International Law*, Vol. 15, No. 3, 2002.

Koskenniemi, M., "Fragmentation of International Law: Difficulties Arising from Diversification and Expansion of International Law," UN ILC Report 2006, Report of the Study Group of the International Law Commission, International Law Commission, fifty-eighth session, Geneva 2006, United Nations, General Assembly, Document: A/CN.4/L.682 13 April 2006.

Kotschy, K., et al., "Principle 1 – Maintain Diversity and Redundancy," in Biggs R., Schlüter M., and Schoon M. L. (eds.), *Principles for Building Resilience: Sustaining Ecosystem Services in Social-Ecological Systems*, Cambridge University Press, Cambridge, 2015.

Kotzé, L. (ed.), *Environmental Law and Governance for the Anthropocene*, Hart Publishing, Oxford, 2017.

Kotzé, L. J., and Kim, R. E., "Earth System Law: The Juridical Dimensions of Earth System Governance," *Earth System Governance*, Vol. 1, 2019.

Krämer, L., *EU Environmental Law*, 7th ed., Sweet and Maxwell, London, 2011.

Kravchenko, S., "The Aarhus Convention and Innovations in Compliance with Multilateral Environmental Agreements," *Colorado Journal of International Environmental Law and Policy*, Vol. 18, No. 1, 2007.

Kuokkanen, T., "Practice of the Implementation Committee under the Convention on Long-Range Transboundary Air Pollution," in Beyerlin, U., Stoll, P-T., and Wolfrum, R. (eds.), *Ensuring Compliance with Multilateral Environmental Agreements – A Dialogue between Practitioners and Academia*, Martinus Nijhoff Publishers, Leiden/Boston, 2006.

Langlet, D., and Mahmoudi, S., *EU Environmental Law and Policy*, Oxford University Press, Oxford, 2016.

Langlet, D., and Rayfuse, R., "Challenges in Implementing the Ecosystem Approach: Lessons Learned," in Langlet, D., and Rayfuse, R. (eds.), *The Ecosystem Approach in Ocean Planning and Governance – Perspectives from Europe and Beyond*, Brill/Nijhoff, Leiden, 2018.

Lebel, L., Anderies, J. M., Campbell, B., et al., "Governance and the Capacity to Manage Resilience in Regional Social-Ecological Systems," *Ecology and Society*, Vol. 11, No. 1, 2006.

Lee, M., "Law and Governance of Water Protection Policy," in Scott, J. (ed.), *Environmental Protection – European Law and Governance*, Oxford University Press, New York, 2009.

van Leeuwen, J., et al., "Implementing the Marine Strategy Framework Directive: A Policy Perspective on Regulatory, Institutional and Stakeholder Impediments to Effective Implementation," *Marine Policy*, Vol. 50, Part B, 2014.

van Leeuwen, J., van Hoof, L., and van Tatenhove, J., "Institutional Ambiguity in Implementing the European Union Marine Strategy Framework Directive," *Marine Policy*, Vol. 36, 2012.

Leitch, A. M., et al., "Principle 6 – Broaden Participation," in Biggs R., Schlüter M., and Schoon M. L. (eds.), *Principles for Building Resilience: Sustaining Ecosystem Services in Social-Ecological Systems*, Cambridge University Press, Cambridge, 2015.

Linderfalk, U., *On the Interpretation of Treaties – The Modern International Law as Expressed in the 1969 Vienna Convention on the Law of Treaties*, Springer, Dordrecht, 2007.

Liu, J., et al., "Complexity of Coupled Human and Natural Systems," *Science*, Vol. 317, No. 5844, 2007, pp. 1513–1516.

Long, R., "The Marine Strategy Framework Directive: A New European Approach to the Regulation of the Marine Environment, Marine Natural Resources and Marine Ecological Services," *Journal of Energy and Natural Resource Law*, Vol. 29, No. 1, 2011.

Long, R., "Legal Aspects of Ecosystem-Based Marine Management in Europe," in Chircop, A., McConnell, M. L., and Coffen-Smou, S. (eds.), *Ocean Yearbook*, Vol. 26, Hijhoff, The Hague, 2012.

Low, B., et al., "Redundancy and Diversity: Do They Influence Optimal Management?," in Berkes, F., Colding, J., and Folke, C. (eds.), *Navigating Social-Ecological Systems: Building Resilience for Complexity and Change*, Cambridge University Press, Cambridge, 2003.

March, J. G., and Olsen, J. P., "The Institutional Dynamics of International Political Orders," *International Organization*, Vol. 52, No. 4, 1998.

Martin, L. L., "Against Compliance," in Dunoff, J. L., and Pollack, M. A. (eds.), *Interdisciplinary Perspectives on International Law and International Relations – The State of the Art*, Cambridge University Press, New York, 2012.

Matz, N., "Financial and Other Incentives for Complying with MEA Obligations," in Beyerlin, U., Stoll, P-T., and Wolfrum, R. (eds.), *Ensuring Compliance with Multilateral Environmental Agreements – A Dialogue between Practitioners and Academia*, Martinus Nijhoff Publishers, Leiden/Boston, 2006.

Mitchell, R. B., "International Environmental Agreements: A Survey of Their Features, Formation, and Effects," *Annual Review of Environment and Resources*, Vol. 28, 2003, pp. 429–461.

Mitchell, R. B., "Compliance Theory – Compliance, Effectiveness, and Behaviour Change in International Environmental Law," in Bodansky, D., Brunneé, J., and Hey, E. (eds.), *The Oxford Handbook of International Environmental Law*, Oxford University Press, Oxford, 2007.

Morgera, E., "The Ecosystem Approach and the Precautionary Principle," in Morgera, E., and Razzaque, J., (eds.), *Biodiversity and Nature Protection Law*, Edward Elgar Publishing, Cheltenham, UK, 2017.

Morrison, T. H., et al., "The Black Box of Power in Polycentric Environmental Governance," *Global Environmental Change*, Vol. 57, 2019.

Natarajan, U., and Khoday, K., "Locating Nature: Making and Unmaking International Law," *Leiden Journal of International Law*, Vol. 27(3), 2014.

Newig, J., Pahl-Wostl, C., and Sigel, K., "The Role of Public Participation in Managing Uncertainty in the Implementation of the Water Framework Directive," *European Environment*, Vol. 15, No. 6, 2005, pp. 333–343.

Nilsson, A. K., and Bohman, B., "Legal Prerequisites for Ecosystem-Based Management in the Baltic Sea Area: The Example of Eutrophication" *Ambio*, Vol. 44, Suppl. 3, 2015.

Oberthür, S., and Gehring, T., "Conceptual Foundations of Institutional Interaction," in Oberthür, S., and Gehring, T. (eds.), *Institutional Interaction in Global Environmental Governance: Synergy and Conflict among International and EU Policies*, MIT Press, Cambridge, 2006a.

Oberthür, S., and Gehring, T., "Comparative Empirical Analysis and Ideal Types of Institutional Interaction," in Oberthür, S., and Gehring, T. (eds.), *Institutional Interaction in Global Environmental Governance: Synergy and Conflict among International and EU Policies*, MIT Press, Cambridge, 2006b.

Österblom, H., et al., "Making the Ecosystem Approach Operational – Can Regime Shifts in Ecological- and Governance Systems Facilitate the Transition?," *Marine Policy*, Vol. 34, 2010.

Ostrom, E., *Governing the Commons – The Evolution of Institutions for Collective Action*, Cambridge University Press, New York, 1990.

Ostrom, E., Gardner, R., and Walker, J., *Rules, Games, and Common-Pool Resources*, University of Michigan Press, Ann Arbor, 1994.

Ostrom, E., and Janssen, M. A., "Multi-Level Governance and Resilience of Social Ecological Systems," in Spoor, M. (ed.), *Globalization, Poverty and Conflict*, Kluwer Academic Publishers, Netherlands, 2004.

Ostrom, V., "Polycentricity," in McGinnis, M. (ed.), *Polycentricity and Local Public Economies: Readings from the Workshop in Political Theory and Policy Analysis*, University of Michigan Press, Ann Arbor, 1999.

Pahl-Wostl, C., "A Conceptual Framework for Analysing Adaptive Capacity and Multi-Level Learning Processes in Resource Governance Regimes," *Global Environmental Change*, Vol. 19, 2009.

Pallemaerts, M., "Introduction," in Pallemaerts, M. (ed.), *The Aarhus Convention at Ten – Interactions and Tensions between Conventional International Law and EU Environmental Law*, Vol. 9, Avosetta series, Europa Law Publishing, Groningen, 2011a.

Pallemaerts, M., "Access to Environmental Justice at EU Level. Has the 'Aarhus Regulation' Improved the Situation?," in Pallemaerts, M. (ed.), *The Aarhus Convention at Ten – Interactions and Tensions between Conventional International Law and EU Environmental Law*, Vol. 9, Avosetta series, Europa Law Publishing, Groningen, 2011b.

Palm, E., "Rättspraxis och tolkningsmetoder i Europadomstolen för de mänskliga rättigheterna," Juridisk Tidskrift, No. 4, 2003.

Phillips, R., Freeman, R. E., and Wicks, A. C., "What Stakeholder Theory Is Not," *Business Ethics Quarterly*, Vol. 13, No. 4, 2003.

Piattoni, S., "Multi-Level Governance: A Historical and Conceptual Analysis," *Journal of European Integration*, Vol. 31, No. 2, 2009.

Platjouw, F., *Environmental Law and the Ecosystem Approach: Maintaining Ecological Integrity through Consistency in Law*, Routledge, Abingdon and New York, 2016.

Platjouw, F. M., "Dimensions of Transboundary Legal Coherence Needed to Foster Ecosystem-Based Governance in the Arctic," *Marine Policy*, Vol. 110, 2019.

Plummer, R., "The Adaptive Co-Management Process: An Initial Synthesis of Representative Models and Influential Variables," *Ecology and Society*, Vol. 14(2): 24. 2009.

Profeta, T. H., "Managing without a Balance: Environmental Regulation in Light of Ecological Advances," *Duke Environmental Law and Policy*, Vol. 7, 1996.

Raustiala, K., "States, NGOs, and International Environmental Institutions," *International Studies Quarterly*, Vol. 41, No. 4, 1997a.

Raustiala, K., "The 'Participatory Revolution' in International Environmental Law," *Harvard Environmental Law Review*, Vol. 21, 1997b.

Raustiala, K., "Form and Substance in International Agreements," *American Journal of International Law*, Vol. 99, No. 3, 2005.

Raustiala, K., and Slaugther, A.-M., "International Law, International Relations and Compliance," in Carlsnaes, W., Risse, T., and Simmons, B. A. (eds.), *Handbook of International Relations*, SAGE Publications, London, 2002.

Raworth, K., "A Safe and Just Space for Humanity: Can We Live within the Doughnut?," Oxfam Discussion Paper, *Oxfam Policy and Practice: Climate Change and Resilience*, Vol. 8, No. 1, 2012, pp. 1–26.

Redgwell, C., "Multilateral Environmental Treaty-Making," in Gowlland-Debbas, V. (ed.), *Multilateral Treaty-Making – The Current Status of Challenges to and Reforms Needed in the International Legislative Process* (Part of the series Nijhoff Law Specials, Vol. 47), Springer Science+Business Media Dordrecht, Originally published by Kluwer Academic Publishers, Kluwer Law International, 2000.

The Revised African Convention on the Conservation of Nature and Natural Resources, https://au.int/en/treaties/african-convention-conservation-nature-and-natural-resources-revised-version.

Reyers, B., et al., "Social-Ecological Systems Insights for Navigating the Dynamics of the Anthropocene," *Annual Review of Environment and Resources*, Vol. 43, 2018, pp. 267–289.

Rockström, J., et al., "Planetary Boundaries: Exploring the Safe Operating Space for Humanity," *Ecology and Society*, Vol. 14(2):32, 2009.

Rosenbloom, J., "Defining Nature as a Common Pool Resource," in Hirokawa, K. H. (ed.), *Environmental Law and Contrasting Ideas of Nature – A Constructivist Approach*, Cambridge University Press, Cambridge, 2014.

Ruhl, J. B., "Thinking of Environmental Law as Complex Adaptive System: How to Clean up the Environment by Making a Mess of Environmental Law," *Houston Law Review*, Vol. 34, No. 4, 1997.

Ruhl, J. B., "Regulation by Adaptive Management – Is It Possible?," *Minnesota Journal of Law, Science and Technology*, Vol. 7, No. 1, 2006.

de Sadeleer, N., *Environmental Principles – From Political Slogans to Legal Rules*, Oxford University Press, New York, 2002.

Sands, P., Peel, J., Fabra, A., and MacKenzie, R., *Principles of International Environmental Law*, Cambridge University Press, Cambridge, 2012.

Sands, P. H., "The Evolution of International Environmental Law," in Bodansky,D., Brunnée, J., and Hey, E. (eds.), *The Oxford Handbook of International Environmental Law*, Oxford University Press, New York, 2007.

Sarma, K. M., "Compliance with the Multilateral Environmental Agreement to Protect the Ozone Layer," in Beyerlin, U., Stoll, P-T., and Wolfrum, R. (eds.), *Ensuring Compliance with Multilateral Environmental Agreements – A Dialouge between Practitioners and Academia*, Martinus Nijhoff Publishers, Leiden/Boston, 2006.

Saunders, C., "International Regimes and Domestic Arrangements: A View from Inside Out," in Young, M. A. (ed.), *Regime Interaction in International Law: Facing Fragmentation*, Cambridge University Press, Cambridge, 2012.

Saunders, F., "Planetary Boundaries: At the Threshold ... Again: Sustainable Development Ideas and Politics," *Environment, Development and Sustainability: A Multidisciplinary Approach to the Theory and Practice of Sustainable Development*, Vol. 17(4), 2015, pp. 823–835.

Schiele, S., *Evolution of International Environmental Regimes – The Case of Climate Change*, Cambridge University Press, Cambridge, 2014.

Schoon, M. L., et al., "Principle 7 – Promote a Polycentric Governance System," in Biggs R., Schlüter M., and Schoon M. L. (eds.), *Principles for Building Resilience: Sustaining Ecosystem Services in Social-Ecological Systems*, Cambridge University Press, Cambridge, 2015.

Schout, A., and Sleifer, J., "Expertise at the Crossroads of National and International Policy Making: A Public Management Perspective," in Ambrus, M., Arts, K., Hey, E., and Raulus, H. (eds.), *The Role of "Experts" in International and European Decision-Making Processes: Advisors, Decision Makers or Irrelevant Actors?*, Cambridge University Press, Cambridge, 2014.

Schrefler, L., "Reflections on the Different Roles of Expertise in Regulatory Policy Making," in Ambrus, M., Arts, K., Hey, E., and Raulus, H. (eds.), *The Role of "Experts" in International and European Decision-Making Processes: Advisors, Decision Makers or Irrelevant Actors?*, Cambridge University Press, Cambridge, 2014.

Scott, J., and Holder, J., "Law and New Environmental Governance in the European Union," in De Búrca, G., and Scott, J., *Law and New Governance in the EU and the US*, Hart Publishing, London, 2006, pp. 211–242.

Scott, J., and Trubek, D. M., "Mind the Gap: Law and New Approaches to Governance in the EU," *European Law Journal*, Vol. 8, No. 1, 2002, pp. 1–18.

Shany, Y., "The First MOX Plant Award: The Need to Harmonize Competing Environmental Regimes and Dispute Settlement Procedures," *Leiden Journal of International Law*, Vol. 17, No. 4, 2004.

Snidal, D., "Rational Choice and International Relations," in Simmons, B. A., Risse-Kappen, T., and Carlsnaes, W. (eds.), *Handbook of International Relations*, SAGE Publications, London, 2013.

Sofrononva, E., Holley, C., and Nagarajan, V., "Environmental Non-Governmental Organizations and Russian Environmental Governance: Accountability, Participation and Collaboration," *Transnational Environmental Law*, Vol. 3, No. 2, 2014.

Soininen, N., and Platjouw, F. M., "Resilience and Adaptive Capacity of Aquatic Environmental Law in the EU: An Evaluation and Comparison of the WFD, MSFD, and MSPD," in Langlet, D., and Rayfuse, R., (eds.), *The Ecosystem Approach in Ocean Planning and Governance – Perspectives from Europe and Beyond*, Brill/Nijhoff, Leiden, 2018, pp. 17–79.

Spiro, P. J., "Non-governmental Organizations and Civil Society," in Bodansky, D., Brunnée, J., and Hey, E. (eds.), *The Oxford Handbook of International Environmental Law*, Oxford University Press, New York, 2007.

Spiro, P. J, "Non-governmental Organizations in International Relations (Theory)," in Dunoff, J. L., and Pollack, M. A. (eds.), *Interdisciplinary Perspectives on International Law and International Relations – The State of the Art*, Cambridge University Press, New York, 2013.

Stec, S., and Jendrośka, J., "The Escazú Agreement and the Regional Approach to Rio Principle 10: Process, Innovation, and Shortcomings," *Journal of Environmental Law*, Vol. 31, 2019, pp. 533–545.

Steffen, W., Crutzen, P. J., and McNeill, J. R., "The Anthropocene: Are Humans Now Overwhelming the Great Forces of Nature?," *Ambio*, Vol. 36, No. 8, 2007, p. 614.

Steffen, W., et al., "The Anthropocene: From Global Change to Planetary Stewardship," *Ambio*, Vol. 40, No. 7, 2011, p.739.

Steffen, W., et al., "Planetary Boundaries: Guiding Human Development on a Changing Planet," *Science*, Vol. 347, No. 6223, 2015.

Stephens, T., "What Is the Point of International Environmental Law Scholarship in the Anthropocene?," in Pedersen, O. W. (ed.), *Perspectives on Environmental Law Scholarship: Essays on Purpose, Shape and Direction*, Cambridge University Press, Cambridge 2018a.

Stephens, T., "Wishful Thinking? The Governance of Climate Change-Related Disasters in the Anthropocene," in Lyster, R., and Verchick, R. R. M. (eds.), *Research Handbook on Climate Disaster Law: Barriers and Opportunities*, Elgaronline, 2018b.

Stewart, R. B., "Instrument Choice," in Bodansky, D., Brunnée, J., and Hey, E. (eds.), *The Oxford Handbook of International Environmental Law*, Oxford University Press, New York, 2007.

Stone, C. D., "Should Trees Have Legal Standing? – Toward Legal Rights for Natural Objects," *Southern California Law Review*, Vol. 45(450), 1972.

Tallberg, J., "Transnational Access to International Institutions: Three Approaches," in Jönsson, C., and Tallberg, J. (eds.), *Transnational Actors in Global Governance*, Palgrave Macmillan, Hampshire and New York, 2010.

Tarlock, A. D., "The Nonequilibrium Paradigm in Ecology and the Partial Unraveling of Environmental Law," *Loyola of Los Angeles Law Review*, Vol. 27, 1994.

Thomas, C. A., "The Uses and Abuses of Legitimacy in International Law," *Oxford Journal of Legal Studies*, Vol. 34, No. 4, 2014.

Thompson, A., "Coercive Enforcement of International Law," in Dunoff, J. L., and Pollack, M. A. (eds.), *Interdisciplinary Perspectives on International Law and International Relations – The State of the Art*, Cambridge University Press, New York, 2013

Toope, S. J., "Emerging Patterns of Governance and International Law," in Byers, M. (ed.), *The Role of Law in International Politics: Essays in International Relations and International Law*, Oxford University Press, Oxford, 2000.

Trouwborst, A., "The Precautionary Principle and the Ecosystem Approach in International Law: Differences, Similarities and Linkages," *Review of European Community and International Environmental Law*, Vol. 18(1), 2009.

Trubek, D. M., and Trubek, L. G., "New Governance and Legal Regulation: Complementarity, Rivalry, and Transformation," *Columbia Journal of European Law*, Vol. 13, 2006.

Ulfstein, G., "Treaty Bodies," in Bodansky, D., Brunnée, J., and Hey, E. (eds.), *The Oxford Handbook of International Environmental Law*, Oxford University Press, New York, 2007.

Underdal, A., "Complexity and Challenges of Long-Term Environmental Governance," *Global Environmental Change*, Vol. 20, No. 3, 2010, pp. 386–393.

UN, Report on Sustainable Development, *Report of the World Commission on Environment and Development: Our Common Future*, 1987 (the Brundtland Report), Transmitted to the General Assembly as an Annex to document A/42/427 – Development and International Co-operation: Environment.

UN, *United Nations Environment and Development Agenda, "Agenda 21,"* adopted at the 1992 UN Rio Conference on Environmental and Development, U.N. GAOR, 46th Sess., Agenda Item 21, UN Doc A/Conf.151/26 (1992).

UN, *The Future We Want*, outcome document of the United Nations Conference on Sustainable Development, in Rio de Janeiro, June 2012, UN doc nr: A/RES/66/288, Section II C.

UN, United Nations Environment Programme, *"Putting Rio Principle 10 into Action: An Implementation Guide,"* Published by the United Nations Environment Programme (UNEP), October 2015.

UNECE 2002, Meeting of the Parties to the Convention on Access to Information, Public Participation in Decision-Making and Access to Justice in Environmental Matters (the Aarhus Convention), "Report of the First Meeting of the Parties," Decision I/7 on *Review of Compliance*, adopted at the first meeting of the Parties held in Lucca, Italy, October 2002, ECE/MP.PP/2/Add.8.

UNECE 2005 Aarhus Convention, Report of the Second Meeting of the Parties, DECISION II/4, Promoting the Application of the Principles of the Aarhus Convention in International Forum, ECE/MP.PP/2005/2/Add.5, Annex, p. 4, article 1.

UNECE, ACCC/C/2008/32 (Part I), Report of the Compliance Committee: Findings and recommendations with regard to communication concerning compliance by the European Union, Adopted on 14 April 2011, ECE/MP.PP/C.1/2011/4/Add.1.

UNECE website, www.unece.org/env/pp/ratification.html (Official UN doc nr: Ch_XXVII_13 Environment, United Nations, Treaty Series, Vol. 2161, p. 447).

Victor, D. G., Raustiala, K., and Skolnikoff, E. B., "Introduction and Overview," in Victor, D. G., Raustiala, K., and Skolnikoff, E. B. (eds.), *The Implementation and Effectiveness of International Environmental Commitments: Theory and Practice*, MIT Press, Cambridge and London, 1998.

von Homeyer, I., "The Evolution of EU Environmental Governance," in Scott, L. (ed.), *Environmental Protection – European Law and Governance*, Oxford University Press, New York, 2009.

Wang, H., "Ecosystem Management and Its Application to Large Marine Ecosystems: Science, Law, and Politics," *Ocean Development and International Law*, Vol. 53, No. 1, 2004, pp. 41–74.

Walker, B., and Salt, D., *Resilience Thinking – Sustaining Ecosystems and People in a Changing World*, Island Press, Washington, DC, 2006.

Walker, B. H., et al., "Drivers, 'Slow' Variables, 'Fast' Variables, Shocks, and Resilience," *Ecology and Society*, Vol. 17(3):30, 2012.

Wennerås, P., *The Enforcement of EC Environmental Law*, Oxford University Press, Oxford, 2007.

Westerlund, S., *Miljörättsliga Grundfrågor 2.0*, IMIR Institutet för miljörätt, Åmyra förlag, Uppsala, 2003.

Westerlund, S., *Fundamentals of Environmental Law Methodology*, Uppsala: Uppsala University, Department of Law, 2007, electronic version at http://urn.kb.se/resolve?urn=urn:nbn:se:uu:diva-258801.

Wiener, J. B., "On the Political Economy of Global Environmental Regulation," *The Georgetown Law Journal*, Vol. 87, 1999.

Wiersema, A., "A Train without Tracks: Rethinking the Place of Law and Goals in Environmental and Natural Resources Law," *Environmental Law*, Vol. 38, 2008.

Young, M. A., "Regime Interaction in Creating, Implementing and Enforcing International Law," in Young, M. A. (ed.), *Regime Interaction in International Law: Facing Fragmentation*, Cambridge University Press, Cambridge, 2012.

Young, O. R., *International Governance – Protecting the Environmental in a Stateless Society*, Cornell University Press, Ithaca and London, 1994.

Young, O. R., "Governance for Sustainable Development in a World of Rising Interdependencies," in Delmas, M. A., and Young, O. R. (eds.), *Governance for the Environment – New Perspectives*, Cambridge University Press, Cambridge 2009.

Young, O. R., "Institutional Dynamics: Resilience, Vulnerability and Adaptation in Environmental and Resource Regimes," *Global Environmental Change*, Vol. 20, No. 3, 2010, pp. 378–385.

Young, O. R., "Effectiveness of International Environmental Regimes: Existing Knowledge, Cutting-Edge Themes, and Research Strategies," *PNAS*, 2011, Vol. 108, No. 50, pp. 19853–19860.

Young, O. R., and Levy, M. A., "The Effectiveness of International Environmental Regimes," in Young, O. R. (ed.), *The Effectiveness of International Environmental Regimes: Causal Connections and Behavioral Mechanisms*, MIT Press, Cambridge, MA, 1999.

Zengerling, C., *Greening International Jurisprudence: Environmental NGOs before International Courts, Tribunals, and Compliance Committees*, Martinus Nijhoff Publishers, Leiden, 2013

Index

For EU product safety concerns, contact us at Calle de José Abascal, 56–1°,
28003 Madrid, Spain or eugpsr@cambridge.org.

www.ingramcontent.com/pod-product-compliance
Ingram Content Group UK Ltd.
Pitfield, Milton Keynes, MK11 3LW, UK
UKHW022231220226
468302UK00017B/245
* 9 7 8 1 1 0 8 7 9 3 8 4 1 *